Noisy at the
Wrong Times

NOISY AT THE WRONG TIMES

Michael Volpe

TWO
ROADS

www.tworoadsbooks.com

First published in 2015 by Matador, Leicestershire

This edition first published in Great Britain in 2015 by Two Roads
An imprint of John Murray Press
An Hachette UK company

1

A CIP catalogue record for this title is
available from the British Library

MME Paperback ISBN 9781473629400
Ebook ISBN 9781473629394

Typeset by Palimpsest Book Production Ltd, Falkirk, Stirlingshire
Printed and bound by CPI Group (UK) Ltd, Croydon, CR0 4YY

Hodder & Stoughton policy is to use papers that are natural, renewable and
recyclable products and made from wood grown in sustainable forests. The
logging and manufacturing processes are expected to conform to the
environmental regulations of the country of origin.

Hodder & Stoughton Ltd
Carmelite House
50 Victoria Embankment
London EC4Y 0DZ

www.hodder.co.uk

For all those who were ever told not to bother.

This book is dedicated to all of those teachers who ever suffered (and tolerated) me, and who made Woolverstone Hall the place it was. In particular, I thank those who recognised what talent I had and tried to nurture it, rather than doing the understandable thing and kicking me out. Perhaps the most profound thanks go to the many post-Woolverstone 'teachers' who, from the rubble of a fractured personality, cobbled together an approximation of a useful human being.

I would also like to thank Helen Hawkins for her help during the creation of this book, for guiding my self-effacement so that it retained a point, and for reining in the worst excesses of someone who never paid quite enough attention in English lessons.

There are countless friends and colleagues who are owed thanks for being part of the protective wall that has surrounded me and allowed me a career in the opera business, in particular James Clutton, Mick Goggin (for kicking it all off) and those colleagues who do so much to make us all look good. All deserve more praise than I can give here.

Above all, this book is dedicated, with love, to my remarkable and indomitable mother, Lidia, my talented and tolerant children, Leanora, Gianluca and Fiora, and my patient, understanding wife, Sally.

CONTENTS

PREFACE

'Michael has made a good start and will do well here.
He may be a bit noisy at the wrong times but I am sure
he will put this right next term.'

In his contribution to my first school report, Woolverstone's headmaster, Patrick 'Paddy' Richardson, quickly identified the first of many weaknesses in me: I was a boy who neither cared, nor was aware, that a correct moment to be noisy existed.

Paddy knew trouble when he saw it, and he certainly saw it when he looked at me, a boy whose inherent goodness was wrapped in razor wire. But then, Paddy had already encountered many similar boys before I sauntered over his horizon, so he had the tools to negotiate the perils. Perhaps, blessed as he was with abundant empathy and forgiveness, 'noisy' was his euphemism for the furious haemorrhage of nonsense – both verbal and physical – that I all too frequently unleashed on his school.

It was 1976 when I first strode into Woolverstone Hall School for boys – a miracle of educational courage and foresight – fresh off my west London council estate. I arrived on the tails of an elder brother, and automatically thought I would own the place. About a dozen of my contemporaries were busy striding in with precisely the same thought at roughly the same time. I was never one for submission to superior numbers, since to do so would have required me to acknowledge that others existed, but we spent the first few months jostling to work out who would get the biggest share of the pie; and after that we just enjoyed eating it together in big, greedy mouthfuls.

I'm not sure when stupidity decided I was a good host, but it certainly made itself very much at home whilst I was at Woolverstone. Garrulous to a fault, I mistook precocity for substance, and arrogance for confidence. Of course, it has taken children of my own and the passage of decades for me to realise all of this, but I can offer the reader this heartfelt guarantee: nothing whatsoever softens the ache of enlightenment.

I can see reports for every year I spent at the school, gathered in one document, and reading it today, decades after Paddy's comment, I flinch. Using the crumbs of wisdom I have since collected from beneath the tables of those I admire, I can see the erratic, but inexorably downward trajectory of a wayward youngster; but as inevitable as the calamity appeared to be, there would be many who tried very hard to prevent it. I insisted, obstinately, that there would be only one direction, not because I wanted to, but because something short-circuited the common-sense proprioceptors that tell of your whereabouts in space.

From one end of my life at Woolverstone to the other, the self-destruct button remained lit, and only occasionally did I resist the temptation to press it. If I had stayed at

Woolverstone long enough, a possibility existed that I would have become a scholar but unfortunately I had only five years.

This book also appears to have become something of a commentary on what it was like to grow up in an Italian family in London in the 1960s and 70s; a family whose dysfunction seemed entirely normal to me at the time, but whose fate has begun to resolve during the course of this book's creation. I may have 'escaped' – my current position in the world of opera is as unlikely an end to this story as it is a happy one – but in many ways it throws my childhood, my family, my roots, into sharper relief. At the time of writing, the maudlin beast of melancholia has me in its grasp, and what writing there was on the wall is revealing itself, line by line, month by month. Brothers die or move to different sides of the world, fathers shuffle off this mortal coil too, without ever redeeming themselves, and a mother knew nothing of her child's death because fate robbed her of memory, meaning that, at her own passing, it was a blessing that she had remained unaware. Who knows where the roots of the poisoned tree were first set down? You, the reader, may draw your own conclusions.

Much of what I recollect may be wrong or unintentionally embellished, but much of it is precisely as it happened. And I suppose I ought to be tactful, which is why so many names are omitted or are inventions. This is a memoir of a fashion, but a regurgitation is a more apt description. I am not a celebrity, so there is no particular reason why anybody should be interested in what took place over five years in rural Suffolk. If I happen across a grand purpose to my writing, you'll be the first to know, but if you need a signpost then I suppose this is also a confession. Goodness knows I have a lot to confess (though my memories don't haunt me as much as mock me), but it would be more my style to sit with a guitar and strum an epic testimony to my life at school and beyond. Even better would be a histrionic opera in three acts, but since I can't play guitar and Mascagni is dead, this bundle of words will have to suffice.

A friend once told me that 'if one doesn't blow one's own trumpet, someone else will use it as a spittoon'. I took her at her exquisitely enunciated word and have been blowing feverishly ever since. It's perfectly acceptable to indulge that urge with short, funky horn stabs, but I've been playing the 'Prince of Denmark's March'. Luckily, in the world of the lyric arts, where, startlingly, I ended up twenty-five years ago, enough people recognise the tune for me to get away with it.

I do intend this book to honour Woolverstone and those who made the school what it was: a place where boys and young men of my background had an opportunity that, like the school itself, exists no more. I just can't promise how the story will all turn out; which is just like me, really.

WHERE WE CAME IN

Sophocles, whose achievements included shortening the play in order to make it more memorable, said that old age and the passage of time teach everything.

Inconveniently, he forgot to say that you don't remember any of it. The specific moment at which Woolverstone first entered my consciousness is hard to pinpoint and I'm attempting to retrace steps I trod long ago, even though at the time I was rarely aware of what I was doing. Pre-Woolverstone, I'm afraid things get even hazier. Throughout my pre-school childhood, I didn't absorb much of what was around me as we lurched from one crisis to another because that obstructed the process of absorbing myself.

I can make out the rough edge of my younger self, but while parts of the world through which I crashed are vivid, others are as if shrouded by an impenetrable London fog of the late sixties, so thick that when walking us to school, my mother could only discern which of her children was on her left or right by the thickness of the bones within their grasping hands. She needed no clear line of sight to tell that my robust hand was the one pulling away from her, its three-year-old owner furious at having to wear a thick, scratchy balaclava, damp with moist smog and cursing breath. Sergio, my older brother by two years, was on the other side, slighter but just as petulant. Such journeys to the place of Mum's work, a nursery in whose care we also spent the day, are among my earliest memories. To Mum, just another day in our troubled lives had begun, refereeing our quarrels and threatening us under her breath so that we didn't shame her. To us, though, it was a bus journey through west London from Fulham to Brook Green, and a friendly chat with the American rockabilly conductor, who wore black silk gloves that matched in lustre his dyed, shiny quiff. He and his driver were the same each day, a familiar and friendly element in our lives, one of the many simple, seemingly unimportant and small constants that live long in the memory of children. Like, too, the woman who would scare me at the bus stop by popping out her false teeth so that she looked like a bulldog, and who inexplicably acted as our savings bank, marking in her little red book the pocket money we gave her as we saved for Mum's Christmas present.

The Doll's Hospital in Dawes Road is another thing that lingers in my memory. So is the barbershop, Patrick's toyshop in Lillie Road and the ABC cinema (now a Waitrose). After it closed as a cinema, when I was around eight, the rock band Emerson, Lake and Palmer bought the ABC as a rehearsal space, and, right about where the vegetable aisle is now, we would hide and peek under the curtain to watch them play, having forced entry through the fire doors. The disappearance of each and every one of these places marked more than the march of progress.

The Doll's Hospital was 'World Famous'. It had those very words written on the sign above its shop front, and people would send their dolls from all corners of the globe to be mended, primped and restored there. And I walked past it every day, waving at the two old gentlemen who sat inside behind their workbenches, lovingly returning pink plastic to former glories. The non-descript bar that replaced the Doll's Hospital was not 'World Famous'.

The cards that my mother kept being dealt left the pack with so wicked a flourish, one might have wondered if they'd been tampered with, but she always did the best she could with it. Mum was the kind of person for whom the welfare state was invented; we had bus passes and free school dinners, and sundry other benefits were bestowed on us. Working as many hours as God sent was her keeping her side of the bargain, and the state recognised that there were people whose labour was no less valuable or dignified because it did not attract a five- or six- figure salary. Mum went out to work at dawn, came home in the late afternoon, cooked a meal and then went out to do an evening job: and whilst there, she would hope all of her children got home alive. Living on an estate, opportunities for misbehaviour were plentiful and readily taken: roof climbing, knockdown ginger, bike stealing, fighting and generally being irritants. Dealing with the aftermath and worry of it all took its toll on her. I suppose it was a life of 'poverty', and although eventually our lives would feature a colour television (rented and on an early version of cable), hot water, heating, carpets and an indoor bathroom, money was a commodity whose presence – or lack thereof – dominated proceedings.

Lidia Perillo and Francesco Volpe – my mum and dad – came to England from Italy in the mid-fifties. Romantically, there was an elopement of sorts, but they were actually invited to the UK along with thousands of others from around Europe and the Commonwealth. They took their opportunity, I suppose, but my mother wasn't to know that embarking on such an adventure with a man of my father's disposition was like trusting a blind archer to split the apple on your head; most of his efforts might fly harmlessly by, but one might be catastrophic. I never asked her if she ever wished that Cupid's arrow of destiny had missed.

Post-war Britain was in desperate need of the skill and toil immigrants could provide but no less suspicious of their motives for being here in the first place, and that schizophrenic approach remains today. My parents were issued with 'Register of Alien' cards and told to report to the local police station of wherever it was they were living. Foreigners, at a time when the Second World War was still fresh and raw in the memory, were largely viewed with disdain and mistrust by Londoners. Well into the seventies I recall shopping with Mum in the North End Road, where barrow boys, irked at her desire to pick up fruit and check its freshness, would snarl at her.

'In ENGLAND,' they would bark, speaking slowly, 'we don't touch until we buy, understand?' A stern look from Mum and a 'FUGGOFF!' would do the trick. It was a theme that I too would encounter right through to adulthood; my ethnicity could always find itself at the heart of a dispute or judgement, and nothing else could evoke the beast within me so easily.

8

When they first arrived, my parents took up residence in various large houses, Mum as the cook and my father as the butler. Early fifties London still had about it the last remnants of the Edwardian age – although few would admit it – but it wasn't exactly *Upstairs, Downstairs*. Foreign domestic personnel were no doubt cheaper and easier to dismiss, but Mum learned to cook roast beef and Yorkshire pudding because there was little desire for gnocchi and pesto. The idea of Dad as a house servant is unimaginable. This is the man who, when taking his London bus driving test, stopped the vehicle in the middle of the road, told the examiner (who he judged was asking too many questions and giving too many instructions) to 'fuck off', terminated the test and left the bus in the middle of Uxbridge Road. This impetuous, compulsive streak is a feature of the Volpe clan, and Dad's ability to stay in one place was forever being tested (he always failed, instead coming and going like malaria). Possibly because of this, their careers as domestic staff ended, and Mum and Dad took various jobs wherever they could find them, their family growing at the rate of one child every two years.

By the time they had three children, they were living in a basement flat in Woodstock Grove in Shepherd's Bush. Dad, using the organ that did most of the thinking for him, left Mum to take up with another Italian woman, who had come to London and had been living with them whilst finding a place of her own. A trusting and good heart such as Mum's is often abused; she used to confide tearfully to this woman that she was convinced Dad was having an affair, unaware that her confidante was in fact planning to trust her own life to him, as Mum had herself once done. At the time it was no consolation to Mum that the woman was actually about to begin the long purgatory of life with Dad, but she eventually believed for certain that she had dodged the most toxic of bullets. Whilst away, Dad and his new girlfriend had a son, but Dad eventually came back again, stopping long enough to get my mother pregnant with me, and I was born in May 1965.

On Christmas Day of that year, seven months after my birth, Dad departed one final time, leaving Mum to fend for herself, which wasn't easy, even without the complication of four children, three of them under five. My uncle Matteo (Dad's brother), who had himself come to England to pursue a better life and who had engineered Mum and Dad's last reconciliation, came to our home for Christmas lunch to find my distraught mother, alone with her four boys. Mum demanded to be taken to the house where she knew Dad would be and on arrival began to scream abuse at the window above, behaviour that brought my father to the street in truculent, righteously punitive mood. My uncle ensured, with equal aggression, that he didn't get the chance to express himself and thereafter remained, for nearly fifty years, virtually entirely estranged from his brother.

Mum went to court for maintenance, but the order of £2 per week was rarely obeyed since it had usually ended up in the bookie's pocket. Over the subsequent decades, Dad tried countless times to inveigle his way back into Mum's life; he needed someone to look after him, to feed him, give him money for the horses, wash his clothes. He would press family members into the pursuit, trying to persuade Mum to take him back. This went on for forty years, and each and every time my mother had only one word for him: '*Vaffanculo.*'

One can only imagine the emotional turmoil of recurring rejection and loss Mum must have suffered during this early period, before her mind and heart were cleared and she saw what she had escaped. In a strange country, her family all back in Italy, living in a two-roomed slum with very little to sustain her family financially, Mum's is a story of stoicism and a relentless battle for survival. If you had seen the conditions she had to contend with, that statement wouldn't appear as melodramatic as it sounds. But soon, fortune smiled on her when she got a job as a cook in the local day nursery in Brook Green. They had a baby room, and, at a tender, still-pink and crinkled age, I was cared for as she cooked in the adjacent kitchen. My brother Serge was also given a place, and our early childhood was full of the pleasures of a well-run council establishment. Council nurseries had lots of staff in uniforms and obeyed strict rules. For the entire five years I spent there, after every lunch, we were force-fed a spoonful of cod liver oil, without fail, no exceptions. We all slept in the afternoon on put-down camp beds, there was a proper pre-school curriculum and the food, on account of our mother cooking it, was the best in the borough – nobody else had the variety we enjoyed. The staff loved the lunches, too, with Mum delivering the full spectrum of southern Italian cuisine. Later, her kitchen assistant, Miriam, who had come to England from the Caribbean, taught Mum how to cook salt fish and patties and gave her the recipe for a spicy crispy batter. Mum's culinary world trip didn't stop there: soon, lunch and tea featured samosas, exotic curries and Jamaican fried chicken to go along with the lasagnes, cannelloni, baccalà and bresaola.

The job at the nursery was a major step forward because it was secure, offered a regular income and carried with it a pension. She would remain in the job for over 30 years until her retirement. But the slum in which we lived made sure life was never simple, even as things began to improve. A one-bedroom basement flat with no bathroom or toilet was home for the first five years of my life. Lino on the floor, baths in the kitchen sink and mice in the cupboards are my enduring memories.

Woodstock Grove, now inevitably gentrified, its large houses re-joined from top to bottom, was the sort of community one rarely sees today. It was a dead-end street (literally and socially), with a BBC complex at the closed end, and cars never travelled its length. Predictably, it had a pub on the corner at the open end, and women had only to step outside their front doors to scream the name of their menfolk, who would wobble from the pub obediently. All doorsteps were painted in that dark burgundy stone paint. It was a place of poor, working class solidity and industriousness, where we could buy fresh eggs from Old Man Lacey, a home farmer with chickens in his back yard and only one arm with which to harvest their crop. Another family bred rabbits in the cupboard under the stairs that were either sold as pets to those with room for a hutch or sent to the pot for sustenance. No doubt those bought as pets would inevitably end up in a casserole too.

The children of Woodstock Grove played in the street together in gangs that seemed to number dozens, all dressed shabbily in hand-me-down nylon and sockless in their tatty shoes. The games featured all of the street's children, of every age. Standing with arms and legs spread in a star shape against a stolen sheet of plywood so that friends could hurl darts like a circus knife thrower was a popular entertainment. One boy lost an eye, and my eldest brother felt the sting of a dart sinking itself into his clavicle. For weeks, wood and flammable scrap would be collected as the kids built massive bonfires in the road on Guy Fawkes Night. Fireworks were a constant thrill and, unlike today, only seemed to go on sale a week or so before 5 November, so there was a real sense of occasion as we pilfered pennies and pooled pocket money for 'bangers'. Ten in a box, these small cigarette-sized exploding tubes with a blue fuse were lobbed at cats, at each other or dropped through letterboxes. On the building sites, we could chuck old milk bottles stuffed with a lighted banger into the air, timing it so it exploded mid-flight. One evening, for some inexplicable reason, my second eldest brother, Matt, lit a Jumping Jack (a special banger that does what it says) and put it in his pocket. It didn't end well. Burns and injuries were a constant menace, some of them serious. But above all else, the bonfires stirred our souls. One was never enough; each section of the street had to have its own pyre so at least three would singe and buckle the tarmac, radiating a brutal heat that singed everything in its path. Given that there was so much nylon around, it is a curiosity that more children didn't spontaneously combust as they were pinned against the houses of the street by the ferocious glow. Every year the fire brigade – most of west London's – had to be summoned. While we're on the topic of our more dangerous pursuits, our other playground was the Central tube line that ran past the end of the garden, which also contained the outside loo. Holding onto the extrusions on the sides and backs of tube trains waiting at red and seeing who could stay on longest as they accelerated away filled hours of time. Incredibly, nobody died.

One summer we all caught ringworm from the neighbour's dog, but Mum refused to let our curly hair be shaved off even though it offered the best chance of a cure. This refusal was completely at odds with the way in which she maintained our much-valued locks, for which she used one of those ferocious combs with an embedded razor, taking regularly to our heads with abandon, turning our hair into feathered mats with a coiled fringe. With mounds of hair at her feet, she would then smother what was left on our heads with *Vitapoint*, a nourishing cream that smelled like cats' piss and had the effect of turning the mat into a greasy brown mesh. Pictures of me as a youngster are an exhibition of wonderfully quirky hairdos, and I half-expect to see a small rodent poking out from behind my ear.

Even as small boys, our pride suffered from having to attend school looking like scarecrows, but Matteo was always at the hospital with real injuries requiring stitches.

We all risked life and limb playing in the local building sites, but Matt would remove the risk by willingly replacing it with certainty. He once turned his feet and ankles into beef jerky by leaping onto a carefully stacked pile of plate glass. My early recollections of Matt include watching him gently pick the stitches from his latest laceration. His attitude towards injury was an early sign of the fearless abandon that would have found better expression had he developed an interest in high finance rather than shop-lifting.

WHERE IT BEGAN

Perhaps the local council was taking notes, recognising the dangers that four young children with a single mother might be in, but more likely they realised the peril our neighbours faced as we grew. Social services were probably less sensitive then than they are today, and in the late sixties and early seventies I suppose many of the social workers would have been war children, when deprivation was genuinely life-threatening. With a world war fresh in the memory, most social workers probably needed the delinquent behaviour of children to mimic the invasion of Poland, or at the very least, the worst excesses of a Panzer division, before alarm bells began to ring. Warsaw felt no threat from us, but Woodstock Grove probably did; and when I was five years old, we were offered the unimaginable luxury of a flat in Fulham Court, a flat, I should add, that had an inside bathroom.

We all decamped to our new duplex three-bedroom flat in June of 1970. Central heating wouldn't be installed for another twenty years, but there was always paraffin. Fulham Court was on the Fulham Road, closer to the fashionable enclave of Chelsea, and Matt no doubt had his own Blitzkrieg in mind; meanwhile I was so unspeakably excited by the concept of a bath that I insisted on sitting in it when we all went to view the flat before moving in.

If this leap in social status was significant to us, it was like winning the pools for Mum. Two bedrooms to share between us children was officially palatial, but Mum had even seen Woodstock Grove as a vast improvement over what she had lived in before coming to England. Her home-town was the mountain top village of Montecorvino Pugliano in Campania, southern Italy. Poverty there in the thirties and forties when she was growing up had a smell and danger all its own, with malaria and cholera haunting the narrow, steep streets of her village. Her younger brother Mario contracted meningitis as a baby and was essentially condemned to death by his doctor, but an old woman, having heard the wails and moans of the family, came to the door with a jar of leeches, offering the last and only hope to my mother's parents. Placing several of the crea-tures around his head, the old woman's intervention was absurd and illogical, but it was a hope of cure in a place without sophisticated antibiotics and, miraculously, the child survived the illness. Mum's childhood home was a lethal environment that sent its inhabitants into the arms of such quackery, but if *Il Dio* ignored your prayers, he'd always send a surrogate with an old wives' tale instead.

It wasn't just bacteria that threated to wipe out the population. In Mum's early teens, war and the presence of the Nazis became the biggest threat once Mussolini had been kicked out. The formerly chummy Germans were an instant occupier when Benito, hanging by his feet, met his gruesome end at an Esso station in Milan. By then the Nazis were undoubtedly on their last legs in Italy, but the continuing resistance action provoked terrible reprisals. Eventually, liberation came, but even that almost cost Mum her life. She, my brothers and I have cause to be thankful for the failures of British munitions workers as a stray Allied shell failed to explode after it crashed through the roof of the bread shop Mum was in, killing the baker as he handed her a loaf. Actually, I don't know the nationality of the shell, but the British were engaged in all sorts of activity in the area as the Allies pushed northwards. The fighting in the region was substantial, and in Mum's municipality, a legend was born when a small platoon of Germans held out for two weeks in a church, fighting the surrounding Allied forces to a standstill. Why they didn't just flatten the church I don't know – perhaps even then there was sensitivity towards religion. Or maybe they did try to flatten the church but the shells kept failing to go off. That munitions factory probably became British Leyland.

I once had cause to experience the indelible mark that the war had left on Mum myself, when we were visiting her family when I was sixteen. Returning late one evening to the home of an uncle in the poor district of Montecorvino (for there were fewer poor areas than others), we had just passed a small block of flats under construction when a mighty, deafening explosion blew us forwards. The blast wave rushed past us, and, before I'd had time even to think, my mother, despite being half my size, had grabbed my hand and begun sprinting up the hill with me in helpless tow. It turned out to be a device planted by the local mafia to remind the builder of his obligations, and if it had exploded when we were passing the building thirty seconds earlier, we would have been turned to mincemeat. But the event had instantly pitched Mum backwards to the days of war, and I had never before even given it a thought.

She was the oldest girl of a large family with an alcoholic father, and it fell to such young women to run the family home. Washing clothes in streams and specially built stone fountains fed by springs is hard graft in the furnace of a southern Italian summer, but working in tobacco fields as she did in her late teens and early twenties surpassed anything for brutal physical drudgery. Her father had been a committed fascist and believed Mussolini to be the great saviour. He had taken up arms abroad and, even more dangerously, at home, alongside the struggling Germans against the Americans and British. With the Resistance so active and the community split, his continuing dedication to the cause had to be guarded and cunning to keep his neighbours in the dark. Money was virtually non-existent, so the richly fertile land and climate was something of a redeemer, but it was an arduous, perilous existence.

Mum's life in London, in Fulham Court with its running water, bathroom and inside toilet was therefore something she could proudly view as the Everest of social improvement. Her regular employment as a cook had indeed rendered her wealthier than most of her kin back home. Despite the economic miracle of post-war Italy, when only Japan and Germany (is there something about losing wars?)

surpassed its growth, the south of the country remained in the relative dark ages for some time. Mum never felt the need to return.

Dad was from the larger town that sat only halfway up the mountain, Montecorvino Rovella. I think this is what led to the elopement: Dad's lot were urban sophisticates compared to Mum's hillbillies, and they didn't approve of his dalliance with her. Class divisions go beyond just rich and poor, something I don't think has ever been properly understood by those who try to alleviate deprivation. All parts of society are sub-divided into almost countless sections, and if you sliced through it, it would have as many layers as a lasagne. My father's dynasty, led by the patriarch Luigi, my grandfather, considered their family to be respected and of high status. Triumphant proclamations by my uncle years later revealed that this elevated self-image was solely on account of Nonno's position as a local government officer and a distant cousin who had become an architect. But such things mattered in Montecorvino.

In fairness, there *was* something a little feral about Mum's clan. Their homes were ramshackle, in centuries-old narrow back streets that still had pigs in sties beneath them. One of her brothers had a miscellany of tiles on the stairs leading up to his house, fruits of the family's gentle thievery. After several years, they had pocketed enough tiles from loose walls or surreptitiously placed majolica slabs from building site entrances into handbags to finish the stairs completely. But they were warm people, and my brothers and I loved our uncles, especially Rolando, who had once run off with the circus to become a famous trapeze artist. He was enormously athletic and strong and could hang all four of us from his biceps. Another of my uncles, Isidoro, used Rolando's strength to help him organise the annual *fiera* because, he said, it was '*come avere quattro uomini*' – like having four men. And when Rolando wasn't carrying half-ton loads on his back for his older brother, he was striking out across the mountains at dawn to collect a cornucopia of wild *funghi* to sell in the market. As far as I could tell, only he had the skills and knowledge to find such delicacies. Knowing which were safe to eat was the golden ticket of *funghi*-collecting talent, so Rolando's arduously harvested produce was valuable indeed. It is impossible to imagine the extraordinary variety of these mushrooms, which Zia Anna, Rolando's wife, frequently served me. Some were like large steaks, slabs of perfumed fungus drenched in olive oil and dusted with Parmesan, rosemary and thyme; others were better fired in the oven with gorgonzola and honey, or wrapped in pasta to make perfect ravioli. It was the southern Italian meadow's meat. Rolando epitomised the simple peasant, wandering the hills with his old, floppy straw hat to protect him from the fierce heat, smoking cigars that hung permanently from his lip. He played the village idiot to some degree, I feel, but with his film-star looks (once captured in an old photograph of him in circus costume), enormous physicality and big heart, he was a bit of a hero to me. This is a man who had run off with the circus against his parents' wishes at the age of fifteen. He was a *trapeze artist* who also did a solo stint on the high swing, possibly the most glamorous act under the big top, for goodness sake! And I had so loved the film *Trapeze*, with Burt Lancaster and Tony Curtis; Rolando was *my* Burt Lancaster. Can you imagine how I luxuriated in this story when in the playground? Nobody in the whole of London had an uncle who was a circus star.

Having a family in Italy was quite a bonus when it came to holidays, because as long as Mum could scrape together the train fare (cheaper than flying in those days) we would get a good long break in the Med. Well, sort of. The train journey was a two-day adventure in choked carriages and stifling heat, but an overnight passage through the Alps is still among the most exciting things I ever got to do as a child. Serge and I, sharing a couchette bed, would peer through the windows into the night, where we could still make out the moonlit crests of the mountains, their villages revealed by twinkling, distant lights. Strikes by railway workers would mean sitting stationary for hours on the tracks, blocked by a handful of disgruntled train drivers who would break out a picnic of bread, salami and home-made wine, sharing it with passengers who would climb down from the carriages. At stations that were loud and chaotic, my brothers would leap from the train to fill containers with drinking water, and amid the pandemonium I would always fret that the train would leave without them. Once, panic and hysteria did break out in our compartment when Matt had failed to return as the train began its onward journey. With Mum flailing her arms in grief and despair, me copying her, and the whole carriage wondering if the Red Brigade was mounting a terrorist attack, Matt nonchalantly wandered into the compartment, explaining that he had merely got on further along the platform.

Italy in the summer meant weeks of freedom in a potent and overwhelming landscape of heat, smells and wild untamed beauty. Even among the poorer members of the family there were lavish late lunches after days at the beach or mornings spent catching lizards in the first rays of the scorching sun. As a youngster I would drive the hot, dusty road between the two towns on a motor scooter, the air soaked with the pungent aroma of wild basil and the occasional open sewer. Halfway up the Pugliano road was a high stone bridge spanning a gorge, and I would stop there and imagine the days during wartime when, with suspicious, paranoid Germans patrolling, my grandfather would sneak beneath it on his way to deliver food to the inhabitants of his town. Inevitably, two soldiers caught him one night, but were persuaded not to shoot him on the spot by the *Fascisti* party card he produced from his pocket. Nonno might have been a fascist, but he still wanted to feed his family. Mum also told me of young women who would be found dead at its base, apparent suicides, but who had more likely been pitched from the bridge by their ashamed fathers and families because of illicit love affairs or unplanned pregnancy. Even today, unwed mothers or forbidden trysts cause a real stir in that part of Italy, but the disgrace it caused in the thirties and forties burned through society like acid. I often think it would be a great subject for a one-act verismo opera; *Il ponticello della morte,* or something equally melodramatic. These were stories of death and dishonour, but they were thrilling.

From the peak at Pugliano I could view, laid out before me, the hot, arid plain between the mountains and the ocean, the landscape filled with mile upon mile of tomato fields, from which my cousins would return every afternoon after picking box after box of *pomodori*, their backs blackened by a day in the brutal heat. The land would stretch out forever, and when the air was clear, you could see the waters of Spineta beach shimmering in the far distance. There was nothing impoverished about the geography of the place, and I can only ever have been enriched by days such as those. It was a long way from Fulham Court.

My time in Italy and the extended family I had there, as well as those who had come to the UK, would always influence the way in which I saw myself. I feel Italian to this day and, as a child, I felt it lent me an exoticism my contemporaries just did not possess. Paradoxically, we were curiosities in Italy too, where most of the town knew who the *Inglese* were. On the warm, humid evenings when the whole town would walk up and down the main street, parading themselves and gossiping about each other, I was always acutely aware of the looks we would get. The only place on earth that I can tolerate crowds is on the 'passeggiata'; the communal gathering that marks the end of the work day, before everyone goes home for dinner. In Italy, the throng of chattering, shouting people who stand in groups small and large to argue and gesticulate vehemently is one of the greatest entertainments known to man. For hours, I would listen to the undulating lyricism of the Neapolitan dialect, which manipulates the Italian language

– already a beautiful thing – into an intricate, acrobatic linguistic feat. It's pure music.

One of my fondest childhood memories (although when I say memory, I mean it to be more visceral than that) is the sound of Italian women shrieking from balconies at their friends, their children or their husbands. Although a cacophony, it still retained a mellifluousness that was full and compelling, a street opera without accompaniment. The complexity of the Neapolitan dialect and the speed with which it is usually delivered gives the language a genuinely animal quality, and as I sat on benches and at café tables with my cousins, I would be gripped by its expression. My spoken Italian is drenched with a strong southern accent; not for me the formal eloquence of the Milanese or Florentine when the inventions and bastard-isations of *Nnapulitan* are there to be washed around the mouth before bursting through the lips with the force of a punch. In the sphere of profanity, the dialect is extrav-agant, and as you might expect, I took to this with gusto at a young age. Swearing in Neapolitan is a cruel art form that spares nobody, where nothing is sacred. It is employed liberally, even in conversations of levity and friendship; a woman would think nothing of telling her brother to go fuck his mother. Neapolitans have words to describe complex realities too: 'The rain is like fine hair', which would properly be something like *La pioggia è come capelli fini*, becomes the much briefer and more evocative 'shul'agaia'. I write the word phonetically because I have absolutely no idea how you might spell it. I am aware that much of this sounds common and peasant-like, but that's because it is. Southerners are frowned upon for such things, but to me it was wonderful and I could cuss, undetected, like no other child at Addison Gardens primary school. In real song, too, the language is bewitching, and *Canzone Nnapulitan* are, in the right hands, and accompanied by guitar alone, a breathless balm for the soul.

Suffice to say, I absorbed every second of my time in Italy and laid it all out for everyone to see whenever it was time to return to Addison Gardens primary school. As an inveterate show-off, I would come back with stories of a lifestyle lived, as opposed to a fortnight in a hotel, although very few if any of my friends could afford that anyway. I could boast of meeting the big man who pushed a dustcart through the slender streets for the municipal authority and to whom everybody would mystifyingly doff their cap. On investigation, I was told that when not tipping the remains of everybody's dinner into his wagon, he would be tipping the remains of the last person he'd whacked on behalf of the local Camorra into a ditch. To my friends back at school, Mafia hitmen were as outlandish a concept as Luke Skywalker; something you only ever saw in the movies.

But while Italy was an incredible place to me, Mum never got over the graft and toil of her early years there, and instead, focused all her efforts on improving our lot back in London. She might have been dealt a dud hand, but sometimes if you wait long enough, a better stack will land in front of you: and it did. When I was nine years old, my brother Serge, the third-born of us four boys, was sent off to a school in the countryside, and the talk was that I would join him there in due course. Being 'sent' somewhere was a significant event in our environment since the word was usually accompanied by another: 'down'. We even knew the names of the beaks at Horseferry Road Magistrates Court who, with their picayune intellects and mammoth prejudices were most likely to give custodial sentences for the most piffling of crimes. The trick was not to get caught, or at the very most, to do only that for which a warning from the local bobby would be the limit. If policemen hate filling forms now, back in the seventies we were still waiting for the paperless office, and they loathed it even more. The only form a copper was interested in was that of the kid they had struggling in their grip, so better to deliver him to his front door with a telling off. It was still the age when trying to knock off a policeman's helmet with a football represented the pinnacle of daring, and the idea of stabbing him couldn't have been further from our minds. Still, Matt – a recidivist who could hit a copper's lid from forty yards, as well as have the watch off his wrist from the same distance – was recurrently dragged off to the local approved school or borstal. Even tolerant policemen have to take action eventually.

I recall feeling especially concerned that I shouldn't ever be committed to the supervision of 'screws' at Stamford House in the Goldhawk Road, with its high fences surrounding the playground and its heavy locks. I'd seen it frequently enough; smelled the tobacco-bleach mustiness of its corridors and experienced the chilling, lip-curled rigidity of its staff as I visited my brother. Being invited through a gate that needs unlocking to see a sibling whose presence at home has become noticeably rare, demonstrates to even the youngest child that a place is out of the ordinary. Matt's captors barked and marched around the rooms and environs like casually attired policemen, and they looked upon me, I was certain, as a future resident. They called Stamford House a remand home or a reform school or some such misnomer; what it really represented was short-stay prison for young teenagers, and character transformation was seldom the outcome. Its gates, grey close-meshed grills and contemptuous care were an option any of us might so easily have taken up. Stamford House or St Vincent's (another such place) had space for any of us Volpe brothers should we so desire it. Correction was the intention, but Matteo learned the art of transgression behind those fences instead.

FIGHT

Criminal activities and fighting weren't confined to Matt's world. One particular incident sticks out in my mind, when I returned to Fulham Court one afternoon after Serge had left for Woolverstone, and was met by the sight of a small crowd gathered in the space between the brick flower-beds and bike sheds that dissected the blocks in which we all lived. Years later, in an act of vandalism, the council removed the flowerbeds but when we had first arrived in Fulham Court they were full of large rose bushes and shrub-bery. Fulham was on the cusp of an affluent flowering that continues unabated to this day. Fulham Court was properly built on the site of an old brewery in the thirties, with old flettons and panelled sash windows, and there was no high rise – three floors at most. Among council housing, it was the pinnacle and not far off being elegant, but most of those it cosseted in faux opulence were far from that.

It was a place where people had a sense of pride in their surroundings but had no idea how to make them, or themselves, much better. Throwing a bucket of disinfectant down the stairwell was simply keeping it clean for the old sofa that would soon follow it, but teenage barbarism was still a marginal and rare concept, and the villains of the place talked of respect and honour when they weren't balancing half-pints of beer on their penises, as one celebrity criminal was wont to do in the local pubs. The estate was a genuine community at a period in time when such micro-societies did not hate and abuse themselves. Avarice was there, but it had not yet become rapacious, cold-blooded or murderous. Material aspiration included the kind of bike you could afford to buy your child; the zenith was the 'Chopper'. We could never afford one (Mum scraped together enough to buy us a small-wheeled bike that we shared), but we could always 'borrow' one for a few hours until the rightful owner, tearful and desperate, discovered who'd taken it and we would give it back. Depending on who it was, we might even convince him that we were doing him a favour by returning his 'lost' bike, which meant we could legitimately borrow it for a few more hours in the future. It was a great system. We had become quickly absorbed into this varied community, drifting, as boys do, towards others of like mind and outlook. We were at home among these people, it seemed.

Half of this population were there in the crowd on the day in question. Mobs, when engaged by exciting events, have about them a character all their own. They don't keep their distance; they swarm in around the incident, seeking to get close to the drama; they hunch their shoulders and implore the subjects of their attention to greater outrages. The crowd that confronted me that day was in their element as they noisily encircled a commotion. I could tell by their intensity and unusual placement in between two blocks that there was a fight going on.

Fight

Nothing could surpass a good scrap on the estate, violence prompted by love, trousers-down guilt or plain old machismo. They could be terribly visceral and frequently drew in a selection of secondary or tertiary combatants such as wives, sons, mistresses. By the end of the drama, several people could be bashing the granny out of one another, screaming and screeching. They were physical soap operas that might run for ages, shifting around the estate, up and down stairwells into the play park or football yard, and those involved might retire to their flats, only to emerge again with weapons, dogs and reinforcements. The police would rarely be called. But if there was anything more spellbinding than a brawl among residents standing up for honour or pride, it was one that involved your mother doing the same. For at the heart of this tumult, in what my memory recalls as a cloud of dust, perms and expletives was indeed Mum, clawing, scratching and slapping furiously at another woman.

My mother was small and Italian. Further description is probably superfluous. Her impossibly tiny waist, seen in old photos, had devolved responsibility for catching the eye to her bosom, which still managed to overshadow her midriff. Mum had succumbed to the seemingly inevitable physical fate that befalls most voluptuously beautiful Italian women. Yet, whilst svelte elegance may have deserted her from her first pregnancy onwards, even at a late age she still possessed the highest cheekbones and a face twenty years behind her number of birthdays. She had diminutive, compact hands of solid granite, honed by years of manual work, forever liberated from manicured elegance or delicacy,

and her forearms were striped with the scars of burns
acquired from sticking her hands in and out of too many
ovens. Her fingers were robust and short; if she ever did
decorate them, the digits looked like red-haired Russian
dolls. Being slapped by her was akin to being shot. So as
I watched the cat-fight I felt some sympathy with the woman
now being clubbed by a furious Neapolitan. I also judged
that Mum's opponent should count herself lucky, for if
there was a coffee table or a vacuum cleaner to hand, my
mother would have beaten her with that.

I don't wish to over-amplify Mum's propensity to
violence, since she wasn't commonly found battering her
neighbours, but her children presented a challenge similar
to that of a lioness keeping her cubs from rushing off in
all sorts of dangerous directions, and she was ever prepared
to roar. Physically keeping children in check was rarely
considered inappropriate in the seventies, either by society
at large or the children being kept in check. Hers was a
kind of behavioural editing, and we were the errant prose.
The desperate necessities of life and the half-panicked
need to feed and clothe us produced a fear for the safety
and wellbeing of her offspring that she was frantic for us
to understand. If she had to, she'd thrash it into us. Italian
mothers are like that: acute worriers whose obsessive
attachment to their children is matched only by the grim
zeal with which they will protect them, even from themselves.
Mum was a worrier from the moment of the conception
of her first child, when, as the first cells divided, she seems
to have grown an extra adrenal gland. The level of cor-
poreal admonishment Italian mothers dish out is directly

proportionate to the dedication they have towards their children; the more besotted with them they are, the more frantic they become when their behaviour is in danger of doing them harm. And Mum really, really loved us.

All four of us brothers were swift to invite punishment, but even swifter to seek to avoid it, so Mum needed strategies and she had to be fast. If she couldn't get herself across the room quickly enough to deliver a manual pounding, she was not averse to broadcasting whatever was within her reach in our direction. Her throwing arm was lethally accurate, and she would launch fusillades of shoes, chairs or ornaments across the room as we crashed through furniture and doors in a frenetic bid to escape the artillery that was exploding off the walls around us. Shoes in the seventies were dangerously synthetic, with thick platform soles of dimpled plastic that could travel through the air at speed. Orthopaedic sandals had wooden soles that could either be used to smack or, better still, cast across the room like pine nunchucks. The heavy glass ashtray on the coffee table was often used, but so was the coffee table itself, which meant you had to dodge both the lump of glass with blue bubbles in it as well as the table. I was forever grateful that we couldn't afford a television with a remote control and the television itself was rented, so she dare not throw that, although she could have if she so desired. The New York Yankees would have taken options on Mum were they to spot her potential. She could curve any object a yard left or right, which meant half-open doors offered little protection; Mum would still hit you with a Mr Sheen tin even when pitched from the unseen corner of the lounge. A curious shortfall in her skill meant she found it harder to score a direct hit the closer she was to you because she threw things too hard. But then, if she was within a yard or so, she had other means at her disposal.

Hands.

I think the expression 'heavy handed' was first coined for Mum. The strike of her hand didn't as much sting as stun. Flesh wasn't flushed with redness from a slap, it was in spasm from blunt force injury. From time to time, when her hands were sore from the latest burn or from hand-washing a full load of boys' clothes, she might corner you as you sat on the sofa, plastic shoe in her grip, in which case the best defensive position was lying on your back with a foot in the air as the first point of defence, very much as a goalkeeper narrows the angle for an attacker. As she flailed away at you with a four-inch platform shoe, you were able to wave the foot about, forcing her to change her slant. After a while, she worked out a new and viciously rudimentary strategy: hit hard on the sole of the foot being proffered so willingly into her firing line. If there was anything more painful than wearing one of those plastic shoes, it was being hit on the foot by one of them, and even as a child, stung into a fit of wailing tears, that particular irony was never lost on me.

Being the recipient of such tough love never seemed to alter our behaviour, but it probably kept its scope to reasonable proportions. Of course, so much of what we did was never tied to us and I will forever be thankful for that. And if we spent a lot of time avoiding a smack from our mother, we exhausted even more dodging one from various characters on the estate. The tattooed loon who was forever doing up his custom car, sullying the tarmac with oil for a ten metre radius from his front door, never found out it was me who smashed the windscreen of his prized asset, for example.

To this day, I have a curious passion for the flight of objects, a primitive pleasure in the arc of a ball or the flat hover of a Frisbee. It is why I can never play ball games with my kids in the garden because I will just *have* to smack the ball into the garden three doors down, just to see it fly. On one hot afternoon, bored and looking for trouble, I sent a stone sky-high with my old tennis racquet, childishly gratified by the gorgeous 'ping' of the strings as the stone hit the sweet spot and I watched, transfixed, as it looped high into the air. After it reached its zenith and began the journey back to earth, I watched it drop behind the block, and for a brief second I was annoyed that my view of the stone's aesthetic voyage had been interrupted. Half a second later I heard the unmistakeable sound of a windscreen being hit by a piece of rock travelling at terminal velocity. Then the shrieks rang out.

'Oi!! What farkin caarnt did that, the farkin caarnts?!'

Nothing my mother could deliver would have matched the punishment he would have dished out and I was sufficiently terrified as to nearly empty myself right there and then. I was already hidden in the stairwell when he, his pals and his large Alsatian careened around the corner looking for the culprit. To be honest he was probably expecting a sniper, so shockingly abrupt was the explosion of glass around him as he fiddled with the wiring in the footwell. Some while later, on one of the Residents' Association coach trips to Margate, I heard him tell this story, and he clearly retained a desire for homicidal revenge within his heart. I tried not to look guilty as his cohorts chorused their disapproval. Apparently, my act had necessitated his pilfering of another windscreen from a similar car.

I was more moronic than malicious in my vandalism, but, like Frank Spencer in *Some Mothers Do 'Ave 'Em,* I could cause pandemonium in a split second of brainless curiosity. Like the time I set the entire adventure playground in Bishops Park ablaze by lighting a mini fire to keep warm under the main climbing frame. Within seconds, the little fire had erupted into a conflagration that began to race up the thick telegraph poles supporting the structure. Four fire engines raced past me to the inferno as I ran sobbing from the park, and I spent months avoiding all contact with the outside world, absolutely sure guilt was written all over my face. For days, soot and minor burns *were* written all over my face. It meant hundreds of kids from Fulham and Hammersmith had to find something else to do while they rebuilt the playground. Likewise, helping a local milkman on his round lasted only a brief time. He'd asked me to drive the float around a small roundabout on a housing estate so that it would face the other way. I overdid the corner, and woke the entire estate as the float, riding on two outer wheels at 45 degrees to the road, emptied most of its bottled load onto the tarmac.

Back at the matriarchal prizefight, there was no hiding for my mother's opponent, but it *was,* as I said, her lucky day. Of course, as her set perm flicked from side to side in time with the blows that were crashing into the side of her head, she would not have seen it that way, but I could honestly attest to it. As it was, my mother appeared to have only those lethal hands and a shopping bag at her disposal. The bag, I noticed, was emptied of milk, pasta and sundry items and was lying crumpled on the ground, evidence that its contents had already been deployed in battle. Had the woman – whose retaliation merely consisted of gripping with despairing, white-knuckled fear to my mother's coat – managed to break free of the rain of blows, Mum would have retreated behind a flowerbed with the shopping and begun to chuck it. The outcome would have been just as messy for the victim.

'I willa fucky killa you!' screamed my Mum as another shuddering clout hit its mark. 'My son issa NOT inna fucky borstal!'

Even amid the guttural squawks of shock and the noise of the baying crowd, the emphasis was resounding. The woman had made the mistake of suggesting to my mother that Serge, rather than being in a school that required an 11–plus pass grade to get in, was, merely by dint that he slept there, in a borstal. If she had mentioned that Matteo actually *was* in a borstal, there would have been no problem. As the sickening sound of another slap resonated between the rosebuds I heard my mother snarl: 'Notta dissa one, anyway!'

★ ★ ★

Mum's fight in the flats ended any lingering doubts I might have been harbouring about the purpose of Woolverstone and the value that it held for her. With an absent husband, two older children on a knife-edge between total apathy and disaster and the lingering threat of more to come, Woolverstone's welcome embrace was something she reciprocated by clutching it in her arms with great pride; you could criticise much about her and her children if you so pleased, but Woolverstone was unimpeachable. The ruckus also meant that my friends became exquisitely polite whenever they called for me.

Politeness on the estate was always for a reason, never natural. We would be polite to shopkeepers if we thought they might top up the bag with a few extra gobstoppers, or we would offer gracious assistance to the porter when it seemed possible he would throw us a fifty pence piece. More likely, the porter would be hurling abuse and fury at us as we scurried from the roof of his workshop. Now, however, there were two very compelling reasons to be especially polite to my mother: the hands of granite. If they hadn't seen the fight then my friends would have heard about it, and, by dint of the estate grapevine, the story would have been vividly embroidered by the time it reached their ears. If they had worn ties, they would have tightened and straightened them as they knocked on our door to call for me.

'Mrs Volpe, can Mike come out to play?'

'No, fuggoff!'

'OK, Mrs Volpe, thanks Mrs Volpe.'

At about that period Serge had been at Woolverstone

for a year or so. He had departed without fanfare, and we would get a phone call from him occasionally. Usually, I would hear Mum trying to reassure him and telling him not to cry with obvious homesickness, but I thought he was being a bit of a wuss and that this was no way to build me up for my intended impending departure. I think he and a friend even ran away once, appearing at home several hours after Mum got a warning phone call from the school. Nowadays of course, a fully-fledged police hunt and an HSE inspection would ensue, but Woolverstone had enough confidence in a boy's ability to find the A12 not to call out the brigades. Despite Serge's desertion, I wasn't spending too much time worrying about joining him and I liked visiting him there, imagining the day when I could sample some of the fun he talked about having when he wasn't despising every waking moment and hitch-hiking his way back to London to escape. I thought that leaving Fulham and replacing my estate for one seventy-four acres bigger and several shades greener would be a doddle, and I was still, at that time, getting excited whenever I saw a cow in a field.

Honesty compels me to say that I really don't remember what I was thinking about the prospect of Woolverstone, but I don't recall being overly worried about it. Given the rebelliousness of my nature and what was becoming an erratic emotionality that was most evident in my tantrums and rejection of authority at primary school, it is reasonable to expect that I should have been concerned by the school's express desire to weed that sort of thing out of its pupils. Of course, I might have been concerned if I'd had any idea what the place was all about, which of course I didn't. The fog of ignorance was evidently a protective veil behind which I merrily carried on regardless. I did often contemplate my impending change of circumstances, and it is possible, I suppose, that I could give a retrospective treatise on the thought processes I was going through, but I would be making it up, just projecting backwards. Applying intelligent analysis to the significantly less-than-bright behaviour of a boy four decades ago can never be anything but revisionist, but if I can't now shine a positive light on what I was up to, I daren't imagine how bad I looked in 1976.

I have struggled through the process of remembering my childhood in Fulham Court. The period from our arrival when I was five to my departure for Woolverstone is muddled and confused and my mind plays tricks with chronology. I remember the *sort* of things we did; particular highlights stand out, as do 'trends' such as our constant presence at Fulham Baths. Swimming was something all of us did well. I think all of us won prizes in the inter-borough championships at Lime Grove baths in Shepherds Bush. I know I did, and somewhere there is a newspaper cutting of my eldest brother Lou with his prize. Swimming was cheap and kept us off the streets – although not necessarily out of trouble.

Fulham Baths were staggeringly beautiful. It was a classical Victorian bathhouse with three swimming pools (Ladies', Men's and Mixed), all with a gallery around them for spectators, old iron pillars, exquisitely tiled walls and mosaic floors. There were also real baths where people could go and get clean, and a huge laundry. All that is left today is the façade, behind which a rump of the entrance hall still stands and in which a dance studio and gym have been created. It's hard to believe that this masterpiece of municipal design could have become the victim of such grotesque vandalism and been replaced with identikit housing without some back-handers. We always suspected corruption at every level of our lives, and we certainly knew of many incidents involving the local constabulary. However, when I was a child, Fulham baths was my church, my playground and just about my everything. Paying a few pence for hours of fun, we would walk the huge corridor that seemed to go on forever and ever to the changing rooms, where baskets were collected, filled with our belongings and then handed back to the attendant to place on a numbered shelf. Emerging through the shallow foot cleaning pools into the main baths was like entering another world. The cacophony of noise that greeted you was thunderous, and in the mixed pool, the biggest of the three, hundreds of people, mainly kids, were busy jumping in and splashing around. Not much actual swimming went on here. My brothers, my friends and I all became familiar with the surroundings and of course, began to take advantage. We let off the big hosepipes and did all of the things the signs around the pool forbade us do: 'No running, no diving, no petting.' The petting part I can't claim to have indulged in fully at that age, but an exploratory fumble of Matt's latest girlfriend's assets with his (if not her) blessing proved instructional nonetheless.

Occasionally, the pool attendants became the target of our japery, and I do recall one day when the head man of the pool was thrown in by a gang of us, only to get out and reveal he had a couple of hundred quid tucked into his short pockets. He showed us the sopping wet bank notes to prove it and barred us all for a week as punishment. They used to throw us in, too, the attendants, disobeying their own rules, and such an incident resulted in a trip to hospital for me and another pool user. Four of them had grabbed me and pitched me backwards into the pool, but as I flew into the water, a swimmer emerged beneath me and my heel connected with his tooth, which tore an inch-long gash into my foot before going through his lip.

Fulham Baths was where we all came together. It kept us out of Mum's hair for a while, and although our hair and eyes were burned by the hours in chlorinated water, it was probably healthy too. But it could only occupy us for some of the time and, naturally, dangers lurked around every corner. Woolverstone was thus a genuine glimpse of hope for Mum.

At this point, you might be wondering what Woolverstone actually *was*. Simply put, it was an experiment, and it sought to prove that if you took under-privileged boys, often from broken homes, and gave them a public school-style education, you would see some remarkable results. In the fifties, the Inner London Education Authority bought a large country estate in Woolverstone, near Ipswich, employed a batch of extremely talented teachers and established a school of three hundred and sixty boys, although that number wouldn't be reached for several years. Children from families similar to mine who had shown academic promise at primary school were put through the eleven-plus test and sent for selection. It was considered to be the leading state boarding school in the country and offered an almost unimaginable opportunity for most who attended. That is, of course, if we ever used our imagination or knew what an opportunity was.

Woolverstone was costly, controversial in its day but, ludicrously, the product of a debate that had people trying to convince everybody else that you needed wealth if you wanted brains. Somebody, somewhere saw that to be the drivel it was and set out to prove them wrong; it was a time when you could do things like that, when the country had imagination and real courage.

The fifties presented boys of a somewhat different hue to those of us born in the sixties, and even the discipline we experienced (of which, more later) was watered down over the decades before I arrived. If the truth be told, most whose fate delivered them into Woolverstone's embrace took the chance with both hands. I would pull mine away at the last moment and poke my tongue out. It has been said of Woolverstone that it took kids from a Labour background, put them in a Tory setting and produced anarchists, but what it actually turned out were many talented and successful young men who went on to great things. Those of us who never progressed to the first rank of writers, sportsmen, actors or academics were satisfied with our success at having made it to voting age both alive and not in prison. Whether it was enough for those who conceived the idea of Woolverstone, I don't know, but it was nevertheless an achievement of which the school could be justly proud.

A teacher at our primary school had put Serge forward for the school. Our two older brothers had attended local comprehensives and taken rather less interest in academia than was felt to be acceptable. I am not sure if there was a social reason for sending Serge, but I am sure it came as something of a relief to our mother. Life was continuing to play silly buggers with her. She had no husband, no money and four energetic, troublesome boys, all of us by sheer necessity latchkey kids. But her devotion to us remained undimmed and, if anything, took on a frenetic quality designed to counter the dangers we continued to expose ourselves to.

By my ninth birthday, the police, porters and sundry other allegedly upstanding members of the community were becoming frequent visitors to our door, reporting daily misdemeanours. The sense of mortification Mum first felt when she realised the authorities were taking a regular interest in her children was soon replaced by a relief that the complainant was not reporting anything more sinister or catastrophic than minor theft. I suppose that's what happens in such families, and why the unalterable decline of a youngster's behaviour establishes itself, because those who might guide him elsewhere become thankful that he is not doing something worse. For our part, we quickly got used to it and soon learned the nature of a knock at the door.

The letterbox doubled as a doorknocker, and a policeman would lift it and deliberately crack it down three times; tension coursed through the house when that happened and often Matt would plead with us to say he was out.

Sometimes he would fly up the stairs and out of the bedroom window onto the parapet high above the forecourt. Girls sometimes knocked for Matt, tearful at the negligence he had shown, and they would produce the same response from him. Porters flicked the knocker up twice in rapid succession, but irked neighbours flapped it repeatedly until the door was opened, often accompanying the hysterical banging with curses and shouting. The impossibly cheerful man from the Pru whistled his way around the estate so you heard him coming before his single, measured snap of the letterbox resonated through the flat. Friends would often dispense with the knocking and just shout our names through the slit in the door. But one day, there came a knocking that we had never before heard. It was a gentle tap on the small square panes of glass that made up the upper half of the door, and the delicacy of this summons disguised a complaint of a viciousness we had not yet encountered. And the messengers were nuns.

With Serge and me, her two youngest, Mum made several efforts to keep us on the straight and narrow, which included sending us to Sunday school, because, despite never going to church herself, Mum was a dutiful Catholic. God existed, the Pope was his man on planet Earth, you go to Hell if you are bad and Heaven if you are good and everyone associated with the Church was beyond reproach. Mum would not be averse to thinking God her punisher when times were hard, and I remember considering how unfair this was, that God should make life so hard for her. Some God, I thought. Eventually I just thought He was a bastard, and it wasn't too long before I rubbished the whole idea completely. Mum's dutiful adherence (for it was never a devotion) was expressed through cheesy images of Christ, which littered our walls or adorned ornaments, none of which, incidentally, would ever be thrown at us. So, even though religion was only something that existed by default in the background, Serge and I would have to get our communion at the very least.

Sunday school took place in a hall at the back of St Thomas's off Dawes Road, a pretty little parish church with a small, eerie graveyard next to it. All who attended disliked Sunday school, but Serge and I loathed it. The nuns who taught us seemed to believe that wearing a habit entitled them to treat children badly, and we retaliated in the only way we knew how, which was to make their bible sessions as chaotic as possible.

To my mother, nuns were one step removed from the Almighty, so having two of them cast small, bottle-shaped Holy shadows across her doormat triggered a most profound horror; policemen were one thing, but two small women in habits was quite another. As my brother and I sat at the top of the stairs, listening to them lie softly through their teeth about what we'd supposedly done, our own horror was turning up in large trucks. Their serene and tenderly delivered fabrication was the smiling assassin personified, as if Carlos the Jackal and Mr Ruby had come straight over from a fancy dress party. I don't even remember what they said, but if it involved the immolation of skewered infants, the defrocking of the priest or pissing in the Holy Water (actually, that one is true) then it featured in their evidence. Mum stood in the doorway, ashamed and contrite, and, when the testimony had ended, quietly shut the door. That's when she began her ascent towards us, and in the mood she was in, there was a real possibility that our inevitable descent to the Pit would begin very soon indeed. Before she reached the door of our shared bedroom, we had managed to throw every potential weapon into a cupboard and were each on our respective beds, a foot waving defensively in the air. Serge was already promising to say that it was me who had fouled the Holy Water, all the while preparing for the onslaught. It occurred to me that in her fury, Mum still might throw the guinea pig's cage at us, but there was no time to hide it. I need not have worried. This was going to be so much more personal. As Mum traversed the landing at the top of the stairs without touching the carpet and exploded through the door, something new was etched into the expression on her face. Accompanying the familiar look of exasperation now was terror; panic at what might befall the mother of not one, but two anti-Christs.

'Mum! Mum! They were lying!' Serge protested with desperate vehemence.

'Nuns donta fucky tella lie, you devil bastardo!' she screamed. And with a bloodcurdling: '*Il dio lo perdona*!' the hands of granite turned into a blur as she went from Serge to me and back to him again, his outrageous slur against Carlos and Jack bringing added reproof. Every blow was an offering to the Almighty, and the harder she smacked, the further from the Inferno she would drag herself. She may well have been reciting the Lord's Prayer too, but I couldn't hear over the sound of our howling.

I have mistrusted nuns ever since. We had committed sufficient crimes to warrant an honest complaint so the embellishments were malicious and unnecessary. The lesson I took from that day was not that I should avoid a beating from Mum by behaving well in Sunday school, but that people, no matter what their apparent status or principles, will always lie. Everyone does it for malignant and benign reasons. They do it to get what they want, they do it to get someone else into trouble, and, of course, they do it in order to avoid getting caught for their own crimes or misdemeanours. I always knew that I told fibs, but that incident shattered the notion that responsible adults are intrinsically trustworthy. Until then, adults had told the truth as far as I was concerned; it was us little buggers who had to do the fibbing, but now I knew differently. For the world at large, that revelation was a bit of a disaster. It tends to shape much of what I do now, too, which is a good thing, I think, because nothing surprises me about anybody.

I learned another lesson that day, too; that lying couldn't possibly be a sin if two of the Lord's most staunch disciples were so accomplished at it. And if it was, there was always confession to fall back on, although facts rarely broke cover in there either. After Sunday school had ended, we were made to line up in the polished pews of the church to which our classroom was attached, and, one by one, we filed into the confessional. As young children, we never fully understood the point of coughing to everything we had done that week, but this was a step beyond even that, since you were supposed to tell a disembodied voice about all those bad thoughts you'd been having about Danielle Pike in the playground. Naturally allergic to the truth, we therefore found confession a difficult proposition. The nuns had spent so much time threatening us with Hell and Damnation, we were sure our misdemeanours would guarantee a ticket to Everlasting Torment. But we weren't impressed by the nun's threat that God would know if we lied, because after their visit to our house we had evidence of their duplicity, proving He could be tricked. And if He couldn't be tricked, then those nuns would be bashing anvils and eating babies alongside us in the Infernal Pit of Anguish. We hadn't yet begun to question the existence of a vengeful deity, though we thought He could obviously be a bit of a spiteful git, but we did doubt His ability to be in several places at once so questions remained. No chances could therefore be taken and we chose not to lie at all. Instead, we simply declared only the mundane.

Taking a seat in the confessional always felt a little threatening, even without Mother Superior's vituperative instruction. It was dark, smelled of old wood and incense and had a grave-sounding male voice emanating from a mesh in the wall, so it was no wonder we felt a sense of foreboding about spilling our beans. But in driving home their threats of Everlasting Wretchedness, the nuns had found no time to explain the whole point of confession, its secrecy and confidentiality, nor the reason we were seeking to confess in the first place. It's no surprise that we subverted the whole purpose of it. The perverse desire to avoid exculpation in a confessional meant the week's adventures were reduced to the completely anodyne and inconsequential. Theft, arson, sadistic torment and getting spontaneous erections during games of kiss-chase were out of the question.

'Forgive me, Father, for I have sinned.'

'Yes, my son, what is it?'

'Errrm . . . I told George Williams to fuck off in the playground.'

'. . . Is that it?'

'Isn't that bad, then?'

'No, no. Have you done anything else, I mean?'

'Umm. I looked up Danielle Pike's skirt?'

I really did look up Danielle's skirt. We were something of an item at Addison Gardens primary school, but I was still a little sheepish about displaying any affection for her. We would all play kiss-chase in the playground and Danielle would lead a posse of her friends in pursuit of me. When they cornered me – and some of them were quite aggressive about it – I would fall to the floor and curl up in a ball to protect myself from the kisses that would rain in. Whilst on the floor, though, I could sneak a peek up the skirts of the chasers, and Danielle's was always a treat because she was the one I loved. And her knickers were always pure white, not grey and rumpled like some of the other girls'. I was heartbroken when she was taken to live in the country somewhere and left me stranded, to be chased by the remnants of her posse, none of whom I peeked up the skirt of with as much relish as I did with Danielle. I knew looking up a girl's skirt was bad, naughty, and probably sinful, but I was unworried by the price I might have to pay for it in the everlasting, so I offered it in the confessional.

I never said the 'Hail Marys' I was frequently ordered
to recite. Our inability to grasp the tenets of the religion
was almost exclusively down to the zealous way in which
the nuns sought to inculcate us with the principles of
Holiness, Goodness, Righteousness Or Else. As with all
fundamentalists, they had neither the wit nor the will to
present the benign face of their religion for fear it would
lack impact. Controlling and turning us into mini-zealots,
afraid of our own shadows was their over-riding aim. Given
the opportunity to be washed of all sin for another week,
we were more prepared to allow it to build up ceaselessly
and hope we could cut a deal with Him when the time
came. I would hate you to think me anti- religion; I'm not
really, but for me whenever I hear a serious debate on one
issue or another, the introduction of a religious viewpoint
has the effect of reducing the matter to silliness, like farting
at a funeral. Apparently sane individuals, with obvious
intellect, will apply the teachings of Jesus to the travails
of single mothers. It leaves me wondering why they even
bothered with an education. Anyway, there you are.

Our seemingly endless capacity for misbehaviour, and
the resultant trials and worries, distressed Mum. It just
wore her down, and there were evenings when it all got
too much and she would march out of the house, vowing
never to return. It would take my brothers several minutes
to convince me that she had only gone next door to the
neighbour to cry and get a break. I'd be crying too,
convinced she had left us.

Woolverstone must have arrived like a beacon of light,
a lifeboat in the storm, a big, whopping helping hand. As

boys at risk of taking several unseemly paths in life, Serge and I certainly needed it – but Mum needed it more. For two years after Serge went away to school, she had the relative luxury of just my two older brothers and me to worry about. One of those – Matt – was providing plenty of anxiety on his own and would continue to do so for decades, but the thought that her two youngest would soon be established, safe and sound, at one of the best schools in the country must have been a balm for her over-worked, on-the-edge life. Of course, I had to actually get into the school and I sat the eleven-plus to that end. I wasn't aware I was sitting the test, nor that it was being used to judge my suitability for Woolverstone, but I did well enough to be invited to meet the headmaster in a room at County Hall. I wasn't daunted by the interview, but I was always wary of being called into offices where stern men would speak to me. But Paddy Richardson wasn't stern at all, and I liked him immediately. The narrow office had a window that looked out onto the Thames and when I wasn't gazing over his shoulder at the Houses of Parliament, I was telling him I wanted to be an astronaut, or failing that, I would be a carpenter. What must have seemed flippant answers to his questions didn't prevent me getting the nod: I was off to Woolverstone in the following September.

It was an easy afternoon, my first encounter with Paddy, an adult I felt I could immediately trust. His good nature and my self-centred approval of him aside, it was his assurance that I would be given a place at Woolverstone that meant the most. So on the warm thermals of Mum's enormous sigh of relief we drifted out of County Hall and back to Fulham where I set about telling everybody I knew that I was going to Woolvo. I told Serge on the phone when he rang soon after; he sounded less than ecstatic, I must confess, but as with everything, I wore my achievement as a badge of honour; something to set me apart. I must have been insufferable.

It is almost impossible to articulate the scale of Woolverstone's *otherworldliness*. I wasn't just going to the good school up the road when everyone else was attending the shit comp around the corner. It was so much more than that. I would be 'moving away', I would vanish from the estate for weeks, months on end and would be entering a world that we couldn't even imagine, save for the old films we had seen, like *Goodbye Mr Chips*. This was interplanetary, by contrast, and if you were going to such a place there was a form of celebrity to be had. It was a distinction that to my mind merely confirmed that I was something indisputably unique. At Addison Gardens, my achievement was announced in assembly; the staff clapped, but the rest of the kids looked terrified, as if I had been sentenced to death. In class, the teacher would say things like, 'For a boy who is going to Woolverstone, this handwriting is dreadful, Michael', or in games I would be told that, 'Woolverstone will expect a little more effort than that young man', and so it went on, endlessly. I became aware that great things were expected of me. At the time, it was water off a duck's back, of course.

GETTING READY

Despite having a posse of friends in Fulham Court, I wasn't overly bothered by the prospect of leaving town for five years, returning only during school holidays. There was certainly a feeling of pride in being chosen to go to Woolverstone, despite the sense of expectation that was mounting around me, and I was looking forward to my departure as an adventure. Probably because boarding school seemed to them a horror of unimaginable scale, or more likely because I was bragging so much that they would be pleased to see the back of me, I am not convinced that my friends were too fussed about my departure, either. We carried on playing together on the estate, but when they talked about going to secondary school, it was a conversation to which I could not contribute – or was never really allowed to. I could tell them the things I knew about Woolverstone from visiting Serge, but they were more interested in life at St Clement Dane's or St Edmund's or, for the brighter ones, the London Oratory. These were the schools where everyone but me would spend their formative years. However, the gentle casting out that I experienced was, in my eyes, a confirmation of my superiority.

The final months before I left for Suffolk were, then, a period of time when I began to separate myself emotionally from my friends. I stayed indoors a bit more than usual and fewer mates came to call for me. On the other hand, I knew they would miss the free ice-creams I could bag for them when my father turned up outside the estate in his Mr Whippy van a couple of times a week.

Dad's departure when I was a baby saw him decamp to Wandsworth, so he was still in the vicinity. He had become an oil lorry driver, and sometimes he'd even take one or two of us out on his rounds delivering heating oil to offices and schools. I always found such days exciting, if only for sitting high in the cab of a lorry. Dad was not very committed to his work, but he did the minimum he had to, and, of course, taking us in the cab of his truck was not particularly legal. The daily drudge was never going to exert much control over him for long; only the odds at Ladbrokes and his overwhelming aversion to responsibility could do that (not to mention the contents of his trousers), so he decided to do something that required less work and, more importantly, did not impose on him a boss to whom he had to defer. However, this repugnance towards any kind of work was in direct and knotty conflict with his love of gambling, so, using an admirably entrepreneurial logic, he bought himself an ice cream van.

Ice cream had universal appeal. It was cheap to produce (he just bought vats of a ready mixed liquid that he poured into the top of a machine), and the demand for a little luxury on the council estates was high. He would only have to work for a few hours a day and could still earn enough in cash to spend a few hours throwing it away again in the betting shop.

The predictability of coming from an Italian family with an ice-cream man for a father was obvious even to me. For a civilisation of the richest history imaginable, Italy does have some unspeakably naff cultural icons. I blame the Cornetto ads for much of that. My Uncle Matteo, who also now lived in London, spent a great deal of time and evangelical zeal trumpeting the delights of Italian art, music, fashion and architecture, and I merely repeated to my friends everything he said. This was when I first began to hear opera and Italian music; my uncle would preach to me about Mario Lanza and play his records. A strange Welsh chap who lived next door to him used to come into the flat and drink whisky; like many Welshmen, he thought he could sing and wailed along to the records in a creaky tenor voice. Mantovani got an airing too, but curiously, so did Bob Marley, who my uncle was very fond of (what the neighbours made of the musical cocktail emanating from his front-room window I dread to think). Frankly, the leap from the reverberated strings of 'The Greatest Gift is Love' to 'Kinky Reggae' is one no man should reasonably attempt to make. Marley and Lanza I thought were cool; Mantovani I placed alongside Cornettos, the circus owner in *Pinocchio* and the arse pinchers in Rome – all of them made me cringe. I continued to regale everybody with outlandish stories of summers in Montecorvino and to advocate the wonders of Da Vinci à la zio Matteo, but the advertising industry was busy dismantling the reputation I was working so very hard to establish for

Italian cultural superiority. It was a rearguard action on my part – one I think may have eventually succeeded – but since Michelangelo, Caravaggio or Verdi rarely drifted through the collective consciousness of Fulham Court's youth, *gelato* would have to suffice as a cultural reference. Simply put, my personal status came before that of the Motherland.

Dad's van generally arrived in the early evenings. Suddenly, from every balcony, mothers would emerge from their doors behind wet dangling washing and scream the names of their children, beckoning them to attend immediately. Usually, the children had already been alerted and were sprinting to the forecourts below their flats to await orders. Coins and notes would rain down from on high as parents babbled instructions to their children who would then rush off to Dad's van. I am not sure why there was such urgency – as with life, I suppose, they thought they might miss out if they didn't get in quick enough.

For me, the arrival of my father was a moment to be relished. Of course, I would have *preferred* him to turn up accompanied by the roar of a Ferrari engine, not the wobbly chimes of his clapped out Mr Whippy van, but those bells were the starter gun for all the kids whose parents had not anointed them from on high with silver coins. Like bees to a honey pot, from every direction they would gather about me in swarms. It mattered not one bit where I was on the estate because I would be hunted down and found. You could hear the relay of shouted enquiry across the forecourts and playgrounds: 'Where's Mike? Find Mike!' I would wait smugly for my coterie to arrive, puffing and panting, eager to impress. If I were indoors, Mum would send me out, if nothing else to consume some time in the company of my father, with an order for a block of ice cream.

'And tella you fadda I'm no gotta ma mentenence dissa week,' she would call as I slammed the door behind me. 'AND NO SLAMMA DA FUCKY DOOR!'

If they had not yet knocked on my door, having fruitlessly searched for me in the Court, my friends would be waiting at the foot of the stairs, fervent, excited and hugely pleased to see me. They would take it in turns to put their arms around my shoulders as we skipped hurriedly towards the chimes, and fights would erupt as kids argued over which of them was my best friend. By the time we reached Dad's van at the Shottendane Road entrance of the estate, we must have looked like the Bash Street Kids, approaching in a comic-book cloud of dust from which arms and legs would occasionally protrude. Peace would return the moment we arrived at the van and I began to bark out orders to Dad, although nothing that my friends asked for was given. You could have a cone, a cone and if you were really lucky, you could have a cone. They came in three sizes, all of them small. Anyone who had the temerity to request red sauce would get short shrift and very likely no cone either. And even I couldn't get a chocolate flake. Tutting and rolling his eyes heavenwards at the demands of us children, Dad was never outwardly pleased to see me. Eventually, I would relay Mum's order and he would grudgingly hand me a small block of ice cream to take home. If his tip for the 2.30 at Plumpton had come in, it would be raspberry ripple. Ice cream was just about the only thing my father ever gave us, but sometimes even that felt like treasure. As we were about to trot off to enjoy the delights of frozen vanilla-flavoured fat, I would remember Mum's other instruction.

'Mum says she wants her money this week.' Often I would have to shout it again, but louder, so he could hear over the large crowd of customers who had gathered.

★ ★ ★

The scorching summer of 1976 also saw me spend two weeks in hospital with an ailment that left the doctors baffled. An agonising pain in my hip and groin left me unable to move during school sports day, and immobility in the fierce sun had led to sunstroke. I ended up in hospital with an acute fever and lots of pain. Putting two and two together and getting five, the doctors suspected rheumatic fever. They took what felt like several pints of blood and, when that proved inconclusive, they took several more, then stuck me on an ECG monitor, X-rayed me, poked me, prodded me and generally acted as if they hadn't a clue. My consultant was the bow-tie-wearing Mr Jolly, apparently one of the world's leading paediatricians of his day. These days I always treat people who wear bow ties with suspicion, and it's common in the classical music industry, but back then it set Mr Jolly apart and I was chuffed when a year or so later I saw him on the television.

'That was *my* doctor,' I would proudly announce to

anybody who was listening, which was everybody if I had my way.

I ought to point out that this was my second stint in hospital; two years previously, I had spent a fortnight in a private room in the maternity unit. I was there because my injury was burns and they had to isolate me as a sterile measure, and the only private room they had was in the maternity ward. I am almost reluctant to relay the cause of my misfortune since it can paint a picture of foolhardy negligence on the part of Mum – but it wasn't really. I was nine years old when it happened, and it was the same hospital, New Charing Cross (as it was then known) in Hammersmith, that picked up the pieces.

Every morning I had a cup of tea. I liked tea. Lou, my eldest brother loved it, so I would too. Mum called us down in the morning, and I stumbled into the lounge in my vest and underpants, half asleep. I came to my senses a bit when Mum brought me the mug of tea, which I took from her, but ten seconds later promptly fell asleep again. The scalding tea was quite an eye-opener, and I sprinted, screaming, up the stairs, sure Mum would wallop me for spilling tea on the sofa. Serge and Lou came charging after me, I thought either to help deliver the walloping or to protect me from it, but it was in fact to assess the serious-ness of my injuries, which they assumed would be bad. They were. The pain was ugly, all-consuming and fright-eningly angry. Blisters began to form immediately, and by now most of the neighbours were in the house wondering what the commotion was. I wasn't happy about that because in my desperation to escape the hot fluid, I had whipped off my pants and vest as I charged up the stairs and was now stark naked, embarrassed that my wedding tackle was involved in the injury. Whilst an ambulance was called, Mum tried to set about me with a tub of butter, which back in the old country she had always thought best for the treatment of burns. Thankfully, Lou was wiser; he stopped her basting me and put me in a cold bath instead.

I was delivered by ambulance and hospital trolley to the room in the maternity unit and isolated immediately. I don't remember going to A&E first. Everybody who visited or came to treat me had to don full gowns, masks and gloves. The first person I recall standing at the end of my bed as I sobbed was a social worker – no doubt alerted by the hospital. She was crying too (more than me, to which I took offence, actually). I didn't know why she was crying. Was I such a pitiable sight? I didn't recognise her so I can't imagine she was weeping on account of my being familiar to her, that I was somebody about whom she cared a great deal. But she was blubbing like a bloody baby, and with hindsight one can now conclude that she was probably more familiar with me than I was with her. *Someone* was clearly paying attention to us.

My lap and upper legs were smothered in blisters and a cold burns sheet had been placed on my injured nether regions. I peeked fearfully beneath it (for even at nine, thanks to kiss-chase and visits to Fulham baths I had become aware of the value of my equipment) and noticed that a blister had formed *right at the tip* of my old chap. Thankfully it was the only one, but it did have a deforming effect that made my willy look like an unpeeled prawn.

Two weeks later three doctors and a nurse gathered around me as if in an operating theatre, with an array of alarming utensils arranged neatly on a steel trolley, and proceeded to pop each of the blisters one by one. Some were huge, and collectively they looked like the cobbles on a street. I remember the warm water running as each was gently sliced at its edge and I recall the stench of the ointment they bathed me in. It was a tough time being alone in that room, but my brothers walked past my window on the way to school and they, along with their friends, shouted and greeted me through the glass. That was something I always looked forward to.

Now of course, this second stint in hospital with a mystery leg ailment meant further difficulties for Mum. Fitting in visiting me was taxing since she had to be in her kitchen at the nursery by 7am and then had a job to go to after feeding the rest of my brothers. Mum would sit by my bed at five thirty in the morning whilst I slept and would then go to work – I rarely knew she was there in the silent, sleeping ward in semi-darkness but she sat there anyway. One morning I did emerge from my deep, medically assisted slumbers and saw her crying. Her tears were not of sadness, though, but of relief; the traction they had put me into the previous day seemed to have done the trick.

I vividly (and with no little upset) recall the day they resorted to traction. They were baffled by my ailment and the extent of my pain. Standing around my bed in a huddle one morning, the doctors discussed many possible options and treatments, but the one thing I latched onto was traction – strapping my leg and tying a weight to my foot in order to extend and stretch it. To me it seemed like the most concrete idea they'd had because it was practical, obvious and tangible. They wandered off to make some decisions, and I began to wail at the nurses that I wanted, must have, just *had* to go into traction. I cried and cried with the pain, and a poor cleaner, a gentle Jamaican woman, tried to comfort and reassure me, eventually dissolving into tears alongside me as she did so. We were quite a sight, and when she could take no more of my pleading, bawling and snivelling she marched off to the nurse's station on my behalf to demand that I be put into traction.

A little later, two nurses, armed with a roll of sticky plaster, some weights and a pulley, performed the duty that in my mind had been demanded and achieved by that lovely cleaning woman. She had got it done, nobody else. And she remains a clear memory for me, that soft compassionate lady whose name I never knew; another of those small but hugely significant people or moments in the lives of certain children that pass by in a fleeting second, yet are burned into their consciousness. Many years later, at the birth of my first daughter, that cleaner sprang straight back into my mind as the Jamaican midwife handed the baby to her weeping father with the words, 'Here you go, bwoy wonder!'

It was the morning after the installation of the pulley and weights that Mum had come into the ward to find me lying, blissfully asleep, on my side – the side of the leg that had been so excruciatingly painful to the merest touch the day before. The mystery had been solved. It had only been a trapped nerve, and so she wept; relieved that from that day forward her mind would no longer be suffused with the worry of what might be wrong with me.

Putting me into traction solved the leg problem, and antibiotics cleared up the chest infection but the sunstroke had struck me quite hard. They wanted to keep me in so that my leg could strengthen and to check there would be no recurrence. I was out of traction after a few days, but I would spend a further fortnight in the ward. Two weeks in hospital turned out to be quite a bit of fun and needing a wheelchair introduced a unique opportunity for mischief. I took the chance with relish and crashed my way around the hospital with a boy whose entire bottom half was encased in plaster of Paris. He was on his belly on a little trolley, and together we caused chaos. His affliction, which made mine look like no more than a verruca, did nothing to prevent his mobility or potential for bedlam. In fact, his arms could propel him down the long corridors at giddy speed; with his legs protruding dead straight behind him and his arms waving furiously beside him, he looked like a lobster on amphetamine. He'd cry at night when his legs were aching, but he was full of beans during the daytime and even cheekier to the nurses than I was.

By the time I left the ward to go home, I was walking normally. I went to the bedside of my new friend, who had fallen quiet as Mum helped me pack up my things for the discharge. He lay there exhausted from the effort of getting up and under his covers, which he always insisted on doing without help. I felt strangely guilty for being able to walk again. We had shared the same inability to use our legs for a short while, but he had been living with it for most of his life. I don't think he minded that I had elevated my own minor ailment to the level of his, but I think he enjoyed the company for that couple of weeks. As I said my farewells tearfully, he smiled.

'Have a good time at that school, wontcha?' he urged.

'Yeah, I will. I'll come and see you before I go,' I lied.

I wish I could remember his name.

★ ★ ★

The end of summer 1976 arrived. The heat wave, which in those pre-global warming days had become a legend, subsided, and Serge was at the end of the remarkably long summer holidays that Woolverstone provided. My confidence about going there was starting to fray at the edges, and I would lie in bed, badgering Serge about the school. What would it be like? Would I enjoy it? Would I be homesick? Occupying me more than anything else was the fear that I wouldn't be the toughest boy in the year – a status I thought I enjoyed at primary school. Because I had visited the school many times previously, I had not been required to attend the open day for new boys, but Serge had been one of those showing people around and he sought to reassure me.

'I saw all of the boys coming in your year, you look harder than all of them,' he said.

It is, I suppose, an indication of what was important to me at the time that I had become concerned about such things. I was obviously sanguine about the academic challenges of Woolverstone, but that could well have been because I never truly realised there were any. It is also possible that of all the obstacles Woolverstone would place before me, the one I feared most was being a young boy who had to compete with other young boys of equal or, heaven forfend, greater potential. Serge took some time to explain the protocols and rules of the school, the regulations forbidding me to walk on the grass, rules insisting I use particular doors to enter and exit buildings and rotas for menial tasks around the house. He pointed out with desperate pleading in his eyes that things would be better for me if I developed an understanding of why these seemingly petty demands had a purpose. Naturally, none of this was making much sense or difference to me, and my brother was transparently alarmed by my imminent arrival; I would surely become a responsibility he could do without and he was aware of the explosive consequences once I was required to conform.

I don't remember being upset at the prospect of leaving Mum, my other brothers or home, but that may have been because I had a sibling to keep an eye on me. That sibling was developing quite a fear of the impending union between his little brother and his school. I was only eleven, after all, a child in all ways, but I suffered from the affliction that many eleven-year-old boys fall prey to, which is the unshakeable belief that they are twice as old. Serge was astute enough to realise that the strength of my conviction in this regard presented him, let alone the school, with complications of an acute nature.

★ ★ ★

Getting Ready

September 1976.

Wearing a uniform only added to the disquiet that was growing in me as we headed to Waterloo to take the coaches to Woolverstone for the start of term: regulation grey trousers, light blue shirt and navy blue crew neck jumper was the casual symphony of colour of the day. Apparently, it had been far more formal in years past, when boys were permanently required to wear ties, shirts and jackets. Now we only had to don blazers for Sunday assembly.

In that preceding summer, I had enjoyed the process of equipping myself for the school by going to the designated uniform suppliers and being issued with rugby kits, shirts, jumpers with the school crest, blazers, trousers et al. I especially loved the fact that Mum had to order lots of name tags with my name embroidered onto them in red, silky thread in a classical typeface. To me those name tags demonstrated why Woolverstone was a school of a different hue from any other I could have gone to. Name tags were so incredibly *posh* in my mind. These items of regulation clothing with graceful little name tags sewn into them were the first sign of Woolverstone's boundaries and expectations. Like all 'public' schools, it was essentially based on the military model and, although over time it had softened a little, there was still a curious and exciting anticipation of this regime.

If I had my way now, all schools would insist that their pupils wore the most exquisite morning suits with brutally strict rules about how to wear them. Today I understand the value of such protocols, like those at Eton, for example. It is not about conformity, this insistence on ultra-formality, it is quite the opposite and encourages the boy to feel proud and to walk tall. Behind the outward appearance of 'uniformity' is the facility for each boy to believe fully in his value within the ranks of his contemporaries. From the point of view of social value and boundaries, a boy's appearance is hugely significant. I think of it as looking after the pennies and the pounds looking after themselves; if the first thing a young man has to concern himself with in the morning is how well his shirt is ironed and his tie formed, his energy for less desirable behaviour might be curbed or diverted. Woolverstone was in no way like Eton from the sartorial point of view, but I wish it had been. In fact, I would probably have babies in nurseries wearing firmly starched nappies. Back at Waterloo on my first day, I think I was at least unconsciously aware of the point.

Anyway, a trunk full of this clothing, shoes and other accoutrements had been sent ahead by road freight, but we still had to struggle with suitcases through the concourse and out onto a small road that ran along the perimeter of the station. All about us was a growing number of Woolverstone boys in the same uniform. I could make out the first formers, who were small, pale and terrified. Well, some were small, black and terrified but there was no mistaking the fear in their eyes as other groups of older boys gathered together, smoked and made fun of each other. Serge was now in the third form and had done this many times, so as we reached the coaches, he began to greet friends, and it became clear he was at least popular in his year, but he was now less my brother and more someone who had been tasked to keep an eye on me, like a chaperone. He had a coterie of friends to whom he could clearly better relate, their shared experience being as obvious as was the lack of it with us new kids. For the first time, I came to realise the distinct worlds he inhabited – home and school. Knowing some of the people for whom he was now so keen to desert me on the pavement was strangely comforting, and I was able to work out for myself that it was only the unfamiliarity of others that was daunting; even Serge's friends would have seemed threatening had I never met them before. I also noticed that some of the kids spoke well, looked clean, very tidy and had smartly dressed parents. Crucially, they had *two* parents. Later I would discover that these boys were fairly rare and were often Forces children.

I'd had wealthy friends in London, and some of them had two parents as well, but they weren't posh. Addison Gardens was peculiarly placed in west London, between Hammersmith, Shepherd's Bush and the affluent, graceful enclave of Holland Park. Wealthy parents sent their children to Addison because it was a good primary school, and so we all mixed happily together, our respective financial positions being largely irrelevant. My best friend for a while was Manus Egan, who lived in a mansion flat in Holland Park that was so luxurious and of such vast proportion that his mother had to gently coax mine through the front door when she came to collect me after a play date. The white pile carpet in the hallway that brushed your ankles as you walked through it had the same effect on Mum that trying to jump off the top board at Putney baths had on me: she would stand at the threshold of the flat and rock backwards and forwards, always just about to take the leap only to lose her courage at the last second. Eventually she would be encouraged to plunge her feet into the shag pile but she insisted on taking her shoes off first.

The most amazing thing about the Egan's home was not the kilometre long passageway, nor the entrance hall that was larger than my bedroom, or even the kitchen that was big enough to have a large oak table at the heart of it. No, what really astounded me was the fact that their living room was so big that the sofas did not have to be lined up against the wall. I'd heard the old fable that *Doctor Who* would get kids hiding behind the sofa, and I had never understood that. My sofa was against the wall in our lounge, so how could one possibly hide behind it? The opening at the back was paper thin, dark and full of things that had been lost for months. It was a genuine curiosity to me – until I got friendly with Manus and we really did hide behind the sofa. And if we felt the need to run screaming from the room, we still had ten yards of Persian carpet to cover before we hit the door to the lounge. The Egans had money, but they weren't posh. They were Irish, and very nice people, too.

At Waterloo, I have to confess that despite my friendship with the Egans, I found many of my new schoolmates very odd creatures indeed, and I chuckled quietly to myself at some of them. Nevertheless, it still remained a little intimidating to be around so many people I didn't know, and I can only imagine the anxiety of those new boys who knew nobody at all. I soon became aware of the sixth formers, who all seemed to have whiskers and in fact looked like fully grown men. Serge's stories about them had rendered some of these aloof, trendy bigwigs as legends, normally of the rugby field. I knew of some who were regularly mentioned as bullies. Some were Good Blokes. Being labelled a Good Bloke was to be welcomed, and Good Blokes in the sixth form were a class above because they did not *have* to be Good Blokes; as seniors, they could have been unexpurgated bastards if they wanted. When you are at primary school, even the older kids still seem like kids, but now I was at school with adults, so knowing that among their number were some nice people offered reassurance. But Good Bloke or not, there was a hierarchy. These sixth formers would tell others what to do, talk to younger boys with dismissive rudeness (except for the Good Blokes, who just didn't notice them, which I suspect is all it took to be labelled a Good Bloke) and everyone seemed to defer to them.

I was largely unaware of what this all meant in real terms, and so it was no surprise that I would fail to take my place when the hierarchy swept me up. Today, I am fully behind the notion of a hierarchy in the workplace because on the whole I think it works as long as you apply scrutiny and equilibrium to what those further up the line are asking you to do. But at eleven years of age, if I had ever been compliant in a hierarchy, it was because I had conceived it, designed it and put it into practice: marbles hierarchies, penny-up-the-wall hierarchies, football-in-the park hierarchies, stunt bicycle hierarchies etc. The common factor was my position at the top of each of them because I had probably initiated the game or pastime. Either you fell into line or you didn't play. Playing alone for lots of the time didn't dissuade me from my stubbornness. At Woolverstone, first formers were at roughly the point on the totem pole where the tufts of grass are growing at the base, but for me, that was a mere inconvenience to be overcome. When, standing on the pavement waiting to board the coach, I felt a shove in the back, it was to instinct that I resorted.

'Get out of the way, pleb.'

What on earth is a pleb? I thought.

The shove shocked me since I hadn't been looking. 'Fuck off, you cunt,' I snarled in a high-pitched voice.

★ ★ ★

It continues to be a trait of mine that I don't really know when to keep a low profile. If there is a parapet, I will perch my head atop it, and if I am in a room full of people whose acquaintance I have never before made, I will still feel the need to point out which of them is an idiot. I do this not in a wantonly rude fashion but by simply persisting in exposing the error of their argument or the obnoxiousness of the way in which they propose it. That my own behaviour is loathsome is not in the least bit relevant since I will have deduced that I'm not the stupid one. In 1976 I also had a notion of indestructibility, despite excruciatingly disproportionate amounts of evidence to the contrary, which consisted mainly of physical or emotional injury mixed with a dash of humiliation.

Exhibit One would have to be Marcia Jones. Marcia was a girl in my class at primary school who also lived close by in Fulham Court. She was bigger than me, but using the logic of a small boy, which is hardly logic at all, I deduced that her size, strength and violent tendencies were neutralised by her gender. My mother's physicality was somehow excluded from whatever fur-brained theory I held on the threat carried by the opposite sex. When, on a warm summer's day, Marcia wanted to drink from the playground water tap, I refused to let her until I had finished myself. In fact, I just pursed my lips on the small upward spout of water and pretended to drink, despite having already had my fill. After a while, during which time Marcia showed commendable restraint, the game was up. Without speaking, she grabbed me by the collar and swung me away from the tap in a move of such breath-takingly effortless speed that my lips were still pursed when I realised my feet were off the ground and my body parallel to it. As I picked myself up, I was still unsure of what had actually happened to me. Before I had a chance to gather my thoughts on the matter, Marcia lunged at me and proceeded to slap me about the face and head, cursing me all the while.

The shock and embarrassment of being beaten up by a girl was cataclysmic, and I blurted something about her being lucky she was female. She and everyone else knew my reluctance to retaliate had more to do with my need to visit the school nurse, who applied iodine to my wounds. It would have needed a vat of the stuff to restore my battered and scarred ego. True to form, I resolved to take nothing of use from the experience, and some while later (a period that had clearly seen me hang on as doggedly to my obstinacy as Marcia had to her irascibility), she asked me to leave a phone box I was mucking around in. I said no.

As with the water fountain incident, Marcia waited patiently whilst I fiddled around pretending to be on the phone. I don't know why she did that: maybe she was giving me the benefit of the doubt? Perhaps she was trying to control (unsuccessfully as it always turned out) the temper that could be unleashed. Neither do I know why I felt the need to persist with what I was doing. In any case, I hadn't learned my lesson from the first time, and I was in all probability more determined to annoy her precisely because she had humiliated me. My resolve also meant that I failed to take note of how much bigger Marcia had become. The old red box shuddered as she yanked open the door and reached in with both large hands. For a second time, the sensation of weightlessness came over me. Familiar, too, was the tempo of the manoeuvre, my hand remaining next to my ear still holding a phantom phone as I hit the ground, landing ten feet away at the door of the barbershop.

Fewer people were present to witness this second assault but Toni, the barber, was enough for me. He knew all of us through my father and was always being lascivious towards Mum whenever we walked past the shop. I looked up at him, his ugly, skinny frame wrapped in his shiny aubergine barber's coat, and my heart sank. His irritatingly Hitleresque 'tache twitched with mirth beneath his ratty little nose as he proclaimed in a voice that could be heard back in old Napoli, 'Fuckinella, you godda beedup bya fucky girl!'

'*Vaffanculo* ya wanker!' I shouted as I walked away.

'Oh! I tella you fadda you say dis!' Toni squeaked.

'Yeah right,' I scoffed, 'and I'll tell 'im you fancy my Mum.'

★ ★ ★

At Waterloo, having been shoved against a wall, I let loose with a stream of expletives. I did so before I had really absorbed who it was who had pushed me, but I didn't really care. Standing there was a large, scruffy sixth former with a jacket that had leather patches on the elbows. I thought he looked ridiculous with his corduroy, lank hair and cheesecloth shirt. I also thought he looked big, but the memory of Marcia was nowhere to be found in my consciousness.

'Don't push me,' I said, undeterred by his size, age, whiskers or cheesecloth. He looked at me for a moment and smiled.

'You'll learn,' he said, before strolling off.

Of course, there wasn't a hope in hell that I would have escaped with anything less than a good hiding had he decided to express his well-practised nonchalance physically, but I didn't really know any better. My sense of indestructibility was indestructible.

★ ★ ★

Exhibit two. Lee Majors, *aka* Steve Austin *aka* The Six Million Dollar Man. Steve was busted to bits when he crash-landed his space-ship-rocket-shuttle thingy. But they could rebuild him. And so they did rebuild him, giving him bionic eyes, bionic arms and bionic legs. They also managed to invisibly repair all of the scars on his handsome face, unless, of course, the crash that took three quarters of his limbs and managed to burn his eyes out of their sockets had miraculously left his fizzer untouched. But I digress. George Williams, my bespectacled best friend *du jour* at Addison, and I were S.M.D.M. crazy. We drew pictures of Steve leaping over buildings and chucking cars, we knew every word of the episodes and we could make all the noises that would accompany his super-vision. We used to run around the playground in slow motion, just like Steve did; cleverly, instead of bothering with special effects, the programme-makers just slowed down the film whenever Steve was meant to be running as fast as a villain's Ferrari. Super-SloMo equals blisteringly fast.

Genius.

Our obsession led us to invent a new game, which involved leaping off the swings from as high as we could, pretending to be Steve pouncing from a building onto the escaping criminal. Playgrounds didn't have soft, Health and Safety-friendly rubber tarmac back then. They just had tarmac. Hard tarmac. Every landing sent a sharp shock of pain exploding through our growing ankle joints. It would hurt for five minutes, but we'd be back on the swing as soon as we could walk again. When that became monotonous (for repetitive pain by itself was never a reason to stop), real rooftops replaced the swings and we would leap across voids, twenty feet above the ground, climb drainpipes or scramble up trees. We risked life and limb, but not for a second did we think of it as dangerous.

I even began to believe that George was as shatterproof as Steve Austin, which is probably why one morning in the playground, when he had angered me for a trivial reason, I clumped him across the side of the head with my donation for Harvest Festival. Two tins of custard in a carrier bag floored George in a heartbeat. I hadn't expected him to hit the ground so quickly. In fact, I thought he would raise his bionic arm and fend off the blow, leap over me, fix me with his bionic eye and finish me off. Instead he fell straight to earth without even a stumble or stagger, his legs dissolving under him. I accused him of being soft. He was still my best friend, but our Six Million Dollar Man games came to a stop because he clearly wasn't up to it.

★ ★ ★

At Waterloo, we had to gather at the coach designated to our House. I was to be in Halls House with Serge. There were sixty boys in each house and six houses – Hall's, Berners, Johnston's, Hanson's, Orwell and Corner's. The latter was based a mile and a half from the main building in an old convent so I was glad I wasn't there. Berners boys were in the main building, and the other four houses were modern constructions arranged in two pairs joined by a long corridor. Aware of the need to develop a history,

Woolverstone named three of the four modern buildings after their original housemasters, and the last was named after the river upon which the school sat. The whole concept of houses to which one gave unswerving loyalty wasn't too difficult to grasp since it was just being a member of another gang as far as I was concerned – or a tribe – someone and something to fight for. What *did* worry me was the urgent need to confirm my place in the pecking order; even then I understood the principle of survival of the fittest.

The pushing episode and the unfamiliarity of so many of those around me were chipping away at my resolve. Thank goodness for Serge and his friends. If I ever acted my age or was ever shaken by the vulnerability of child-hood, if I had ever wanted to run and clutch at my mother's apron, it was at the moment I took my seat on the coach with boys known to each other, noisily notifying us newcomers that we were at the bottom of the pile. The Six Million Dollar Man had vanished. If I could, I would have run in Super-SloMo off the bus, leapt Waterloo in one huge bound and scurried off to Fulham and my ice-cream kingdom. I wished George Williams were there. I wished Manus Egan and Danielle Pike and the boy in the plaster trousers were with me. Hell, I even thought I'd like Marcia by my side.

Saying goodbye to my pals had been a cursory exercise, to be gotten out of the way so that my adventure could begin, but at that moment I had my first ever real lesson in the value of friends. Gazing through the window at the scuffed and dirty pavement of the Waterloo side street, wondering what was to come, I was even prepared to allow George a free whack with a couple of tins of Batchelors soup. I longed for my *fuck-yous* and *bollocks-ya-wankers* as we escaped the porter's angry grasp, and I pined for our frosty bedroom with its torn wallpaper and rickety headboards. I knew something exciting lay ahead of me, that I would begin new friendships, have adventures maybe, but what would replace the sweet home comfort of Mum's post-bath pasta fagioli, served up in the hot glow of a two-bar electric fire just in time for the latest episode of *The High Chaparral* or *Star Trek*? What would stand in for the inky smell of the paper shop, whose sweet stock we so frequently raided, or the rancid stench of the overflowing bins or the strange hybrid aroma of piss and bleach that filled the stairwells in Fulham Court?

What arguments would replace those between my oldest brother and us when we wanted *Star Trek* and he demanded the news? There would be no more football in the estate playground, no more clattering across the rusty rooftop of the covered car park and no more being chased by the unruly estate dogs who were let out like children, to play and return home when hungry. Who would sneer disapprovingly at the policemen who came to arrest my brother? Who would help Mum at five in the morning when she took the washing to the local baths to use the industrial sized laundry there? What would become of the flat on our floor in which a fire had taken the lives of three of our playmates after their mother had locked them in to go to the pub? Would other children take up residence in its rooms, which had seen their horrific history brushed away by a tin of cheap council paint? Who would play with *them*? Who would teach *them* to climb roofs, or get *them* free ice-cream and tell *them* of the ghosts that haunted their house?

All these things spun around my head as I shrank inside my bulky school jumper, feeling lost and alien. All that I had been so eager to replace with Woolverstone I began to cherish and desire like a hungry man craves stale bread. Neither the petulant, ungallant water hog nor the phone box staller was anywhere to be seen. Gone were the nun-baiter and the roof-climber. All of them had run off with Steve Austin. There were others on that coach in the same position, yearning for a thousand similar things, but knowing that offered scant consolation. Later that night I would share a dormitory with nine other new boys. Each of them had left behind lives they might have taken for granted as much as I had mine, and, at that moment, the spectacular opportunities of Woolverstone that should have been, but never would be, offered to all like us, were buried beneath the apprehensions of us lucky few. On that first frightening night in Suffolk, many unfamiliar and threatening miles from home, all ten of us sobbed quietly into our pillows.

* * *

It is strange looking back on this now, in a different decade, and a father myself. Soon after my son, Gianluca, was born, I recall the wife of a wealthy Opera Holland Park sponsor excitedly telling me of a brilliant school I ought to consider for him. She was Eastern European, I think, and had heard I lived in Maidenhead and Windsor and thought the coincidence too great to leave unmentioned.

'Oh, Michael!' she cried. 'That's so convenient. There is a fantastic school near you, and both of our boys went there. It's called Eton, have you heard of it? Get his name down now because it is very popular.'

She was a lovely woman and meant well, but I think she found it hard to believe that anybody sharing dinner with her would be unable to afford such a school's fees.

Anyway, my son's choices of secondary school ranged from the merely poor to the unspeakable. I considered not sending him to school, making a stand and going to prison for keeping him away. They do that now, don't they? Put the parents of truants in prison? If you stay there long enough you'll meet your progeny in the slopping out room. Apparently, our schools are so good, we shouldn't dare think badly of them.

Cutting a long story short, I managed, through a combination of undignified pandering and something not dissimilar to begging, to exploit the last vestiges of the poor man's quality education system and got him into a local grammar school that has been going since the seventeenth century. It has the sort of anachronistic traditions that Woolverstone had and although it is not a boarding school, when I read the school booklet it took me back a bit. Another obvious difference is the social status of the intake, which is exponentially more wealthy and middle class than Woolverstone's was. At any rate, the point of this diversionary guff is to say that I went to pick him up after his first day and I felt *nervous*. I was more intimidated by his school than I thought possible. I thought back to Woolverstone and imagined how he must have been feeling as he took his first steps into this new larger, more demanding world, and I remembered Waterloo in all its visceral, heart-stopping mystery and anticipation. When I was eleven I thought I could take on the world, and would have tried given half the chance, but I saw my son as a little boy. Did he feel like one or was he just the same as me inside? When he approached me, smiling, I breathed a sigh of relief, and whilst driving him home I peppered him with questions, trying to discover how he had dealt with the day. Brushing each away nonchalantly, he did at least agree that the sixth formers looked like adults. But apparently the prefects were helpful, and nice.

Is nothing sacred these days?

RULES, RULES, RULES

Secondary school is daunting for all children, even those at ordinary day schools, and so that first night at Woolverstone was always likely to feel like the last night on Earth. We had excitedly discovered our dorms, chosen beds, lockers and sets of drawers in Hall's house, a modern prefabricated two-floor affair that was clad in wood from which the paint was peeling in parts. It had a strange smell too – disinfectant, musty blankets, and, occasionally the sticky aroma of municipal food that emanated from the kitchens located in the corridor connecting Hall's with Johnston's house. It didn't smell a *lot* like Stamford House, the borstal, but there was a faint recognition, which didn't do much for my impression of the place. It was both exciting and frightening, and on that first afternoon we buzzed around until bedtime – a moment so ordinarily mundane, but which was as profound an introduction to independence as any of us had previously experienced. This was for keeps, and almost to a boy we would be spending the first ever night away from home without a parent. But young boys are adaptable if nothing else and the acute anxiety soon subsided. After a few days, things were a little different. Better. Now we had to get our heads around the regime of the place.

We had two or three days of orientation, were given our class diaries, had the rules of the house and our duties explained to us, were told of the meal schedule, our responsibilities in the house, when we had to change laundry and our bedding. It was a whirlwind of times, rules and regulations and it was perplexing. We were made aware of the punishments for certain misdemeanours, like walking on the grass; received reports of the legendary examples of slipperings or canings; and had it pointed out which masters possessed the strongest arm. Corporal punishment very quickly emerged as the great unseen demon lurking in the shadows, and one several of us would soon provoke.

We discovered that there were not one but two types of detention: the Saturday afternoon Masters' detention and then the Sunday afternoon Prefects' detention, which was the first sign of the self-policing strategies that Woolverstone had in place, that and Prefects were to become the bane of our early Woolverstone life. We also learned that lights went out in the dormitories at a certain time for each of the year groups and that talking after lights out was not permitted, a rule that was especially difficult either to obey or understand.

We were subjected to a framework of control that hardly any of us had ever experienced and thought only existed in the army. You might expect that imposing such a regimen on children like us would be akin to containing anchovies in a tuna net, but I often wonder why it was we fell so easily into line – for into line we most certainly did fall, despite the grumbling and the grizzling we were prone to.

Maybe it was peer pressure, a self-policing routine that meant second formers policed first formers, third formers policed second formers etc. *We did it so YOU have to do it* and so on. Perhaps it was the new boundaries we had never before lived within. They do say children like boundaries, but I am inclined to think we were just a bit stunned, too afraid of this new world to countenance even questioning it. So much was unknown; we knew nothing of what was to come and how it would feel when it arrived.

Every day there was a chore to be done. Sweeping, mopping the showers, swabbing the tables after meal times, etc. I had a peculiar loathing for the milk collection in the mornings. The milk was given out at break in small individual bottles with foil tops, and the milk truck would deliver the crates to a bay at the back of the building where Hall's joined with Johnston's house. On cold, frosty mornings blue tits would descend in great numbers and peck holes in the foil tops, sucking out the creamy head, and if you were too late, the boys performing a similar duty for Johnston's would have got to the crates first and left you with only those filled with the perforated lids. That's when you could get in trouble with the older boys, because few wanted to drink from a bottle whose milk had first been violated by a tit. I had less trouble with the sweeping of the hallways but despised the mopping of the showers and the cleaning of the boot room. The worst chore of all would come in a year or two: laying up the dining room for breakfast was horrendous since it meant getting up earlier than everyone else.

Getting up was difficult enough at the normal time,

and the master on duty would do it in the style of his choice. Suffolk mornings in the autumn or winter were unforgiving things; frost and mist and, above all else, cold would greet you when you opened your bleary eyes and cast a look across Berners' field. If you had games that day, you would know what suffering lay ahead from that first glance. John Morris, the formal housemaster of Hall's, would walk quietly through the house, pulling open curtains and rhythmically intoning, 'Wakey, wakey, rise and shine, time to get up,' as he went. He would give the bell to an individual whose duty it then was to go through the house ringing it every five minutes to ensure all were finally awake and at breakfast by the given time. Bell ringers, without a choice in the matter, were deeply unpopular. We ring a bell at Opera Holland Park when we need the patrons to get to their seats, and we send a steward around the theatre to clang and cajole people out of the public spaces. It has the same irritating effect on them as it did on the boys in Hall's house; the familiar sneers and gruff voices following every bell ringer have probably been the same through all history.

Mike Coulter, John Morris's deputy, took a different tack. He would sneak up to the door, silently release the catch of the handle, stand back and then launch himself feet first through the door bellowing: 'Get up! Get up! Come on, come on! GET UP!' Sometimes you would hear him coming if you were already awake, and I would never fail to be shocked by the deviousness of his technique. I once suffered a serious crick in my neck from having lifted my head suddenly from the pillow as Coulter traumatised us into life. At weekends, when rising time was a bit later, Morris would occasionally bring his young son with him, and the child would ring the bell gleefully all through the house, which is the worst possible way to be awoken. One Sunday morning, the child took the bell to within an inch of the face of second former we shall call Big Dez, and began to ring it loudly in the sleeping behemoth's ear. Like an ogre beneath his bridge rather than the big teddy bear the child obviously saw him as, Dez opened one eye, checked that Morris had gone ahead to the next dorm and then delivered a sharp smack to the mini bell-ringer's head, his huge hand shooting out like a chameleon's tongue. As the child ran off screaming, Dez went back to sleep.

During the first weeks, some of us had begun an uneasy acquaintance. Of the ten first formers in Hall's House, there were at least three of us who obviously fancied ourselves as year leaders, but we had sense enough to just accommodate the competing egos. I had instantly warmed towards Rob Smith, who was seemingly prepared to indulge in rule breaking. Then there was Seaton, who by coincidence lived near to me in Fulham and whose estate used to regularly get into fights with ours. The second formers, who shared a dorm with us, were keen to assert their newfound authority, having been the recipients of the standard bullying the year before. I was soon to learn that Serge's year had given them quite a hard time and they were looking for revenge. Big Dez, who had an afro the size of a small bay tree, was worrying me a great deal, and we first formers quickly learned the art of quiet submission. Even my instinct to retaliate for the most minor affront was somewhat curbed – there were ten of them in a largely unsupervised dorm, and even I didn't think I could take them all on at once. So cuffs, shoves and name-calling were the order of the day for all of us. I was being singled out for an extra bit of verbal attention because Serge had obviously been a bit of a bastard to them in the previous year. But it remained verbal precisely because Serge had been a bit of a bastard in the previous year.

Those early days were characterised by the uncomfortable feeling of being out of our normal element. It was *discombobulating*.

The comforts and certainties of home and familiar surroundings were torn from under our feet, and the exigencies of our new world of rules, which smothered us like cling film – with beady eyes on our every move and no end of people ready to correct our behaviour – pulled many of us up short. Every day a new protocol would present itself: don't use that door, use the one ten feet away; don't stack your shoes like that, stack them with the heels showing outwards; only hang towels in the drying room, not in the dormitory; fold the corners of the bed sheet thus. I list but a few of the orders we were obliged to obey on a daily basis.

'It's like a prison in this shithole,' I would mutter under my breath almost every time I received a command. It got to the point where I would want to dig a hole whenever I saw a sixth former or a master approaching, to hide in dirt and muck, if only to avoid the next piffling demand or needless errand.

I simply found it difficult to obey orders without a bit

of a fight. I'm still like that. I knew these boys were bigger and older than me and had the 'right' to tell me what to do, but I found most of them unworthy of the role. Some were moderately cool, sixth formers with long hair who played guitar or were top rugby players, but too many were obviously relishing their power over us; and almost without exception, they would be the nerdy ones, those who from time to time you would hear being mocked by their peers. It was an early lesson in insecurity. So, when an order came, I wouldn't disobey, but there would be a momentary pause, a glance, a look away and then a quizzical look back, a question perhaps. I would then comply with a wry smile. Sixth formers would rarely beat up the smaller boys, so I had worked out that I was in little physical danger. They must have hated me.

'Volpe! What the fucking hell are you doing using that door?'

'I'm going into the house.'

'Why?'

'Because it's cold.'

'What fucking door is it?'

'The door to the house, where it's warm.'

'Is that the junior's door? Is it?'

'Errm, I'm not sure to be honest.'

'No, it isn't, you little shit!'

'Oh, OK.'

'The one *next* to it painted blue is, so use it. You are in prefect's detention for two weeks, one for using the wrong door and one for being a cheeky little fucker.'

'Oh fucking hell!'

'Make that three weeks for swearing.'

The power always resided with the sixth former despite my notions of rebellion, but if I could exasperate them, delay them or simply annoy them to a point just south of a punch in the head, I was satisfied.

It wasn't just the outlandish idea of rules and regulations, or order and command, duty, responsibility and deferment that challenged us – or, more specifically, me. Our environment was unspeakably taxing too. Even the good stuff like rolling hills, trees and grass carried a threat of a kind to us city kids. The sky was enormous, the night was as black as ink and the air could be so cold it would burn your nose. Where was the light and roar of traffic I was so used to? Noise accompanied my every waking and sleeping moment in Fulham; with a fire station to our left, a police station opposite and a railway line to our right, we were surrounded by sirens, clatter and din. At Woolverstone, if you sat on the grass and listened, you could just about hear the pulse of your own blood over the squeaks, tweets and squawks coming from the shrubs and bushes. If Fulham was the dissonant croak of a punk band, Woolverstone was Sibelius as played by the Berlin Philharmonic conducted by Furtwängler. And I hated it. I couldn't cope with the silence at night. Or the darkness that might conceal a prank or devious bully who could, unseen, pelt you with spiked horse chestnut husks as you ran corrective perimeters of the school road for using, yet again, that wrong bloody door. On a clear night, the purity of the darkness meant I could see so much more of the cosmic ceiling; I had only to go seventy-five miles to render twice as beautiful things that were millions of miles away.

I had never imagined a life in the countryside, and here I was, about to face at least five years slap bang in the middle of it. I couldn't see myself ever adapting to the mud, the cold, the wetness, the wildlife or the distance between everything. There were fields all around us, cattle in the paddock next to the cricket pitch and there were warnings about the foreshore, the irrigation ponds and about keeping off farmland. I had no idea what an irrigation pond was but was assured it was deep and exceptionally deadly if you fell into one, and we had three at the bottom of an adjacent field. Wherever you were, there was *always* an adjacent field. There was a field to cross before you could do anything. Usually there were several fields, and you were never sure if you were permitted to cross them, in which case you might have to walk around them and that doubled or trebled the distance. If you risked it, you invited the possibility that a gravel-voiced farmer with a dog that doubled at Pinewood as the Hound of the Baskervilles would chase you away. The farmers hated Woolverstone boys because we always damaged crops; as far as they were concerned, we all belonged back in the city with the rest of the scum. Their dogs, which were frequently more intelligent and erudite than their masters, hated us even more than their primped, subsidised owners did. They could happily walk past a hundred people, waddling and snuffling cutely at small children and rolling onto their backs for a tickle, but the slightest sniff or sighting of a Woolverstone boy and they would turn rabid.

But there was no escaping the truth that Woolverstone was a fine-looking place, even if it did at first feel as though I had landed on Mars. When gazing from the back of the main house down to the Orwell river, you saw a patchwork of early autumn colour and mile after mile of trees cladding the rolling hills of the river valley. The foreshore of the wide Orwell was fringed by a substantial open marsh dotted with boggy pools, and it gave off a smell that drifted up on the crisp air. Before that was another seam of thick verdant ferns in summer, golden bracken in autumn and flat frosty saw grass in winter. Large cargo ships would chug up the river to Ipswich through the forest of small bobbing yachts and fishing boats that cowered in their enormous wake. Seagulls and their distinctive cry filled the air, crows cawed endlessly in the morning mists, and when it shone, the sun was bright and sharp on the eyes. And there was quaintness aplenty: in the chocolate box prettiness of St Michael's church up beside the First XV playing field; in the tiny picture-postcard villages of Woolverstone itself, as well as Chelmondiston, Shotley and Pin Mill.

We even had archetypal groundsmen, whose local brogue meant I couldn't understand a word any of them said. I don't think they truly qualified as 'quaint' per se, especially not with their grizzled syllables and big, gnarly hands. There were four of them, led by Dickey Mayes, a former Kent cricketer and creator of a wonderful first class wicket on Berners' field. Digging beds, driving tractors, pulling small carts of plants, mowing lawns or the playing fields, the groundsmen were wizened, weather-beaten and Suffolk residents through and through. One always had a pipe in his mouth and a happy demeanour. That is to say, once you realised he wasn't growling at you, it was easier to see his happy demeanour.

'Yaargh roit, g'daaay boy. Naarh be waaarg'n on thart there graaas wool yaarh?'

He didn't as much speak as *vocalise*. After a while, you could determine when he wasn't telling you off and could make out a few words from the inflection he used or the look in his eye. The groundsmen never moved very fast. If you passed one on the way to a lesson, he might be replanting a flowerbed at a speed where movement was barely perceptible. However, when you came back, the previously empty wasteland of the bedding plot would look like a gold medal display at Chelsea.

Paradoxically, despite considering myself to be in a surreal place, I do remember feeling smug when I thought how jealous my friends would be if they could see me, although I see now that this was peculiar, since the idea of boarding school filled them with dread. But at primary school, we had twice gone to a farm in Beaconsfield (a mere hop, skip and jump from west London) and the journey out to the farm was always suffused with glee on account of our passing fields full of cattle and sheep. The farm itself was little more than a shed with a pair of Friesians in it, but the ground was muddy and the aroma was that of dung – fruity, herbivore dung as opposed to the effluvia on London's streets. I think we associated the countryside with wealth and posh people, and believed everyone had a car in the country. And a house. Usually a large house. I'm not entirely sure what was so exotic and exciting about the green spaces around London, but we would be beside ourselves with the exhilaration of it all. Now, my entire playground was a hundred times better than that, I would awaken to the mooing of cattle, and their smell would hang in the air permanently. Only to an urban child could the type and smell of shit be a status symbol.

It seems to me that my education – in a more global sense – began in those first few days of life at Woolverstone. If the environment was part of the plan when the brave and brilliant individuals who created Woolverstone first drew up their ideas then they chose the crucible for our instruction well. A child's environment has a huge part to play in his development, and it's not just the *social* influences. If heightened aspiration was the driving engine powering the school, both the sculpted lawns and uncontrolled wildness of the land upon which it sat was the exquisite bodywork. Our school offered us space and wide horizons; I am not so trite as to make the obvious correlation here, but education needed to provide us with more than the vocational or merely prosaic. It was not immediately obvious to me that the Suffolk countryside was more than a geographical location, but it is certainly clear to me now that I had a great deal to adapt to when I arrived at that place, and coming to terms with this beautiful but nevertheless shockingly new and unfamiliar world was all part of the learning. This forced emergence from our personal little castles extended to everything, including the ability to share our worlds with those around us.

I had been used to sharing sleeping space at home, but it was a very novel experience having to do so with nineteen others. They all had their habits or did annoying things; I would roar internally at the variety of irritating bedtime rituals. Some of them farted a lot, had rancid feet, talked in their sleep or just plain got on your nerves. One boy even slept with his eyes wide open, which was unsettling if you happened to glance at him as you returned from the toilet in the middle of the night. If you were in a bottom bunk and the person on top fidgeted a lot, the creaking and squeaking of the metal netting above would drive you to despair. We shared everything; sleeping space, toilets and showers, mealtimes and duties, so our new world was certainly going to test us all.

The anticipation of being at the school was mixed with the inevitable homesickness many were feeling, but soon, chatter replaced sobbing in the dorm after lights out, despite our knowing it was *verboten*. Conversations were laced with ninety per cent untruths as boys sought to establish their credentials. Brothers would become gangsters, sisters would be beauty queens and, for those of us who had them, dads would be businessmen or spies. Many of us had been champion something-or-others at primary school, and *all* of us knew what it felt like to touch a girl's bits. Slowly but surely, a pecking order was forming among the first formers, based on who was the loudest, had the best stories or who claimed to have won all the fights he'd ever had. It wasn't entirely surprising that we saw our physicality as the passport to status, and it is something Woolverstone would come to harness and channel very effectively, but it was also a measure of where our priorities lay.

Later, we would discover many boys in the school had commendably glamorous parents who, strangely, we all took some sort of credit for in our growing camaraderie and solidarity. There was the boy whose father led the Red Arrows and the boy with a dad who was props master on the James Bond movies. We had a friend whose mother was a model, known to all for her part in a famous Levi's advert and whose best friend was married to Eric Clapton, which meant the boy spent Christmases playing snooker with superstars of the rock world. The boy himself went on to fame and stardom for a time as a pop star. Another schoolmate had a famous disc jockey for a dad. Several boys had about them the demeanour of laid-back hippies, a mood absorbed from liberal parents who smoked lots of weed. We were a diverse bunch for sure and I was quite often struck by the ordinariness of my own family when compared to this alluringly bohemian, Arts and Crafts menagerie.

My plain background didn't stop me basking in the reflected glow of these colourful lives, but the truth was that there were many who knew the caustic dangers of inner city London as well as I did. In time, we would come to know more of the lives of our school friends, and all too frequently it was easy to discern crushing difficulties. In my memory, most of us had fractured families and those who didn't were usually among the small intake from military families. Conversely, of course, there were boys who had stories they never wanted to tell, or felt unable to, for fear that they could not measure up to the elevated bloodline of the heroes and hard-nuts who now surrounded them. We must have appeared absurd, terrifying or both, but these boys would nevertheless remain quiet and probably frightened.

I haven't until now thought much about my own homesickness in those first few weeks. I don't recall it, although I must have felt it somewhere along the line. I was quite an independent child; my mother always recalled the time she took me into hospital at five years old to have my tonsils out, but getting me settled in was cut short by my excited invitation for her to leave and let me get on with the adventure. But whilst I don't recall ever crying down the phone to Mum (no doubt helped by having an older brother there), I did miss bits of my life at home, and I also believe I was already feeling the weight of expectation. The fear of failing was getting to all of us because we were surrounded by those who were just so bloody good at stuff. You couldn't escape them: the rugby players, the musicians, the real eggheads who were talked about in hushed tones. We had a lot to live up to, and it took some time to work out which behaviour was appropriate in order to step onto the track whose destination was 'success'. It would normally begin as silliness and bravado, but the crucible for building self-image was at first the dormitory or the house, not the classroom, and the first seam that male adolescence usually mines is machismo.

Small boys, when they first encounter other small boys, act in a way that is the human equivalent of a peacock showing his feathers. In a normal day school, there are often mums and dads to add character and status to an individual, along with the size of car or house. There are the reassuring comforts of home, and an evening in the bosom of family can revive the flagging spirit of a child who has had a bad day among his peers. In a boarding school – or, more specifically, in a closed, darkened dormi-tory – it is, even in a benign form, a case of kill or be killed. There is no comforting hug from mother to soothe a furrowed brow, nor is there is any escape from a bully or a tormentor in a hall of residence. There is just the daily grind of the effort to get up the pecking order and to achieve, at the very least, a position no less than halfway up it. I fought my way through force of personality to what I believed was somewhere near the top, and in truth I was more force than personality, but I felt as though I was making progress.

Many did not relish the post lights-out humdrum, but it was certainly a time when we could get to know each other and for friendships, such as they were, to emerge. (Rob and I formed an alliance in those early weeks that lasts to this day.) It was also a time for the second form to have their fun, forcing juniors to run 'dares' or ordering one of us to 'run the gauntlet', when everybody waited at the foot of their bed with a pillow as the chosen one ran between them, taking blow after blow. Dares were often exciting, but none of us wanted to have to do them, and we dreaded the nights when the second formers decided it was to be such an evening.

Our dorm looked out across Berners' field towards the old pavilion, so when a nervous first former was ordered to run to there, we could see the events unfold in front of our eyes. The boy had to get out of the house first, usually at a time when the house was in full functional flow, so his furtive escape into the night was laced with danger. He could be caught by anyone walking through the house, or by a senior watching TV in the dining room. Worse was to get caught by a master on duty. A frisson of excitement would ripple through the dorm as we saw the boy appear on the lawn in front of the house, creeping, hiding behind pillars, crouching below windows. Once convinced that the coast was clear, the boy would set off sprinting across the open ground with his striped pyjamas flapping in the breeze. Pyjamas were almost universally striped and too large for the boy. If they did not flap, it was because it was pouring with rain and the fabric was clamped against his skin: meteorological considerations were thin on the ground between empowered second formers. Other dares were more epic and involved bringing back evidence such as a sign or piece of wood. When they got really elaborate, boys doing the dare could be out for half of the night, returning to a silent, sleeping dormitory.

Sex, or the prospect of it, was never far from our minds, and usually the general discussion in the dorm would turn to it. Opinion polls would be held on the various wives of masters, pop singers or newsreaders, and we rued the fact that matrons were never attractive (probably a deliberate decision on the part of the school). After long talks about the virtues of various girls of our acquaintance, many of them inventions, the unmistakable sound of twenty boys wanking (impossible to describe) would fill the air.

So the dormitory became the centre of our worlds in the first few weeks at Woolverstone. It is where you would retire to if weary, to lie on your bed and read or wonder about home; and I suppose, despite occasional dangers, it was a place of safety. The small, two square metres of bed were your sanctuary, and nobody was permitted to cross the threshold; nothing provoked ire as fiercely as seeing somebody lying on your bed. But your bed didn't protect you from everything, as Rob Smith soon discovered.

The dorm was in three sections, with panelled walls dividing each of them. The middle section had the toilets, and at each end were the doors onto the landing outside. I was in an end section on a bottom bunk, and Rob was in the middle section. We were all busy after lights-out telling various lies about ourselves, excitedly talking about the rugby careers we were soon to embark upon, when John Morris, the housemaster, quietly opened the dormitory door and stood listening.

John 'Musher' Morris, as he was known, was a calm, religious man. He had a young family and, in fact, looked a little like Bobby Charlton with glasses. He was a man who commanded respect by virtue of his quiet moderation and reason, and was a fully paid up member of the hierarchy and played us well in this respect. In order to stop someone like me from bullying, he knew immediately to send me on an errand to stop somebody else doing it. Morris epitomised confidence of a more modest and self-contained kind, and although I never thought to emulate him in this respect, I was sufficiently aware of it to moderate my more strident side whenever he was around.

He taught history and was a very fine rugby player and coach, so I spent lots of time outside of the house in his company, but I wish more of his manner had rubbed off on me. I thought him a brilliant man. And I quickly came to know where his line in the sand was; as it was described to us, he hated many things, but he hated swearing and rule-breaking more than anything else. Rules were there for a reason, they brought order and discipline, and it was no surprise that he held such a view. Nor was it a shock to learn that profanity offended him more gravely than if you had run him through with a scaffold pole. Swearing was a crime beyond almost anything else we could commit; to swear was an offence to oneself, to others around you, to God too, I suspect. It was not something we ever philosophised with him about, we just did not do it when he was around. Oddly, I suspect my memory of Morris as a trenchant, God-fearing man is probably as a result of school embellishment, but when we arrived, this was the caricature painted by our contemporaries, and it took hold.

Rob Smith, being in the middle section of the dorm did not see him come into the room and as we all fell silent, Smith continued his pursuit of an answer to a question he had asked me.

'Volpe? Volpe? Answer me, Volpe!'

The silhouetted housemaster stood still, listening. And then he spoke evenly and in a menacing monotone.

'Smith. Go and stand outside my study.'

There was a collective lurching of stomachs. Even at that early stage, we knew what that meant. As Smith

climbed out of bed and trudged out of the dormitory clad
in nothing but his pyjamas, we suddenly all realised that
henceforth, life was going to be different. As Morris left
the dorm, he reminded us sternly of the no-talking direc-
tive and closed the door. The second formers were beside
themselves with mirth and excitement at Smith's imminent
beating. We novices weren't sure what to make of it, but
it was certainly dramatic. I should think all of us had
received a good hiding from a parent before, but formal-
ised punishment has gravitas precisely because it is
controlled and by design. We did not know what to expect
from it all. Would we hear Smith's screams echo through
the house? Would he come back howling and crying? Would
he need hospital treatment? Would he ever be the same
again? How the world outside drifted further away at that
moment, how our cockiness evaporated and melted into
the thick, tense air of the dormitory.

Pound to a penny, Rob would piss his pyjamas, I thought.

* * *

The first time I had received a whack from a teacher was
at Addison Gardens when I was five years old. The headmaster had been called to the classroom because some
boys were getting unruly. He came in, asked the main
culprit – who was unmistakeable on account of his being
half-buried in the beads and counters he had been chucking
everywhere – for the names of his accomplices, and the
bugger had named innocent, uninvolved and oblivious *me*.
Almost before I could raise even a yelp in protest, I was

pitched across the headmaster's knee, right there in front of the whole class, and given a hand smacking. And I pissed in my pants. Some weeks later, the teacher called me to the front of the class and scolded me for something that, again, I hadn't even done. She ordered me to put my hand out, which I did, not knowing why, and from behind her back she produced a thick wooden ruler and attempted to bring it down across my knuckles. I moved my hand. She grabbed my hand and rapped me across the knuckles anyway. I kicked her in the leg and ran out of the classroom. Mum visited the school to speak to the headmaster about that one and told the teacher, 'Iffa you touch mya son again, I fucky killa you.'

* * *

Ten minutes after leaving the dorm, Smith shuffled back in quietly. Nobody spoke to him and none of us asked what had happened. We all just went to sleep and if he had pissed his pants, he wasn't telling.

In the morning, we were eager to talk about the previous night's drama. I don't know what we expected, but Smith looked pretty normal; there were no bruises on his face, no tear-streaked cheeks, no plaster of Paris or blood or crutches. In fact, I think we were disappointed to see no signs of injury *at all*. Had he not just been slippered by the legendary Musher Morris? Why was he still breathing? Walking? Alive? But injury he did, indeed, suffer. Smith told us how Morris had wordlessly ushered him into the study, took him by the back of the neck with his right hand, encouraging him to bend at the waist and with the left delivered four thwacks with a rubber-soled plimsoll. These being pre-Nike days, plimsolls were not the light athletic constructions of today, but canvas and rubber bludgeons. The shoe in question was a Dunlop Green Flash. The sole was at least one-inch thick rubber and into it were moulded hundreds of small lightning flashes. Smith reported that it was at least a size ten. It hurt, apparently. A great deal. Rob, as we had now taken to calling him out of sympathy, showed us his arse and in the middle of a sickeningly large contusion that covered his entire posterior, we could clearly discern the word 'Dunlop' in reverse, and scores of small lightning flashes bruised into the skin. Right there and then, we all vowed to avoid a 'kippering' from Morris. But there was no doubt that we admired Rob for taking the beating and not crying his eyes out twelve hours later. It was a badge of honour of sorts, he had broken his cherry and the knowledge of how it felt to receive a slippering was his to impart. It would never surprise him again.

Astonishingly, I do not remember any of us complaining that the punishment had been disproportionate to the crime. At home few of us would tolerate such discipline, would never consider a bruised and wounded arse to be anything but an outrage. But there, then, we had bought almost completely into the regime that delivered said indignation. We did not examine or wonder what on earth would happen if he'd hit a boy or stolen some bread from the kitchen or disobeyed an instruction. The truth was that for all those things he would have received the same punishment, which was exactly the point. Maybe a suspension would ensue if he burned the house down, but crimes both minor and major were punishable by the same thing. And we seemed to know it, even if it was subconsciously.

Despite Rob's slippering and the resultant collective determination to avoid the same fate, it was inevitable that I would soon suffer something similar. In truth, perhaps I was hoping to earn some spurs myself, but the way in which I did so was entirely unintentional and wholly unexpected. It was barely a week before I too was ordered to the study, and it was Rob who caused it.

Our friendship had continued to grow along well-marshalled lines; conservatively offering olive branches to each other whilst remaining aware that at any time there might have to be a summit to decide who would become top dog. Since we had decided we liked each other, we thus spent a lot of time hanging out. It also meant certain facets of our personalities were becoming more evident and Rob's most manifest personality trait on the fateful day was thinking it was hilarious to see how people reacted to pain. Walking across the concrete paving outside of the master's dining room, he was waving a large, flexible branch in the way that young boys do, for no reason. We like to hit things with big sticks, but we don't like being hit with them.

Well, I don't.

Inevitably, Rob waved his big stick at me. This is no euphemism; he really did have a big, wooden branch from which he had stripped all twigs and leaves. Even more inevitably – and fate intervened here, I am sure – it connected with the back of my leg. The sting brought white light and tears to my eyes, and from deep within, a boiling eruption of invective issued forth into the Suffolk countryside. In an instant, several 'fucks' and at least one pair of 'cunts' had rung like a klaxon through the crisp autumn air. Unfortunately, at that moment, Morris happened to be breathing the same air. Indeed, so close was he, he could probably smell the foul language. Halfway through my third 'you utter fucking bastard Smith', I noticed him staring at me, his eyes livid with rage, and I can't swear to it but I am sure he was trembling too.

Gulp.

'Volpe, go and stand outside my study,' he growled.

I mean it, he really did growl and I was almost sick on the spot. As Morris turned on his heels, no doubt eager to get back to his study for a quick warm-up, I wobbled, stunned and shaken, numb with fear. I thought of how hugely offensive Morris would have found my outburst.

I knew.

I thought of Rob's bruised, mangled buttocks and contemplated how much more angry Morris must now be, having been assaulted by my broadcast of almost the entire lexicon of Anglo-Saxon profanity. Perhaps I *would* need hospital treatment? Maybe, this time, there surely would be blood? I walked towards the inevitable agony and considered my options. Refuse to bend over? No, he'd make me. Get a book and shove it down my trousers? No, someone had once tried that and been given twice as many whacks as a result. I know; I could run away, hide and never come back! I would live off the land forever, eating bugs, squirrels and fish for my supper. Anything seemed possible as I thought of what was to come.

In truth, I had no choice, but it was not for want of considering every outlandish route of escape. As I approached the open door of Morris's office, I did so in what felt like slow motion. I had been used to getting a good hiding from Mum, but this was entirely unlike anything I had felt before and I kept thinking – hoping – that maybe he wouldn't slipper me, that I would get a good talking to instead. As I passed the dining room and saw a dinner lady, I wanted to run to her and hide behind her. If there was going to be a saviour, then they had better arrive soon because I was just feet away from the threshold of Morris's study. My legs were turning to jelly as I reached the room, and Morris was waiting for me, standing by the side of his desk, the files he had been carrying placed roughly on the otherwise neatly stacked papers. I saw this as a sign of his anger. Anger, or any form of outward emotional dynamism, was uncommon to John Morris, so when it appeared, you bloody noticed it, I can tell you.

★ ★ ★

It was a warm summer day, and Morris was taking a history lesson in the classroom that had once been a large drawing room of the old Berners House. There was an authentic Adam fireplace behind protective glass and elegant cornices framing the room. Large curved windows faced out onto the Orwell side, with views across the river to the north. Suddenly, a boy motioned to the window and asked, 'What's that, Sir?'

Morris strolled to the window and so strange was the sight, we all rushed to the windows for a closer look too. Over the hills across the Orwell was a large black cloud, and it was moving towards us very quickly. Morris scrunched up his face in thought as he gazed at it. We all hung from the open windows trying to work it out too.

'Close the windows please, boys,' Morris said, without a shred of dramatic inflection.

As we did so, the cloud grew angrier and larger and seemed to cover the entire playing field outside. Soon it was upon us, and the windows were covered with thousands of bees. They buzzed furiously at the glass for a few moments, and then this swarm of biblical proportions moved away as one, no doubt following their Queen. Within a miraculously short space of time, they formed a huge teardrop of teeming, squirming, vibrant life hanging from the lower branch of the great Cedar of Lebanon tree that sat below the building.

'Back to your seats, please. Right, where were we? Ah yes, the Somme . . .'

* * *

'I will not tolerate the kind of language I just heard, young man. It was disgraceful,' Morris said, his voice steel-edged with indignation. The usually laconic Morris had also become comparatively verbose.

'But Sir, Smith hit me with a stick and it hurt and I couldn't help it . . .'

I trailed off pathetically. I had nothing more to say since

what I had already said sounded hollow, and I could see in his face that it was worthless trying to explain what had been a torrent of adolescent, potty-mouthed petulance. I was also starting to hyperventilate, and even if words had been ready to come out, they would have perished on the arid carpet that was my tongue. To Morris's right hand, I could see a basket of sports clothes, bits of equipment and, lying threateningly on top, the upturned sole of a Dunlop Green Flash plimsoll. I stared at it, my executioner, my nemesis and the most famous plimsoll in all of Suffolk. If inanimate objects can take on a personality, the Green Flash was the Daddy of them all. It had character, reputation and a degree in torture to its name.

Morris said something about teaching me a lesson, but by now, I wasn't listening. He slowly picked up the Green Flash and came towards me. I remembered what Rob had said about the hand that forced him to bend. My fear had clearly not totally dispossessed me of my belligerence, and I bent, as nonchalantly as my growing terror would allow, offering Morris my behind in defiant invitation. Unfortunately, I had bent down facing the wrong way – Morris was left-handed. He told me to stand up and then took hold of the back of my neck anyway.

I will always place John Morris above nuns, but to him swearing sat at the top table in the Hall of Beelzebub. There was no place for it and argument to the contrary was never brooked or tolerated. It was hard to contend that earthy colloquialisms were common in religious practice, but at primary school we gloried in the rhyme, 'Bloody in the Bible, Bloody in the book, if you don't believe me, have a Bloody look!' However, 'fuck', 'shit', 'tosspot', 'wanker', 'cocksucker' and all the other words I had shouted at Smith that day are not in there. Look for them yourself, I promise you won't find them; neither a tit nor an arse will you encounter in the Old or New Testament. Not even Happy Clappy churches indulge in cathartic, satisfyingly mouth-filling imprecation. I still find that a shame, but bent double at the waist, waiting for the Dunlop hammer to fall, I just thought it was deeply inconvenient.

I got five whacks, each of them feeling harder than the one before. On the first, the shock propelled me forward, and I hit my head on the piano in the corner of the study. Such was my convulsion, Morris had lost his grip on the back of my neck and as my cranium connected with the corner of the keyboard, the guts of the piano gave a sharp note, like a sleeping dog being trodden on. Morris was quick with the strokes, and there was no sense that he was enjoying it. I was to learn later that some masters most certainly did enjoy it, but Morris displayed a rhythm and technique that managed to maintain whatever sense of propriety such an event could muster. It was formal, controlled and painful. It was shocking, too, since there was an inherent violence in the act, but I never held that against him, essentially because I was in no position to do so with my arse prone, a strong hand holding me down and half a pound of rubber giving my school trousers a polishing.

By the fifth strike, the sting had become a blunt pain that radiated into my legs and up my lower back, but the relief of being able to stand, knowing it was over, was colossal. Morris seemed calm and composed, which is somewhat different to how I felt. The sweat that had broken out on my skin was being burnt off by the energy the beating had transferred into me – I was in danger of generating cumulonimbus in the study. Morris allowed me a moment before telling me to leave, and as I limped out of the office, doing everything in my power not to 'crack' (a cardinal sin) I heard the kerfuffle of laughter from the shower drying room that was next door to the study. I went in to find several of my housemates, quickly gathered together by a gleeful Rob, sniggering hard, clutching the glasses they had used to listen through the wall.

I went on to be slippered by Morris many times and for what one might consider greater crimes. None, however, came close to that first occasion for sheer intensity. Morris's strength was never so provoked as it was by a c-word. Climbing roofs, disobeying teachers, leaving school without permission, beating up a smaller boy, strangling his wife, kidnapping his children, disembowelling his dog: nothing I could have ever done would have summoned forth fury like a 'fucking bastard' did.

PRESSURE COOKER

The pressure of life at Woolverstone continued to build with every one of those first days. There was layer upon layer of expectation, duty, responsibility and rule. It felt relentless at times and our individual personalities were being moulded and crafted, if not extinguished, by every single one of those regulations. I'd love to have heard the view of some of my primary school teachers had they been observing this remarkable transformation. It was not so much a change in me, but in what I was apparently prepared to countenance. Every event, from assembly to detention to prep and breakfast, was sacred; we had to be in the right place at the right time and be wearing the correct clothes. The rules felt trivial, pernickety – hysterical even – and we had noticed how certain individuals enforced the hierarchy with particular zeal.

The whole process of integrating into the life of the school was made more arduous by these endless regulations and some of the frightful people who revelled in enforcing them. Yet all of these pressures, palpable even in the first week, were nothing compared to the looming reality of the sport that Woolverstone excelled at and which would expect more of us than almost anything else: rugby.

None of us had ever played rugby at primary school. All of us were football mad, and some had played cricket, but I was again at some advantage having had Serge give me two years of reports on the game and how important it was to the school, yet I had never held a rugby ball in my hands. I remember being told repeatedly that Woolverstone was 'one of the top three rugby schools in the country' and woe betide the intake that broke the sequence of achievement. Our first sporting test was looming over us like a great shadow; all the talk was of the impending event, from which no first former could escape, one for which the whole school turned out and for which we would wear our new rugby kit and steel-toed boots for the first time. It was an event of magnificent conception, the most popular match in the school rugby year, and it was called *Stonehenge*.

Stonehenge was brutally simple. Sixty boys split into two teams with one team in blue and the other in white. Something in the order of five balls would be thrown onto the pitch, and each team was told to touch balls down behind the try-line at the end of the pitch they were facing. They should try to pass to a colleague in the same coloured shirt and 'tackle' anybody they saw with the ball, and the team that scored the most 'tries' would win. That was it. No structure, no rules, no referee. It was carnage, but there *was* a point. As boys flailed and charged at each other, chasing bobbling balls around as if they were pursuing chickens in a farmyard, several masters and a couple of members of the first fifteen stood on the touch-lines with clipboards, noting the naturally talented and determined players. From this sixty would come two groups of thirty, divided into A and B group. The A group would then produce the school under-twelves team. Even at that young, tender age we would be playing competitive matches with the same level of expectation as any other year group.

Knowing this fact was quite a spur to those of us with egos that had followed us to Woolverstone, and I had the added incentive of knowing that Serge would kill me were I to fail to be a half-decent rugby player. If there was a miracle at work at Woolverstone, it was its knack of finding boys of ferocious competitiveness (or injecting it into them), and I have often wondered how it did this. I doubt many of us had glittering academic careers mapped out for us by our parents, who in most cases hoped for a trouble-free adolescence, a successful arrival in the lounge marked 'adulthood' and then perhaps a decent, sustainable job. Woolverstone didn't comply with such a lowly ambition, and there was a belief that all could achieve great things. That, after all, was the point of the school, surely? And Stonehenge was the first opportunity to show some mettle – with the entire school watching.

Preparing on the pitch, surrounded by bewildered and frightened kids, I was aware of the gathered throng's collective mirth at the appearance of several of the participants. What went through my mind at that moment is forever etched in my consciousness, and if my mind had teeth it would have gritted them as it thought *those fuckers ain't laughing at me*. And then the balls were kicked into play and pandemonium took over. So did the ferocious competitiveness I mentioned, and I firmly believe that just the first five minutes of that game would have thrown up those who would make it in rugby and those who wouldn't. (Indeed, several were very soon just throwing up.)

From my house, I knew that Rob, Seaton and one or two others would be in the thick of things, but I simply had no time to look about admiring the skill of others. A ball spilled from a boy's hands close to me, and I picked it up. I was near the touchline and there was a roar; 'Run, you silly bugger,' or words to that effect, probably shouted by an individual but to me it seemed as if the whole of Suffolk had screamed it into my ear. So I ran. In fact, I ran over a small boy in my way. I seemed to know that putting my hand into the face of someone trying to stop me would help in getting past him, and I managed to resist the temptation to close it. I heard the boy whelp like a small dog, and everyone on the touchline laughed. I approached another boy, squatting before me, arms out wide as if to bar my way. No chance. I slapped him too, which this time brought gales of merriment from the crowd.

I was beginning to enjoy myself just as a large mass landed on my back and began choking me. Even I knew that this wasn't allowed – was it? I began to object violently, but with a half-closed windpipe and crushed vocal cords, this was difficult, and 'Get off me you fucking cheat' came out like 'Geghh fme yaow fuurghi sheet', at which point I landed face down in the dirt. I swung around with my arm to hit him, but he had run off to throttle someone else. Now I had a taste for running with the ball, but when I next gathered one under my arm, I ran with one eye glancing behind. And I scored. I scored many times, in fact. I realised something else: I was stocky and quick and people had trouble stopping me. By the end, most were scared, and when they saw me chugging towards them with a grimace, they just waved a cursory hand in my direction and let me by. I had also taken to adding vocal effects since I remembered reading how the Vikings did this to instill greater fear into their opponent.

'Aaaaarrrgh!'

'Grrraaarggh!'

And even, once or twice: 'Chaaaaarrge!'

It took me a while to lose the habit actually, and right up to my last playing days, when I ran with a rugby ball I would emit a low growl that rose in volume when I crashed into someone.

'GrrrrrrRAH!'

Then it happened. It wasn't cataclysmic or particularly unusual or a rare thing, but it was unfamiliar, exciting and confusing; after a while, the laughter and mirth on the touchline turned into what can only be described as *admiration*. When a try was scored in a particularly exciting or impressive way, the crowd would applaud and shout, 'Well done'. To have this come from older boys whose reputations, at least, I had already started to admire carried more weight than any praise I'd had in the past from teachers. I was genuinely excited by the idea of being good at this rugby lark. Naturally, you will have deduced by now, I would never really learn to keep my pride in check, but Stonehenge felt like the moment I believed I might just be in the right place.

By the end of the match I was knackered. The nervous tension of the first fifteen minutes or so had taken its toll on us, but my chest remained puffed out. I was in love with the game already because, right there and then, I was good at it, or so I thought. There were boys who had skill, speed, courage and strength, but as long as I convinced myself I had some of those qualities too, I realised I would eventually be chosen as one of the fifteen to represent the school. The day was wet, the ground was muddy and I remember the cutting edge of the wind that blew in from the North Sea a few miles away. But I was hot under the collar, flushed with the effort of slapping and bouncing past people, running with three kilos of mud stuck to my boots. I was exhilarated by the entire experience.

Stonehenge was a crowning glory. I had never before been so totally immersed in a visceral battle on a sports field, and the collective approval of a crowd, albeit one of boys of varying ages, was an entirely new experience. At primary school I had always been a performer, a show-off, had always been in school plays and choirs. This, too, felt like a performance, and immediately it became clear what being good at rugby meant at Woolverstone. It gave you a starting point in the hierarchy, a gloriously physical form of showing off, and it signified that you could survive the first year among your peers. I think Serge breathed a sigh of relief as he saw me repeatedly cross the try-line.

My exertions in Stonehenge would duly reward me with a spot in A Group, as was the case for several of my new pals in Hall's House, including Rob and Seaton. That first hurdle was negotiated, and you could tell how relieved we were as we traipsed back to the house, tired and sore with the autumn mist descending and the light dimming. We had risen to Woolverstone's first challenge. Fish out of water we may still have been, but we had started the process of conversion. Maybe we would never make fully-fledged middle-class public schoolboys, but we would be rugby players. Round One to us, then. And since Round One was rugby, the most credible thing to be decent at, there was respite in knowing that even if we only stumbled clumsily over the other hurdles the school would put before us, rugby would offer a salvation of sorts. We couldn't wait for the real training to begin, and our self-esteem had inflated two-fold. The outcome for the boys I had been trampling on was less clear, but at that moment, I could not have cared less.

★ ★ ★

As that first term wore on, for some of us it began to feel normal. The slipperings, which continued with close frequency, felt normal. So did not walking across a patch of grass, the use of specific doors to enter the same hallway, lining our shoes up with heels out and all the other regulations we had not so long previously been exasperated by. We settled into the system. That's what happened, we just accepted things.

Normality, I regret to convey, began to include punching any boy who upset me, for soon I began to throw my weight around a bit. It was bullying, but I convinced myself that it wasn't and that I only responded to provocation. Furthermore, I had figured out that at Woolverstone you were either the type of boy who got punched, or the type who did the punching, and I was inclined most fervently to the latter. I am happy to report that I curbed this behaviour pretty quickly because I loathed causing other kids to be upset. I can honestly confess to this because when I took a decision to land a blow, I did so fully expecting retaliation. Once I'd punched them, I usually realised that there was little chance of their doing the same in return. I didn't much like the way it made me feel and I often apologised. (How big of me, huh?)

It is easy to condemn myself for being so inclined, but if I have a defence, it was merely the way in which I was brought up; or more accurately, the way in which I had to grow up. Hit first, hit hard. Goodness knows how silly and loutish I feel as I write that, but it was nevertheless true and necessary. At six years of age, I vividly recall being in a pushing match with a boy I was supposed to be playing football with. One of my brothers emerged from the doorway of a flat we were visiting and said, 'Just hit him, Mike!' And I did. His collapse to the ground, blood leaking from his nose, surprised me, as did the whack he got for fighting when his mum came out to investigate his howling. I merely continued with the policy as I grew up, and it felt perfectly natural to bring it to Woolverstone with me. Other boys did not have such a feral approach to confrontation, so it would naturally appear as though I were the aggressor or, indeed, bully. This all sounds like an excuse doesn't it? Oh well, so be it.

It would be ridiculous to suppose that there was no ritual bullying, particularly from those in the older age groups, but it never felt particularly malignant in most cases. It was standard stuff that those in the year above us felt they had earned, and we in turn looked forward to when we would be able to do it ourselves. But quite soon our year and that above us began to merge and become closer friends. There were few whose hearts were fully in it, and so this rite of passage, for which they had waited a whole year, was temporary.

Although spikes of genuine cruelty would occur, the whole edifice of power and control over younger boys was pretty well self-regulated, with distinct boundaries and rules. It could be intensive, persistent and unpleasant, and for some it was unbearable. It was that hierarchy thing again, lots of eleven and twelve-year-old boys, struggling with an alien environment, hormones that were starting to flow and a fear of falling behind their peers. Rogue – and rare – bullies visited a fair degree of violence on younger boys, but they would generally get their comeuppance, whilst physical assaults by seniors on the first years were exceptional. Suffice to say, I ensured my experience would be of the atypical sort.

I only recall ever being hit once in those early days, and it was by a pupil so much older than me that I almost considered it an honour. Sitting in the dining room watching *Grandstand* one Saturday afternoon, a few of us from the first form had just finished delivering a pounding on the rugby pitch to a poor bedraggled group of public schoolboys from Norfolk somewhere. *Grandstand* and *World of Sport* with Frank Bough and Dickey Davies were a treat on a wet Saturday afternoon, getting the scores of our respective football teams or watching the ludicrous wrestling with Mick McManus, Big Daddy et al. We would all gather with chairs beneath the television in the dining room and joke and laugh, revelling in the moving white streak of Dickey's coiffure. They were wonderful, comfy, warm-as-toast afternoons, all of us fresh from the showers after the match, aching slightly but glowing with the healthy exertions of the day. I recall them with huge fondness and can remember how it felt; winners again, feeling strong, watching the winter gloom gather outside and looking forward to the Saturday evening teatime. Later that night, we might be allowed to stay up to watch *Match of The Day*, so best behaviour and no mistakes.

It was into this happy world that Thompson barged and switched the TV channel. A sixth former entering a room like that would have a monstrously demoralising effect on the younger boys gathered there. He intruded, did what he wanted, put us in our place – and we never liked being put in our place. Doubtless full of the bravado that adolescent testosterone creates and stung by a strong tweak of indignation, I challenged Thompson. It was one of the few occasions we got to be ourselves, free and relaxed, among others of our age, and Thommo's arrival was, to quote Billy Connolly, about as welcome as a fart in a spacesuit.

Thommo's friends called him 'Sabot', but I don't know why. In any case, the emphasis is on 'his *friends* called him Sabot', certainly not eleven-year-old big shots.

'Oh, fucking hell, Sabot, don't turn it over!'

If you have never seen a square fist, I can tell you it is a remarkable thing. I mean a square block of flesh and bone the size of a bag of sugar. It doesn't narrow from the large fingers down to the little finger; it remains constant, with a flat front surface, and is, in point of fact, frighteningly *square*. The really astonishing thing is that the knuckled plane of the clenched fist is almost three times the width of the wrist it is attached to. Thompson had square fists. He also had wide wrists, which gives you an impression of the clubs he wielded at the ends of his arms. Before he popped me on the chin, knocking me backwards off my chair, he gave me a quizzical, half-smiling look that seemed to ask, 'Did you just call me Sabot?'

Similar to the way a batsman of quality meets an over-pitched ball with a gentle swish of the willow, Thommo didn't put much effort into it but, rather, timed the strike to perfection. He didn't even get off the seat he had taken in front of the TV: I was directly behind him so he needed only to turn on his chair. The punch appeared to me to be in slow motion, and although his lazy, unruffled style meant that I saw the fist coming, I was mesmerised by its size as the light began to dim in its shadow. It was so large I think I was caught in its gravitational pull, for I can think of no other reason why I remained stock still in its path.

'Crikey, that's a big . . .'

The thought was pinched from my mind as stars erupted into my peripheral vision and continued to rotate as I gently keeled over. Looking up at the ceiling for a moment seemed to bring me round and I would like to report that I sprang to my feet and took an eight count, but I fear I more likely just emerged slowly and in installments from the lino. I righted my chair and asked, quite as if nothing had occurred, 'So, Thommo, what we watching then?' Anyone else would have learned a valuable lesson about his own limitations. I, on the other hand, resolved to pay no attention to it whatsoever.

The centre of house life was, for the entire time I was at Woolverstone, the common room. A large open space on the ground floor, with an anteroom for reading newspapers or books, the common room had a table tennis table in it. All of us would gather there in the evenings after prep, on afternoons after rugby and at weekends. It was the hub of our social life, where we argued, took the piss out of one another, bullied or got bullied, had fights and, best of all, learned to play table tennis.

For hour upon hour, we would play tournaments and epic matches, usually topped out by a game of Round the Table. Round the Table involved lots of boys starting at each end, hitting a ball across the table and then running up to the other end for the next turn. Round the Table was funny and dangerous after a while but what we loved, adored – were fanatical about – was a one -on-one match. We all spent money on quality bats with dimples, padding and rubber sheets of varying thickness. We learned how to spin the ball, swerve it, smash it from below the table top itself, and some boys developed a serve that sent the ball gyrating over the net in a supernatural arc so unpredictable that sometimes it was almost impossible to return the ball as it pinged wildly off your bat in every direction. Our epic competitions could last hours. Sometimes, seniors would come into the room and demand the right to use the table, which in the middle of a tournament could be soul-destroying. Off we would trudge, our delirious fun ruined by a couple of seniors who couldn't have cared less. From time to time, a rebellion would erupt, usually when someone only a year or so older than us would try it on. As we grew bigger and more confident, the worm would turn. Des launched himself at one such bully who crashed through the table, with Des beating him senseless, but the table was knackered after that and we couldn't play anyway.

In the anteroom, I first began to read newspapers and heard about Thatcher and her rise to power. I remembered Thatcher from her days as education minister and the time she stopped primary children getting daily milk. My political opinions began to take form in that anteroom, and I even wrote a letter to Thatcher, telling her what I thought of her. The soft chairs would become tattered and torn from the lack of care we gave them, and many a long argument would evolve, especially on freezing winter days, when we stayed in the warm, waiting for tea time to come. Some of us loved to argue for the sheer hell of it and Woolverstone gave us what ordinary day schools couldn't: time.

Time together, just being growing young men. Today, when on holiday, I love more than anything the pointless but hugely entertaining sit-down; drinks in hand, blathering about nothing in particular. We get so little chance for such pleasures these days. I can smell that common room and I can see its walls, the low radiator that ran around the edge of the room, the table tennis table and the chairs. I can hear the laughter of my friends as though they sit at my side now. I learned as much in that room as in any classroom.

Music was a passion for all of us but, oddly, our group

had rejected entirely the growing punk movement and was obsessed with the likes of George Duke, Narada Michael Walden and many other jazz-funk pioneers. Black music, groove and soul were the heartbeat of our generation, or so we thought, not the gobbing, ugly, scruffy dirge of the Sex Pistols. My own tastes were eclectic, to say the least, for not only did I love the jingly funk grooves of Herbie Hancock, but I also adored the pompous rock of Genesis, Yes, Emerson, Lake and Palmer, Steely Dan and many others. I was in love with the Music of John Martyn, too. Later, he and another of my favourites, Phil Collins (because of his drumming prowess), would collaborate on one of the greatest albums of all time, Martyn's *Grace and Danger*. I loved to listen through headphones to the live grandiosity of Genesis and Phil Collins' drum solos. I dreamed of playing them and adored the extravagant scope of the music – almost operatic, I suppose. It was ostentatious bollocks, of course, like much of opera, but neither is diminished for being so. Hours could be occupied listening to and arguing about albums.

Our quarrelling was a constant but never malignant habit, and was another aspect of a life at Woolverstone that could provide so much more in the way of time to indulge our pleasures. Friendships grew and flourished and sometimes died in those hours spent doing nothing but hanging out, listening to music and mocking each other. The love of a good ruckus has never left me, and I find dispute necessary and entertaining; not many people agree with me on this, which means I can have a good argument with them.

I have recently finished reading Stephen Fry's excellent autobiography *Moab is my Washpot*. The trials and tribulations of his school life are rendered in language that only he could hope to get away with, but I was struck by the similarities between our respective schools – his and Woolverstone. They had the same rules and regulations, systems, hierarchies; and the boys seemed to have the same concerns with it all. Fry, of course, came from a healthily middle class background with a high-achieving father. The problems he encountered in his life are well documented in both the book itself and elsewhere, but his fairly privileged background did nothing to prevent his thieving tendencies or generally bad behaviour. He talks of his home life in his large Norfolk mansion, and it seems a million miles from my own experience. When, however, he talks of his school life, he could easily be talking about Woolverstone, and it illustrates to me quite what a gift Woolverstone was to most of us, since it was not something our sort was commonly offered. Fry's book proved something else too, which is that boys will be boys, whatever their background.

Being exposed to your peers for twenty-four hours of every day, whilst challenging at times, did teach us other things, and I don't just mean how to make a bed or sweep floors. I believe I learned about empathy at Woolverstone, and how to discern the hurt behind bravado. A boy's emotions would vary through the course of a full day, after which there is no going home to Mum. That immersive experience is profoundly affecting, whether the mood is a good or bad one and I recall occasionally feeling very

alone at times, despite Serge, and despite my new friends
and the hubbub of house life. What you do at such times
is, I suppose, the key to how you turn out in the end
because it forms you, equips you. None of this is evident
at the time, of course, but my tactic was sometimes to
slope off for a bit to be on my own, though more usually
I would just bounce into the dorm and annoy someone.
I think it was Woolverstone that gave me the ability to
assume the pose of engagement with those around me, to
be the loud one, the entertaining one, the gregarious one.
At school, it felt as though one had to be so to compete
and to survive, but even now, after decades in the working
world, including jobs that require me to be at the centre
of a room full of people, I often feel like a performing
seal who would so much rather just disappear, slink off
elsewhere and be alone. After a long evening of company,
when the party is still going strong, I get a powerful urge
to vanish from the throng and frequently do, without
fanfare or even a 'goodbye' sometimes.

There were rewards at Woolverstone, some carrot and
not all stick. On Saturday evenings, there were film shows
in the school hall, either junior films or more violent or
racy senior films. Usually it was some war movie or other,
like *The Eagle has Landed*. Richard Harris was always in
them. I do remember once seeing the first reel of an Indian
porn movie that had been sent in error by whichever organ-
isation supplied them. It was called *Arabian Nights*, and
I think the master showing it expected an oriental fantasy
of a different kind. We howled our protest at his desperate
lunge for the off switch, but he only succeeded in stopping

the reel, not turning off the hot lamp, and the still phallus in the frame quickly burned away on screen.

You could be deprived of these evenings by a prefect, who might sometimes be deeply annoying and bar you from the event, but the booty offered for scoring well in 'Standards' was most important. I call these 'Standards' because I cannot precisely remember the real name, but that might be the right one. I think we also knew them as 'pluses and minuses'. Whatever; it was an end of term exercise in which masters from each of your subjects would award a plus for good work and effort or a minus for less than satisfactory endeavour. I think you could get nothing, i.e. just satisfactory. About a week before the end of term, a great big matrix of names and boxes would be posted on the house noticeboard, and we would eagerly gather around to see the results. Three pluses and you got a reward, which was either a day in Felixstowe at the old funfair there or a trip to Ipswich to see a movie. In the first year at Woolverstone, I would frequently get three, four, five and even, once, six pluses. Later, six minuses were more common.

Felixstowe is most famous as a shipping port, and whatever you can imagine about a port on the east coast facing the North Sea is nothing compared to the reality. The wind blew, the sun hardly ever shone and people were rare. Grey was the prevailing colour; of the sky, of the sea, the pallor of the locals. Well, actually, that is my memory of it, but I fear I do it an injustice because I recently had reason to visit the town again and there is a pretty parade of colourful homes and establishments on the sea front. But the *memory* is the vital thing, I think.

Crowds never overwhelmed the old funfair, even in summer, but there was the immeasurable excitement of a go-kart racing track and we tended to spend all of our money there in the first hour of the day. Irrespective of the grimness of the surroundings, it was, above all, a group day out, a release from school and its routines. However, the very first time I scored enough pluses was when the movie *Rocky* had just been released and the prize was a trip into Ipswich to see it. People often forget that the very first low budget *Rocky* film was actually an Oscar winner, and we were knocked out by it, if you will forgive the pun. When we left the cinema to walk back to the school bus, we all jogged and jabbed our way along the pavement, exhilarated by Sly's magnificent success in the ring. I had a sneaky Italian pride thing going on, too, but I never articulated it. Boys *en masse* shadow-boxing their way back to the car park and the old LCC School Bus must have appeared threatening to the locals in Ipswich, but we were only being silly. I also recall being energised by the notion of exclusive reward; twenty boys seeing *Rocky* meant that forty others in the house hadn't, and all this just because I did my work in lessons. Though clearly, I quickly got bored with movies.

Sport was a huge part of Woolverstone life, as was practising to play it. Cross country runs, circuits and two hours of training twice a week on the pitch and then a match on Saturday. We also had the chance to partake of other sports such as fencing, badminton, squash, orienteering, canoeing, archery, sailing on the marina at Woolverstone and a seemingly endless number of physical activities. Physical expression is appealing to most young men, and to young men whose academic dedication was questionable it offered a route to success. Boys who were simply not physically inclined were never excused participation, but they were never drilled excessively. Woolverstone would seek other outlets for these kids. I enrolled in the gym club in the second term and discovered that, despite my stocky frame, I was good at it, being able to walk the length of the gym on my hands and perform a double somersault off a springboard, although I rarely landed on my feet.

It was about this time that we all began to discover the nooks and crannies of the seventy acres of land upon which the school sat. Every night and weekend was spent playing in the woods, wrecking the lawns by sliding down the hilly ones on our arses when the rain fell; or we ventured down to the foreshore, trudging through the thick mud or leaping into it from the apex of a rope's swing. British Bulldog was, however, the great craze of the day, and scores of us would hone our rugby skills on the terraced lawns below the main house of the school. But in that second term, my sporting ways were to cease for a period after a miscalculation at gym club.

Executing a straddle vault over the long box, I calculated that *not* taking my hand off it before swinging my legs through behind me would be fine. This was a miscalculation, and I broke my arm. Not that this was immediately apparent, not even from the howling and screaming I was engaged in. Indeed, it was my thumb that hurt the most, but my bawling was not going to spoil the humour in the moment for my gymnastic colleagues, who all laughed like drains. I actually consider it to be to my credit that, despite my condition, I still tried to punch one or two of them before Kev Young, one of the sports masters, grabbed me and sent me the short distance to sickbay.

Sickbay was a small house behind the gym and music blocks. It had an examining room and several small dorms upstairs that acted as wards. Sister Allen was in charge, and she looked pretty concerned when I arrived clutching my arm. She examined it quickly in her jolly-hockey-sticks manner, which is to say that, unless the limb was hanging by a thread and pumping blood she took a very pragmatic and unfussy approach to things. In the absence of exposed sinew and spurting claret, she wrapped my arm in bandages and sent me up to one of the rooms to lie on a bed 'to calm down'.

Sickbay was Sister Allen's domain and it was like a tiny cottage hospital over which she held complete sovereignty. Although obsessed with cleanliness she still kept a dog in the building, and Jasper, a huge standard poodle, followed me up to the small dorm. I was whining and whimpering when Jasper lifted his huge bulk up onto the bed and spread himself across the lower part of my legs. He was as heavy as ten sandbags, but he began to lick my swollen, damaged arm. It must have cut quite a scene, like something from a dreary Swedish drama, that empathetic dog and the snivelling boy. I suppose it was the sort of thing weird people who obsess about the paranormal drone on about in late night satellite TV programmes; the intuition of animals or whatever. Personally, I think Jasper liked the taste of bandages. I would love to say it soothed the pain away but in truth his committed, rough slurping hurt like hell; yet it was a touching gesture from a dumb animal and I appreciated it. Plus, it was melodramatic, and I liked that. After an hour, Sister Allen sent me back to Hall's, telling me to return on Thursday afternoon when the doctor came for surgery. This was Monday night so I had to last almost three whole days and nights.

This wasn't easy.

Sleepless, unable to eat, I quickly became sickly and exhausted, the pain throbbing relentlessly in my arm. When my sprained thumb had halved in size, the pain in my wrist and arm doubled. There were no painkillers, I still had lessons to manage and it was at one of those that my first real loathing was born. It was for a maths teacher; a former rugby legend at the school and a cussed, cantankerous bugger. He taught in one of the Nissen huts that were first built at the school when it played an important part in the RAF's communications system during the Second World War. Sitting at the front of his class was a pre-requisite for me because I had been disruptive in my first lesson. My arm and lack of sleep were taking their toll on me; I felt nauseous and wretched, and so I was resting my head on my good arm when he saw me. Suddenly he had snatched my geometry set from the table and flung it through the window he always kept open, even in winter. Such was his rage at my inattentiveness, he then landed a kick on the front of my table that in turn knocked me off my chair, causing me to land heavily on my injured arm.

Even though we had become used to the concept of

physical admonishment from masters, this, even to us, seemed to have crossed the line. It was not the controlled punishment of the plimsoll, a situation where a sort of deal is struck between punisher and punished. I was prepared to succumb to the system to the extent that I would play my part in that agreement, but this was just vicious and spiteful and I never forgave the teacher for it. Several boys, including Rob, voiced their disapproval but focused more on preventing me from lunging at him.

Thursday and the doctor's surgery took an age to arrive, and when I walked in and showed him my deformed and heavily bruised arm, he ordered I be taken to hospital immediately. Our matron at Hall's House was responsible for taking me by bus to Ipswich, and she wasn't pleased about it, marching as quickly as she could, chiding me for falling behind. She never realised that the more she displayed her annoyance, the more I sought to add to her irritation. I dragged my feet, winced at every step and generally played silly buggers. I was very put out by what seemed a total lack of sympathy, and decided that if I could prevent her finding time to pop into her favourite shop, I would.

Matrons at Woolverstone were as varied as were the masters. Their role in the house was to arrange the laundry, take care of personal needs, injuries and minor illnesses and generally 'mother' the younger boys when they needed it. Our matron was not unpleasant, but she was a pragmatic, Presbyterian type of Scot, which meant there was little natural sympathy about her. If you know the sort of formal Scottish woman I am talking about, you will understand what I mean. She was prim, proper, neatly turned out and solved everything with a matter-of-factness that meant, for example, that any injury or ailment could be solved by soaking it in hot then cold water. She was a mixture of Miss Jean Brodie and Mr Mackay from Porridge, just not as benevolent as either. I never thought she liked boys much, and although she was generally kind, warmth was never the first thing to emanate from her. This last-minute demand on her personal time went down like cold sick, but I was acutely aware of her discomfort and resolved to make the day as difficult as possible, though the extent of the unease I would cause her came as something of a surprise to me too.

At the hospital, a pipe-smoking doctor nearly had his block knocked off when he insisted on twisting my arm during his examination. Why do doctors do that to injured limbs? He was gently holding my arm and feeling the limb softly with his fingertips. I was twitching and jerking with every press and palpation, but he suddenly took hold of my hand and turned it quickly. The world came to a stop, the light became blinding and the room turned as four hundred knives were thrust through my bone. I took a swipe at him with my good hand as the pain seared through me in a sudden, sickening shock. Indeed, he was lucky that the shock didn't make me sick all over him. I was unable to scream or utter a single sound.

'Oh,' he said, 'that would appear to be a bit painful, young man.' He hadn't yet bothered to look up at me to see the bulging eyes and distress etched on my face. You had to get up early to catch this fellow out, I could tell.

As the wave of pain hit the summit and then subsided, I was able to muster the breath to give my opinion of his diagnosis.

'Of course it's fucking painful! Why the fucking hell did you fucking twist it, you fucking bastard!?'

To be fair to him, he hardly flinched at the tirade, but Matron was almost choking, and she staggered backwards a little, buffeted by the force of my fulmination, as if an unseen sniper had shot her.

'Michael VOLPE!' Matron intervened, 'you will NOT speak to the doctor with such FOUL language!'

'I don't fucking CARE,' I screeched, the word 'care' coming out so high-pitched that it was almost inaudible to humans. 'He just twisted my arm, and it fucking hurts like fucking fuck, for fuck's *sake*!'

While Matron nearly passed out, the doctor sat quietly, sucking on his pipe. With a warm smile and a nonchalance he could only have honed from twisting lots of broken arms and seeing the reaction, he said, 'Let's get an X-ray and see what's going on. I don't think we'll worry about the bad language too much.' As a nurse gently coaxed me through to the X-ray suite, I was grateful that the doctor had taken the onslaught so well, but the method of his diagnosis had returned to me the violent hurt and trauma of the moment when the injury had first occurred. Matron's indignation was the least of my concerns.

The episode of the broken arm was all a bit traumatic when I think about it. The three days of agony had left a deep mark on me, and I felt terribly homesick during those awful seventy-two hours, but for some reason I never once used the payphone in the hall of the neighbouring house to call Mum. I can only deduce that I did not want to worry her. Actually, as I write, I am not sure that anyone ever informed her of my injury. It is possible I just turned up at home with my arm in the plaster, although I doubt it somehow. It created a sense of vulnerability, a feeling that my tough skin had fallen away.

Did I feel sorry for myself? I honestly don't think I did. I was in too much genuine pain and felt too dreadful for that, but I cried quietly into my pillow every single night as the pain intensified with darkness and the loneliness I felt in my bunk. I thought about my friend in the plaster of Paris trousers and how he suffered pain every night, and I tried to draw some strength of character from his memory, but it never worked. Only Rob would drop from his bunk to see how I was. Empathy is a quality Rob has always possessed, and he had it even at eleven. Some years ago, he and I went skiing in Italy, where one morning I slipped on ice and crashed to the ground, wailing as I tore several ligaments in my ankle, but Rob's discomfort and trauma was greater than my own. I don't think he felt quite the same way in 1977, but he was sensitive enough to appreciate what I might have been feeling and he would look genuinely troubled when he saw my pain. But in my memory, at least, he was the *only* one.

Maybe it was no more than I deserved.

It occurs to me that maybe the tough guy persona I had been cultivating since I had arrived was now coming back to haunt me; either my other pals were too uncomfortable to show sympathy or they quietly relished my suffering, but I'll never know. I haven't yet decided whether Woolverstone's hard-nosed approach to injury and self-preservation was a good or bad thing. No doubt, its effect differed from character to character, yet, as odd as it sounds, to cry in public, even at so tender an age, was not advisable at Woolverstone. I mean, I might have shed a tear when screaming obscenities at the maths master who booted me from my chair, and I certainly sprang a leak when the doctor performed origami on my forearm, but I never just whimpered or wept at the pure undiluted pain of it all. For the three days before seeing the doctor, I wandered around with a fixed expression of misery and a substantial element of grumpiness too. I don't think I invited sympathy, and I'm not sure I wanted it anyway, but I never bawled.

It turned out that I had a serious fracture and was put in plaster up to my shoulder, which drew the curtain on my rugby for the year. But it did not put a stop to my British Bulldog career, which continued with renewed vigour now that I had a weapon. The vulnerability I had felt needed exorcising, so I crowned many people foolish enough to try and halt my passage across the lawn and shattered the plaster twice. When I broke the cast, Matron had to take me back to Ipswich. On neither occasion did she make it to her favourite shop. That says something about me, but I think it says more about her.

TOP OF THE SLOPE

Life back at home for Mum was marginally improved by not having to worry too greatly about Serge or me. Matteo was his usual self, though; his banditry wasn't getting any better and one drama or another frequently blemished holidays. He was sixteen by then, was still into girls and had begun to dabble in harder drugs. A policeman kicking the door down at dawn was becoming a frequent event, as were visits by Mum, with Serge and me during school holidays, to various borstals and detention centres. Lou was eighteen, and a photographer's assistant to Rodney Wright-Watson, a famous art photographer who catalogued the great collections in museums and large private homes, including those of Her Majesty. The job also meant Lou got to use the big saloon that Rodney owned, and he would occasionally drive Mum up to Woolvo to visit. I never told anybody that he did not own the car.

When I ponder those days, when my brothers were all teenagers, it strikes me how different we all were and still are. Lou was the quietest and most shy, and although he wasn't an angel, being a persistent truant, he generally kept himself to himself, never wanted to be the centre of attention and could not have been more the opposite of my demonstrative, attention-seeking incarnation. He is probably also the brightest of all of us. Serge was more like me: he too was a show-off, a performer, and was quickly developing a Woolverstone 'face' and a fiery temper – more fiery, even, than mine – but he had a better attitude to academia than I did.

Matt had his own problems but was a bit of a cad, a real London boy. I think I would probably have turned out most like him had Woolverstone not intervened. Matt was effusively attached to Mum, and though his 'issues' were to be a lifelong burden for her, she never gave up on him. She once recounted to me that when Matt was born, she and my father had been desperate for a girl that they could name after my nonna (Lou is really Luigi, named after my grandfather). Matt appeared and there was, she said, a sense of disappointment. She carried the guilt of that reaction and blamed herself for how he was appearing to turn out. She certainly paid her dues in that respect; when I was in my late teens I remember the telephone ringing one night and hearing Mum erupt into hysteria. Matt was in prison at the time, and the caller, claiming to be an officer of that establishment, was regrettably having to inform her that Matt had died in his cell that evening. I took the phone and the person hung up, but a few calls to the prison established that Matt was fine, and the call had been a hoax. I have no doubt that such episodes (and there were many) ate away at Mum's spirit relentlessly. In reality Matt would actually die of a sudden cerebral event, in May 2013, at the age of 52. Such events are supposedly random, but it is hard to discount his life of excess as a factor. He was complex, troubled but enormously good-hearted until the end, and his death was a real blow. When he died, I wrote about the events of a week that still haunt me, and I reproduce it here because I can't go through writing about it afresh.

★ ★ ★

It was a late Saturday afternoon when the hospital called me. My brother Matteo, the voice said, was in intensive care after a bleed on his brain, and his wife, Nikki, had asked them to contact me. 'He has had a very significant haemorrhage, Mr Volpe. It's very grave and we can only offer palliative care,' she said, with a professional sweetness I still find remarkable. She had done this before.

Having rushed to Charing Cross hospital, just two hundred yards from my house, I felt in familiar surroundings, because Matteo had been in their intensive care unit twice within the past four years; first for an aneurism and, later, septicaemia. But whilst he had reason to thank his lucky stars for surviving both, this time it felt different. I met with a stern but gentle consultant who showed me the CT scan they had done of Matt's head. Even I could tell that the bloom of brightness that permeated most of the left half of his brain equated to a colossal event that, if he survived, would render him seriously disabled at best.

'Have you ever seen anybody live through something this big?' I asked. After a long, thoughtful silence, she replied, 'Yes', but she was offering no solace, just stating

a fact, and her pause was designed to test my intuition. My intuition passed, telling me everything I needed to know.

If A&E is the 'poor bloody infantry', then ICU is where the SAS reside. In a dazzlingly equipped ward of just four patients, Matteo, in a coma, was tended constantly by a nurse in scrubs, testing, examining, watching and entering figures onto a metre-wide chart of bewildering complexity. Matteo was taking his own breaths, but a ventilator was helping him. A good sign? Automated syringes pumped constant streams of powerful sedatives into him to keep him asleep; their withdrawal would be the first big test for him. I was a constant source of questions, wanting to understand every drug, every machine, every bright, flashing and multicoloured reading on the screens. I would look at the charts, trying to work out the meaning of the vast matrix of measurements, vital signs, blood and chemical analysis. And not once did a professional in that ward prevaricate, nor did they lose patience or turn their eyes heavenwards. In the past, I have always found doctors and nurses to be reluctant to engage in anything more than rudimentary, patronising chitchat. This time they indulged, offered more than was asked for, and I knew, deep down, that they were sorry for us, pitying us, perhaps knew that this was all a short road to the inevitable.

Matteo had got through the first twenty-four hours. He was taken off the sedative for the first time on Monday, but a while later it was reintroduced as he showed no sign of awakening and his blood pressure began to fluctuate dangerously. He had reacted to a pinch: a natural reflex, but still a small sign of hope. My conversations with the doctors took on a slowly increasing clinical quality because I wanted to understand and I had to report developments to Serge and Lou in Scotland and the USA. I needed infor- mation and wanted to know outcomes. I was in and out of the ward several times daily and I got to know the nurses and doctors. By Tuesday they tried to withdraw sedation again; this time he lasted an hour before desta- bilising. Still the doctors indulged me, still they answered my questions. By now I was discussing the options with my brothers by email or Skype. Along with Nikki, we had to make decisions on resuscitation, on what criteria we would base a decision to withdraw Matt's life support; a sense of conscious thought being present, even if seriously disabled? Nikki said cremation had always been Matt's choice, and I found myself thinking about music for his funeral. I called a soprano friend to ask if she would perform.

At midnight on Wednesday night a doctor I had come to know well telephoned me. Since Saturday I had been waiting for a call to say that Matteo had given up his fight, but this wasn't quite as dramatic – yet it was the first, painful step. Matt had 'blown a pupil' and his blood pressure had crashed. This was the first sign that the bleed was affecting his brain stem, from which there was no return. I sent emails to my brothers. Serge wrote back, 'Go and sit with him, talk to him, tell him we love him, that it is going to be OK, that we are all with him and not to be scared.'

And so I did. I whispered in his ear, in the darkened

ward, accompanied by a symphony of bleeps and quiet alarms, and sat with him all through the night, sustained by tea, made for me by his nurse. At 7am, I returned home; Matt had made it through the night.

Later at midday of Thursday I returned to the ward to be told that his other pupil had blown and that there really was no hope. The neurological teams had assessed him again too, and their view was the same. So we retired to a private room with two doctors and the head of nursing, a new face. Nikki and I fired questions, and the doctors deflected any that required a definitive timescale or which might offer hope. They handled it beautifully. The head of nursing was also the transplant coordinator for the hospital, and he asked if we would consider donating Matteo's kidneys. A burst of something resembling joy filled me; yes, that would be something wonderful for Matteo. It would take twelve hours to identify potential recipients, to line up the processes and they explained how it worked, how Matt would be taken to theatre, how in the anaesthetic room next door his support would be withdrawn. After death, five minutes would be allowed to elapse before going into theatre to harvest the organs. The twelve-hour timescale meant 2am for this to happen but Nikki was adamant he would not die during the night because since his aneurism operation, he had become afraid of the dark. Graciously they all agreed this would be fine, and we bartered about whether it should be 8am or 9am. We went for 9am.

I returned to the ward and saw his nurse attaching a bottle of something brown and milky to one of the tubes leading to Matt's nose. It was his feed, and I at first wondered what the point was, given the conversation I'd had a few moments before. And then I understood.

Matt needed to hold on now so those kidneys could be given to someone. Some family members visited that evening to say goodbye to him and I went home to try to sleep, my appointment with my brother's death made. Sleep didn't come easily, but when it arrived, it bludgeoned me, the previous night's vigil having taken a toll. The meeting with Nikki at 8.30am for coffee was as normal and as benign as any ordinary day but played out with a surreal soundtrack, a numbness and clinical monotone. We went to Matt's bedside, to be told the two potential recipients had been tested but that tissue typing had revealed there could not be any organ donation. They were sorry, and we were crushed. We resolved that it was 'not to be' and proceeded to ask more questions about the mechanics of Matteo's death.

We were asked if we would like to be with him at the moment of passing, but after some thought decided against it. Would he suffer? No. He was requiring ever-increasing levels of support and it would be swift. Would they give him some morphine just in case? 'Yes,' said the doctor, 'I promise. I will do it myself.' I stroked Matt's head and said, 'See you later, Matt.'

And then we went for a coffee. After twenty minutes I telephoned the ward and asked if Matteo had died. 'Yes, he passed and we are giving last offices. You can come back.'

And so we returned to be with Matt for the last time,

only now with no tubes, sallow of cheek, quiet and the machines weren't purring and chattering, their screens dark. He went very quickly, they said, within five minutes, peacefully, with no struggle. He just stopped living. I can't yet articulate what I felt on seeing him then, I simply don't have the words, but it is in my mind's eye constantly still.

With our NHS under threat, it takes an episode like this to realise what we have. Those doctors and nurses fought for Matt, even though they held little hope of a positive outcome. The treatment would have cost a great deal of money, and during one of my many conversations with doctors, a consultant had said she had only seen one patient with a bleed this extensive leave the ICU alive. With those odds, how many bean counters might baulk at the efforts made to improve on that solitary statistic?

The medical team gave him a dignity it is hard to fathom and harder to describe, unless you have seen it given. In all truth, Matt left us on that first Saturday, but had he simply died then, I would not have been there to walk him to his end, to see him living and fighting and being given that chance. And we were, I suppose, more gently introduced to the notion of his passing, spared the suddenness and shock. Hospitals are there to save lives, but they can also help people like Matt to their end whilst performing heroically to try to prevent it. The great monument to our civilised values that the NHS represents is perhaps even more evident in their 'failures' and their vainglorious attempts than in their successes. And that is a thing of great distinction that cannot be qualified by cost nor visualised in profit terms.

We asked those mourning at his funeral that donations should be made to the Friends of Charing Cross. They had performed miracles twice before for Matt, but in the caring and dignified process of not doing it a third time, they – and society – had possibly made their greatest gift to him.

* * *

My life at the school was settled. I always bemoaned the return from holiday, but in reality I was drifting away from friends at home anyway, so it was nice to get back to what had become my first-choice gang. I liked the sport at school, too, and was forever keen to get back into it. Autumn term was the time for normal fifteen-a-side rugby, spring term was for sevens and summer was for cricket. Amid the sporting endeavour, it had not really dawned on me that Woolverstone was, above all else, a scholastic enterprise. I *knew* why I was there, but the hours of sport were when I felt most at home, and to academia I found it hard to apply myself for more than the bare minimum of time. I knew what I was good at and paid more attention to that, but I was insufferably difficult to reach on other topics. I did not find the work difficult; I just had a lot of chips on my shoulder and was busy establishing whatever reputation I believed would deliver the status I thought I deserved. It never occurred to me that masters had seen it all before, but I sensed they were not unduly worried. In any case, I was unused to people showing any sort of concern for my welfare beyond that of my brothers and mother, so I probably liked the negative attention I would frequently provoke.

It is easy to see from here that I was an angry boy with an inflated sense of what was right and what was wrong. My being in charge was right; anyone telling me what to do was unequivocally, indisputably wrong. We were still settling into the routines of daily life, working our way through the system, absorbing the constant expectation and trying, ever trying, to rise up to the required level, and occasionally failing to do so wasn't held against us too fiercely at that stage. Egos are not supposed to amount to much in young boys but mine could have floated one of those cargo tankers on the Orwell.

The school day at Woolverstone was long, finishing at 5.30pm with the end of the final double period of one subject or another. It would all begin with an assembly that took the form of most school assemblies; masters on stage, announcements, hymns and occasional 'thought for the day' type pronouncements from Paddy, followed by lessons, lunch at 12.30pm, and then either a couple of hours free or, if a Tuesday or Thursday, two hours of rugby training, which meant no late lesson. Assembly was always where a feud of one kind or another might get resolved as all the protagonists came together in one place, and it was common to see a good scrap in the hallway after assembly. Assembly was also a time to fear if it was your birthday, because the swimming pool was next to the assembly hall and getting thrown into that on your birthday was a tradition that didn't care what season it was. A celebrant broke ice on his way in once.

I always remember the hymn singing as being full-blooded and actually very accomplished. All the old favourites were there, but in common with almost all schools, it seems, 'Jerusalem' was the big stirring number. 'Bread of Heaven' was a favourite too, the 'Feed me 'til I want no more' chorus being fully rendered in harmony and voice section. It was terribly showy. Sunday assemblies were more formal, and we had to wear blazers and ties for these. Guest speakers would appear, or musical guests, most notably *Cantabile*, a vocal group featuring an old Woolverstonian that had found some fame and success, who would give a short concert. We were told that our speakers would be fantastically interesting, and sometimes they were announced with the sort of fanfare that suggested we were in the presence of greatness, but I cannot remember a single one of them by name, or of what they spoke. On particular festivals such as Easter and Christmas, Sunday assembly was in St Michael's Church, and I was frequently asked to do a reading. I'm not sure why at that stage they had decided I was a performer of some fashion, but it always seemed to be me. A few verses from the Bible were the normal way of things and I loved seeing my name printed in the Order of Service:

Reading
by Michael Volpe, Hall's House
15:7 Benevolence

The power of print began there for me, the reading I would scarcely acknowledge, meaning and reason flying over my head. As I took my place at the dais to read the selected verses, I was only relishing my fame, smug and trussed up in blazer and tie.

> *If there is a poor man among your brothers in any of the towns of the land that the LORD your God is giving you, do not be hard-hearted or tight-fisted toward your poor brother.*

I might not have been paying attention to the sentiments of the New Testament, but I was able to bring nuance and emphasis to the moments that required it. Or at least the moments I thought needed it. I understood emphasis. I was *always* insufferably, voluminously *emphatic*.

A day of lessons was long, to be sure, longer than we would ever have expected at an ordinary London school, which we knew finished at about 3pm, but academic activity was most attentively observed during prep. For prep, all boys in the school were either closeted together in their house dining room or in their small dorms and rooms for the older boys. It was two hours every night for us first formers, and we would sit with twenty others from the second and third forms doing our homework. A sixth former would supervise the prep, and talking or any kind of communication was forbidden. Most sixth formers had their own work to do and would look up occasionally when some misdemeanour was committed, in which case, the miscreant was put into prefect's detention. The head boy would read out the names at Friday assembly, and we would always hold our breath, hoping that the senior who had threatened us with PD had forgotten to put our name down. Usually the bugger remembered. There were no emails or mobile phones back then, so a prefect had to make a bit of an effort to lodge your name with the head boy.

Prep was among the greatest cultural shocks Woolverstone presented. At home, after school, I would normally have been straight out into the estate to muck about or get up to no good. It was my time, and I recall no homework being given to me at primary school. A long day in lessons followed by hours doing prep was something of an outrageous new development for most of us.

Some of the sixth formers who supervised prep saw it as a wonderful opportunity to torment us because they simply had nothing better to do. Ask to go to the toilet and you would be made to sit in front of the senior as he poured water from one jug to another. If you looked away, you would get a 'head dot', which was when the knuckles of the clenched fist would be brought down sharply onto your skull. For really serious fuck-ups, you would get a 'bowler'. This was when you got a head dot, but only after the sixth former had run the length of the dining room and performed a bowling action as you stood, head bowed, waiting for the crack.

When prep was peaceful, I managed to get lots of work done, but I was choosy about what I paid most attention to, lavishing loving care on biology, for example, underlining headings in red and taking ages over technical drawings of cells and pictures of stamens. For this purpose, I had a full case with tools and coloured pencils. I loved exercise books – still do – fat and crisp and clean at the start of term and becoming more ruffled and grimy as the weeks progressed. My writing was quite neat, but my hand was heavy and would put a thousand tiny creases in the paper, making each page dimpled and crunchy. But there were boys whose elegant hand flowed across the page delicately and cleanly, and their books were filled with even, fluid text, punctuated by neat, forensically accurate monotone diagrams. Not a superfluous underlining or piece of colour would be found anywhere, and the pages of their books never became crinkled or crusty. I envied their effortless precision and intelligence – I still do.

I treated English prep with a certain reverence, but maths and most other subjects got short shrift. We were studying interesting books in first-year English, most memorably for me, *The Catcher in the Rye,* a book I suspect many of us identified with closely. Holden Caulfield's rage and angst was a challenging subject for eleven-year-olds, but I recall agreeing with lots of what he said, despite thinking him a bit of a whinger. Indeed, assigning the book to eleven-year-olds is an indicator of Woolverstone's ambition for us, and I doubt the school thought any of us would go on to assassinate a pop star.

I greatly enjoyed essays and reviews since I had a chance to vent spleen or offer an opinion that I had probably already presented loudly in class. I wasn't, however, particularly good at them. Essays would begin well – my hand would be scrupulously tidy, my analysis thorough. By the second or third page, both calligraphy and scrutiny were going south. Maintaining a patient approach to argument, contemplation, vocabulary or writing style had always been difficult for me. Often it was because my thoughts would race ahead and I'd be trying to articulate them from their slipstream, as they disappeared off into the distance. Invariably and inevitably, I would struggle to make out their full form as they drifted away, but no matter, some new ones would be along in a minute and maybe I would keep up with *them*. It is why my work was always only two-thirds finished. If I was lucky, what I managed to get down on paper would roughly approximate the point I had set out to make (as long as you could read the handwriting, of course). Usually, the relevant master would be able to mark me well enough to convince me it had not all been a total waste of time and if astute enough, he would decipher for himself the point I was trying to make. Brilliant teachers can do that, and I was fortunate to have many of those.

So, I was doing OK.

If that sounds a little underwhelming, it shouldn't, because, even by Woolverstone's standards, a boy like me doing 'OK' should be viewed with unconfined admiration, if not for the boy, then most definitely for the school.

It was at this point in the first year that the headmaster, Paddy, started to pay more attention to my development. Throughout my school life, there was always at least one teacher who has seen through me and found a way to control my temperamental unpredictability. At Addison Gardens, it was Rhiannon Morris. I met with her after many years, and she recalled how she could be sitting drinking tea in the staff room when a fellow teacher would put their head around the door and demand her attendance

My mother, Lidia

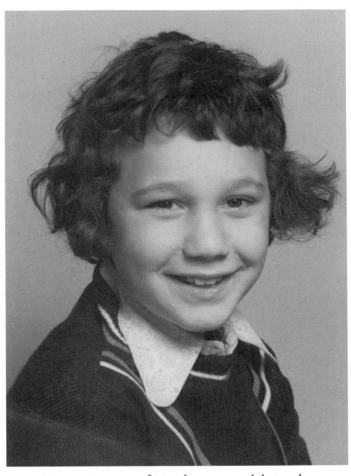

Me, sporting one of Mum's razor-comb hairstyles

Mum and Dad with toddler Lou and baby Matt

Me, Matt and Sergio

Me at school, by the squash court

School photo, 1977. I am far right, seated on the ground.
Immediately behind me is David Hudson, and to his left,
with hands on his knees, is Paddy Richardson

My father's family
with nonno Luigi
at the back in the
white shirt

Mum, with the sort of
look we knew well!

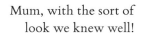

Mum with all her boys
in Ravenscourt Park

Zia Anna and zio Rolando, the circus star

Mum (second left) with her sister Ines, and brothers Rolando and Isidoro

Matt

An early interest in photography did not last long

at an incident involving me. She would rush to the playground, to find me ranting and raving at all and sundry, the result of some insult or injustice. She would just have to bark my name at me, and I would be subdued, whereas countless other teachers trying the same thing had abjectly failed.

Paddy Richardson had the same effect on me. He sometimes called me into his office in his house and would ask how I was getting on, which I never really understood. It was very benign and low key, but he might then fling me a nugget of advice or wisdom.

'I hear you have had some problems with Maths, Michael?' he would enquire gently.

'Well, the teacher doesn't like me, Sir,' I would reply. This is how I *always* replied.

'Do you think he might just be tired of your being disruptive in class?' Blaming me was a risky tactic, but he managed it without sounding as though he knew the answer.

'No, Sir, I don't think it's that, because I only become disruptive when he has been horrible to me or blamed me for something I didn't do.' I would be careful to affect a wounded tone because after all, I actually believed what I was saying.

'Well,' Paddy would sigh, leaning back in his chair, 'I think you may have a point when you say he doesn't like you very much, but it's not his job to like you. It is his job to teach you maths, which you won't let him do. Why not try to let him? Maybe he'll like you more, hmm?'

It was hard to argue with Paddy for long. I never wanted

to get into disputes with him anyway, because I had obviously afforded him the status of 'adult who understands me'. Added to that, agreeing that I was right about the teacher's allergy to me was an exceedingly good tactic, and he did it in a way that still left the onus on me to do something about it. As long as I could tell myself I was right, perhaps I could find the good grace to give the teacher a chance. Paddy was no fool.

In the matter of people not liking me, I am an expert. A young boy is rarely aware of the spikes of his personality that hollow out the flesh of those around him. If those close to me complained, I would more often than not do whatever possible to confirm every negative thought they had. Today, it is still the same inasmuch as some people are inclined to instinctively recoil from me, but now there is a difference: I know precisely what is causing discomfort. Moreover, I have come to realise that when a thorn does penetrate, it is usually because a weak, tender spot exists, and I don't think it is too malignant an idea that I should exploit that from time to time. Woolverstone didn't want to knock those spikes off me: it just wanted to teach me to be more careful when brushing up against others. I find that the world is full of people who love to brandish their personalities like weapons in the pursuit of dominance but who are at the same time totally unprotected from retaliation. Not only that, they are frequently surprised that a riposte should come at all, so it does them no harm to feel a sharp jab in the ribs from time to time. At school, you are not really supposed to probe the emotional or moral weaknesses of your teachers, but I tried my best.

Paddy obviously knew all of this about me before I did (self-awareness was a late-blossoming friend of mine), but getting me educated was not compatible with allowing me to experiment on the psychology of teachers whose default position, after all, was one of dominance. I just had to get on with it and play the game. It was his experience that allowed him to negotiate the minefield that he had almost certainly mapped out immediately after he'd met me for the first time. I quite relished being sent to him by other masters; I knew he would indulge me, and even when he wore a stern look he never let me down in that respect, always doing and saying the right thing and never turning on me. He was fair and understanding in a manner that the *Daily Mail* would ridicule today (you know, enlightened management of difficult adolescents). This is a skill that I am convinced only a few have. The subtle difference between command and encouragement – but encouragement laced with expectation – is what set people like Paddy Richardson apart. Too often, I would detect too little expectation and too much command. Emotionally complex boys are manageable in a way that is not as difficult as it at first seems, and I think that people look more deeply into the problem than is necessary.

Paddy wasn't alone in making a connection of sorts with me. My year card shows that very early on the school had assessed me as 'a very opinionated, emotional boy who is prone to be argumentative'. There was no real secret to dealing with me, and several masters managed to grab my attention whilst delicately tiptoeing around my personality traits. But the school could not afford to be soft, and few masters were.

Paddy certainly wasn't the sort to mollycoddle his charges. One afternoon whilst walking around the circle of lawn between the two wings of the main building, I got into a kicking match with a friend. We swung kicks and lobbed abuse at each other for no particular reason, but I was at a disadvantage since my opponent, the euphoniously named Adebola Adelano, was wearing violently tapered winkle pickers. As I carelessly drew back my crepe-soled beetle crusher, I left myself open to counter-attack, and, while my stance resembled a runner caught on camera, Ade snapped out his foot in a heartbeat. I saw it coming and knew the extent of my error almost the instant my foot left the ground, but I was frozen mid-kick as I thought, 'Oh no!' With perfect accuracy and deceptively terrifying velocity, the honed tip of his shoe connected with the underside of my scrotum, sending each testicle in opposite directions. If I'd had my hands in my pockets, I would have been able to catch them. Readers who have a scrotum will know immediately what happened next. During the time it took for my balls to settle back into their natural position, I stood in stunned, silent expectation of the exquisite pain that would inevitably visit me. I bent at the waist with hands on knees, suppressing the urge to vomit until I softly keeled over onto the floor, where I lay motionless and dribbling. Testicular trauma, along with childbirth, is probably the most profound pain from which survivors emerge, and Paddy, being a man, must have known this. Ten yards away, from his study window, he noticed me prone on the floor in what he must have thought was a most unexpected place. He came out and walked over to me.

'What's wrong with you, Volpe?' Paddy enquired.

I took a while to answer and when I did it was with something like, 'Ki . . . Ade . . . balls . . . Sir.'

'You've been kicked in the balls? Volpe? Is that what you said? You were kicked in the balls?'

'Ye . . . (long pause) Sir.'

He laughed and walked back to his house.

I liked my headmaster a great deal. It isn't easy to explain this relationship – or my view of it at least. I don't know about other boys from a similar background to mine, and I don't want to be overly emotional about it, but I used to single people out as mentors and then proceed to put them to the test; to challenge them, to see if they would stick with me or just give up on me. Of course, it would often be a self-fulfilling prophecy. With Paddy, I had a conditional relationship that I would have set aflame and destroyed had he taken the wrong turn, but I went out of my way not to let him down, and if he praised me after a rugby match or some other minor achievement, it would be the praise I valued most. His was a guiding hand, and whenever Mum came to school for open day, Paddy would reserve some special words for whatever I had done that year. He never made a big deal of my misdemeanours, even though I was sent to him several times for such, and the sullenness that I liberally deployed in dealings with other masters, would evaporate on entering Paddy's large study.

I realised later that he was not singling me out and that he did this for many boys. I suppose that is what made him such a good headmaster. If anybody performed the role of father figure in the absence of the real one, it was Paddy Richardson. To my mind, the lack of a father was never too great a burden for me; mine had made a run for the high road early so there is no significant moment of his departure. Nevertheless, our family's subsequent belief that his contribution to our lives would likely have been minimal and destructive didn't detract from the reality that there was nobody to set me straight, set an example or provide a security framework for life's vicissitudes. When he did pay attention to us, Dad was never very good at it; had he taken a similar approach to me that he chose for Matteo, the outcome would have been catastrophic, I suspect. Responding to a call from Mum, who was becoming desperate about my brother's delinquency, Dad's benighted answer was to give him a kicking in the Fulham Road. Such a course of action may have worked with someone else, but Matteo's nefarious ways were never to be diverted by a thrashing. I can just picture Dad's face as he delivered each corrective blow, and I can well imagine what was going through his head too: the boorish self-satisfaction of a man who hadn't a clue who his son was or what he needed.

How Dad's absence was affecting me I cannot, even now, say. I think it may be too easy to blame my father for the recklessness and unruliness we all showed at one time or another. Fatherless I may have been, yet my reparative approach towards key individuals suggests that I knew the value of a surrogate. There was nothing new in all this for Paddy, who was in charge of many boys like me and who, I later discovered, experienced the divorce of his parents at the age of twelve. I know it's dot-to-dot behaviourism to suppose that the roots of Paddy's *simpatico* reached back to his own family's fracture, but I think a life of fatherless existence allows me such romantic, rosy-tinted speculation.

* * *

The summer of '77 arrived and with it cricket, late evenings and ever more mischief. Rob and I had become firm friends by then and we spent much of the school holidays together too. Rob lived in a large flat in Battersea with his Mum and two sisters, and there were frequent parties and get-togethers. All of us salivated over the blonde bombshells who were his older sisters. Actually, come to think of it, Rob's world was a couple of times removed from my own, although he too had grown up without a father's regular presence. Compared to me he was well spoken, and his Mum's flat, which overlooked Battersea Park, was enormous. I'm not fully aware of what made us so compatible as friends, but we had got over the early pecking order stuff and were getting on with the business of sitting at the top of it together. As a part of that process, we had also developed into an enforcement squad, encouraged by our housemaster to sort out those kids who took bullying too far. Transferring to us the responsibility for protection was part of Morris's clever plan to keep our minds off persecution. Our hearts were unequivocally in it, too, because by that stage, we had grown conscious of the effect our darker behaviour could have. When we realised that being bullied in a place like Woolverstone was hellish, we soon developed empathy for our fellow boarders. It might have made us feel warm all over to reprimand the bully, but it also gave us the opportunity to bully *him* officially. It is no laughing matter, of course.

I hate to think that once I might have been a bully: if I committed crimes against anybody on account of my ability to punch harder than they could, I apologise profusely. But I will claim that my days as a threatening, antagonistic ruffian ended in about April 1977. I loathe bullies of all kinds, be they workplace bullies, people who gang up on others, racist bullies, political bullies, queue jumpers. I might so easily have continued to be a bully if something, someone, whatever or whoever it was, hadn't diverted my undoubted capacity for aggression and violence onto the side of the victim. And I think my zeal is born of the fact that I do indeed understand the emotional poverty that drives a bully to do what he or she does. Of course, back at Woolverstone, I would still tease and assert my authority of sorts because I could never be expected to relinquish that in an environment like that one – *Lord of the Flies* was horribly accurate. Later, as a teenager, my propensity to meet fire with fire was unbounded, as a pair of skinheads following me in a Fulham street discovered late one evening. Their merry abuse of me, encouraged by their superior numbers no doubt, led to an explosion of violence that found its target on the first of them I could lay hands upon. I was enraged not by their abuse, but by their cowardice. At school, as a reformed bully, I felt sympathy for those who before had been my 'victims', and my righteous hostility spelled trouble for any middle-ranking tormentor looking to cut some teeth.

It wasn't as if there were scores of helpless, pitiful boys wandering around the school like starving, abused refugees, but it didn't take much for a boy to fall prey to more than just a bit of teasing. In most cases, the worst kind of bullying came from boys who were in the middle of the natural hierarchy, not at the top. They seemed to be motivated by bitterness and resentment that they themselves were from time to time bullied, and it provoked some viciously sustained cruelty. One victim in particular was crippled by an affliction that could not have been worse in such a place – he had trouble controlling his bowels, which meant from time to time he would have about him a pungent smell. At first, we all joined in, unfeeling and callous in our torturing of this unfortunate boy. But at some point during the year, probably after witnessing another spiteful and heartbreaking example of his misery, we started to line up on his side. I could no longer take his wobbling chin as he fought back his tears, his bowed head and the look in his eyes that cried out for his mother's protective arms. He was weak and vulnerable, but I have never been called upon in my entire life to muster the kind of courage he had to summon up every day. We should all feel shame at how we treated that boy and eventually, after a year and a half, he left the school. What troubles me is that such boys may remember me for the times I taunted them rather than for those when I protected them, since I had been very good at the taunting. At eleven, who knows these things? We were thrown into the pot and stirred, and few of us could resist the power among peers that suddenly became available to us.

* * *

Woolverstone sits to the east of Ipswich on the river Orwell. A visit today does nothing to diminish the beauty of the place, which the memory can often embellish over the years. It is an exquisite part of the country. The climate in winter was harsh and damp, with easterly winds blowing off the North Sea, but in summer – and my memory may well be embroidering here – it was full of golden light and morning mists. Woolverstone in that first summer was a paradise for us urban boys. The evenings seemed to go on forever, and at dusk, swallows would swoop and sway across the playing field in front of the main house. I could spend hours watching them and when, years later, I heard Vaughan Williams' 'The Lark Ascending', it conjured the image of Woolverstone's swallows. As a piece of music, it perfectly encapsulates the English countryside, but it positively produces a living, breathing hologram of Woolverstone for me. The chorus of birdsong on a warm summer evening was intoxicating, with wood pigeon, cuckoo, house martins, blackbirds and so many others I could never identify. The sun seemed to take an eternity to sink behind the hills flanking the Orwell, and when it finally dipped, ushering in the half-light, the bats would come out to feed, chittering and flapping around us as we smoked in the ferns. At eleven, boys rarely appreciate what they have, but from time to time it did dawn on us that we had been blessed with a gift. It might have been expressed in harsh London vernacular, but the sentiment was straight and true.

Boarding schools thrive on tradition, but they thrive best on routine, and Woolverstone was no different. Routine at home didn't exist for me, and neither did normal things like eating at a table or being tied to a schedule. School life therefore had a structure, but our twenty-four hour presence there also created opportunities that London life simply couldn't. Of course, these structures might appear mundane to any outsider, and they certainly weren't always popular with us, but the life of the school was busy and provided endless activities for boys to pursue. The clubs were endless, and alongside being in the junior choir I enjoyed puppetry, pet club, fencing, sailing, debating, orienteering, cross-country, nature, gymnastics – and even go-karting for a period, when a metalwork teacher named Mr Farley-Pettman taught a group how to build a real, engine-powered go-kart. They used to drive it through the woods; although it frequently broke down, I always thought it a very cool club indeed. Farley-Pettman was famed for setting himself alight when, during another of his mechanics-related clubs, he accidentally punched through the petrol tank of an old banger with his welding torch. Fortunately the metalwork shops were close to the swimming pool, and he extinguished himself in that, suffering no more than lost eyebrows and burns to his arm.

I find it ridiculous to recall, but I took a lot of pleasure from the Cadets, which was run by a couple of seniors who came from military families. Dressing in fatigues and wearing calf-high, steel-toed army boots as we charged through the countryside smeared with camouflage cream never ignited a desire to join the army, but it was great fun. We even got to shoot a pair of old.303 rifles at targets down in the cellar of the main house, and once we acquired some cheap cigars from Chelmondiston and spent the evening chewing on them like Rutger Hauer.

Woolverstone also had a very fine library in the elegant downstairs rooms of the main house that contained over 8,000 books, most of which went unexplored in favour of the pile of Asterix annuals it also featured. There were a couple of macabre photo books of the First World War, and we would pore over the extremely graphic and gory pictures they contained – some unimaginably grotesque. I spent quite a lot of time in the library and from time to time would even choose something enriching to read from the walls of shelves stuffed with exceptional collections of poetry and literature. I once saw a sixth former reading a red bound book with a Latin title, and I sought out something similar: I sat reading page after page of Latin text phonetically, understanding only one or two obvious words, hoping one of my friends would come in and see me. Because I had found *The Canterbury Tales* so engrossing, I even once pulled Chaucer's *The Legend of Good Women* from a shelf, mainly because I imagined it might contain more smut, but I didn't have the application to get beyond the first few pages. There were more modern novels that could be scanned for passages of sex, and we scoured many in search of such.

Extra-curricular activity was consequently where one often found most joy at Woolverstone, but routine life in the house was rigidly observed and frequently bemoaned. Laundry days and bed-changing days were tiresome, though it was always nice to get fresh, crisp sheets and a new pair of clean underpants. This story was repeated throughout the six houses with little variation to the routine; it had a rhythm, and it is not too trite to say that we eventually found a sort of security in it.

★ ★ ★

Cricket became the sport for the last term and I took to that with the same gusto and attack that had characterised my first, albeit truncated, rugby season. I would be a fast bowler. Nothing else would do.

Deciding that guile was for pansies, every ball I chucked down the wicket was intended to scare my opponent, rather than just get him out. A mile-long run-up was a prerequisite because I'd seen that Aussies Denis Lillee and the wonderfully quirky but devastatingly fluid Jeff Thompson had one. The school's head of cricket, Pete Sadler, had taken us on a visit to Chelmsford to see Essex play the touring Australians, and on the bus had made a point of telling us never to try to copy the bizarre action of Thompson, but a long-run up was common to all great fast bowlers, so I simply had to have one. I did not grasp that the run-up was about generating speed, which I was supposed to transfer smoothly into the action and thus the ball. My run-up was well measured and long, but when I arrived panting at the crease, I performed a shimmy, executed a little leap and slammed my front foot into the crease, heaving the ball from my shoulders. Any impetus developed in the run-up was lost on arrival at the wicket. Other than the last couple of strides, the tactic was completely worthless. I'd have had more luck if I'd whipped out a pair of maracas and forced the batsman to drop his guard through laughing. Later in my school career, that action would give me a bad knee, but I had powerful enough shoulders and eventually I developed a rip-snorting delivery that could take wickets. It was a bit wild at times, but I learned how to swing the ball by the midway point of the season. Any decent batsmen on the other side worked out that my bark was worse than my bite and would cane me to boundaries short and long, but enough were intimidated by the aggression. I approached the bowling crease in very much the same way that I charged over the try-line from ten yards out, grunts, grimaces, growls and all. In fact, with that mighty approach, I think I ran further in a cricket match than I ever did in rugby.

Many summer nights were spent in the cricket nets at the far end of Berners' field, practising the run-up and perfecting my salsa at the crease. It also meant getting to hit a few balls too. Typically, when I batted, my aim was not just to work on strokes, perfect my timing or learn how to send a ball skimming along the ground to square leg; inevitably I always tried to slam the ball out of the net and as far away as possible. There was an aesthetic quality to a cricket ball arching high into the air that I enjoyed immensely. More specifically, when the ball is travelling away from you, there is a beauty to it, but when it is sailing back over your head, it is deeply demoralising for the bowler who has to retrieve it.

'Oh, for fuck's sake, Volpe!' the bowler would whine as he trudged off to collect the ball that might come to a stop a good 150 metres away.

Pete Sadler lived in the main house and would spot anybody using the nets. He was very possessive of them and would march the couple of hundred yards across the field to remonstrate with anybody who was using them without his permission. 'Get out of my bloody nets, Volpe' was a common refrain. We considered it a privilege to be admonished by a master in such a way. When we were not being chased out of the nets, we discovered the slips cradle, which looked like the bottom of a small rowing boat. One person stood at each end and threw a ball at the cradle, off which it would fly at all angles, and the fun of diving about catching it was endless. When I say we did this for hours, I mean it. And whilst we were having fun, we developed very sharp slip fielding skills. It was like that for most things at Woolverstone and, by accident or design, most of what we did turned out to have a purpose for cricket, rugby or something else. With the training, practice and access to equipment and facilities almost twenty-four hours a day, we were becoming fine athletes and sportsmen. There is certainly a lesson there for modern education.

As a cricket team, we were good but not spectacular.

We had fine players and some of them shone more brightly with willow or leather in their hands than they could with mud on their boots in rugby. Every negative character trait I had was expressed in cricket. My impatience meant I slogged my way through an innings, forever on the edge of letting a ball slip by my guard or falling victim to a catch. My propensity to whack the ball as far as I could in the nets meant I never spent enough time working on my ground shots, so more often than not I was getting caught on the boundary. I can assure you there is no more irritating way to get out, and I would storm back to the pavilion, swearing and groaning under my breath. My urge to show off made me a decent slip fielder, always playing to the cameras had there been any, diving hither and yon to intercept a fizzing ball. Flinging howitzers down the wicket at people sated my aggression. We lost about as many matches as we won, but I always had a good game in my mind.

Pete 'Fart', as he was known, was passionate about cricket and taught history. I think the nickname came from a one-off release of gas during a lesson on the Tudors, but I can't be sure. That was just what we called him, and it was in use long before I arrived. Like many of the masters at Woolverstone, he never seemed to get angry although irritation was easily discerned. He also had three daughters, two of whom were of sufficient age to be the subject of much lecherous pursuit. I liked Pete. He, on the other hand, loathed me with a passion, I think. This was becoming a theme among masters. They were roughly divided along a very clear line: either they had a soft spot for me or thought I was the devil incarnate. Confusingly, I believe a couple of them had a soft spot *because* I was the devil incarnate, but I would hate to speculate as to how many were on either side of the line. Perversely – although for me, maybe not – I quite enjoyed irritating the masters who disliked me. It meant I was making an impression, and I always sought to make an impression, whether metaphorical or physical.

★ ★ ★

Speaking of impressions, it was the entire body of Timothy Creswell that made an impression on the stinging nettle bush he had fallen twenty feet into. His calamitous and entirely unintentional descent was a result of failing to hold on tightly enough as an enormous rope swing reached its optimum point before swooping back through its colossal arc. We found these rope swings all along the foreshore, tied to large trees near the steep banks. Climbing the bank to the top, we would survey the ride ahead, and it was often terrifying. I have no idea who tied the ropes in the first place, but the swings were like a free ride at Alton Towers. We soon developed games of 'boarding', in which as many boys as possible would launch themselves at the returning swing until a pack of up to eight or so clung for dear life to any inch of rope they could find.

Creswell was riding solo when he fell, and I think it was the sheer horror of reaching the zenith that did it. For no discernible reason, he just let go. He seemed to hang terrified for a moment in mid-air, like a squirrel monkey caught in the dappled light of the forest canopy, before somersaulting and plummeting to earth. I would be lying if I said there wasn't a certain visual beauty to the fall. He landed flat on his back in a thick clump of the evil little plant, the impact sending clouds of dust into the air. We all choked the instinct to laugh as he hit the ground with a sound somewhere between a thud, a splat and that of an elephant charging through the bush. His sharp exhalation as the air was bashed out of him sounded like whooping cough. Silence descended as we waited for signs of life, but he lay still – until he slowly rose to his feet. That's when we laughed, despite his appearance, which, with angry outbreaks of red bumps covering his arms and face, was similar to that of a smallpox victim. Not many falls matched that for aerial ballet, but scrapes, bumps and burns from the rope were the currency of bravery.

That is how the summer progressed: cricket, swallows and river swings. There was no inch of the grounds left unexplored, and we went at the country life with the feverish abandon that only children who get excited at seeing a cow in a field can. The dark, threatening country-side of the winter had blossomed and expanded in our view. Whole new areas of Suffolk came within our range, and we roamed everywhere. In the foreshore verges, high with unfurling, pungent ferns, we would flatten small clearings and lay chatting and smoking, new tins of Old Holborn collected from Chelmondiston's 'Orwell Stores' cracked open along with bars of chocolate. It was the idyll that you only truly recognise in reminiscence; but I can smell those ferns and that chocolate and that 'baccy', I can feel the gentle crunch of the flattened leaves beneath my back as I lay squinting at the sun, musing on girls, football, masters and all the things that occupy the minds of eleven-year-olds. The contrast with our home milieu was profound, as was the miracle of our now immersive comfort with our surroundings. Coarse Cockney cries that rang out across the landscape were merely a reminder that everyone and everything is adaptable.

There was a set time to be back at the house, and we frequently missed it. But we lived by the light – when it started to dim, it was time to go. Pushing our luck as the dusk drew in, we usually misjudged the distance we had travelled, leaving us significant hikes back to the house. Being late for tea was punished with extra duties, but worse, no tea at all. We would return filthy and stinking from mud, dirt, undergrowth and, for a short period, pig shit.

We had found an enormous mound of pig dung in the woods behind the marina hard. It was blended with straw, and it was hot and steamy from the composting process. Startled by the location, we nevertheless considered it of huge potential. I think it was Rob's idea, but we decided to build a pig shit igloo. Then someone suggested building a tunnel to another igloo. Then another. We ordered ourselves into teams, relaying the movement of dung, passing it to other teams who were to build the walls or the tunnels. Soldier ants would have envied our precision and industriousness. Soon, there was a complex of pig shit igloos in the clearing covering many square metres.

We reduced the huge pile to nothing as we developed our new compound. And then we would sit in them and smoke roll-ups. It was a terrifically creative enterprise that lasted days until one of the igloos collapsed, engulfing several boys in manure. Not being familiar with structural engineering, we failed to build supports, thinking the curvature of the walls would work along the lines of real igloos or the vaulted ceiling of the Duomo in Florence. However, pig shit has different properties to that of ice and fired brick, and the inevitable happened when the moisture had mostly evaporated from the sticky goo of the building material. When we had dug our friends out, we decided to find something else to occupy ourselves. All good things come to an end, even ones made of pig shit.

Our summer passed from craze to craze. We would lock intensely into a particular activity and exhaust its entertainment value completely within a few days. Diving into the bamboos that surrounded the biology pond took care of a few days, but too many of us got stabbed by ground level stumps for it to continue for too long. Climbing down into the voids inside huge unhealthy trees occupied our attention for a while, until someone fell off a branch and injured himself and another got stuck in the hole in the trunk. Our biology master had told us that there were lots of rabbits afflicted with myxomatosis in the area; deaf and blind with bulging eyes, they were pitiful. We were instructed that if we came across one, it should be killed humanely and put out of its misery. Killing it humanely did not, I suspect, involve creeping up behind it and booting it' ten feet into the air. Nor did it require us to tie the carcass to the crossbar of a goal and throw homemade bamboo spears at it. We spent hours hunting and 'humanely' slaughtering rabbits in this way, but it ended when Rob took a large stick and whacked a dead rabbit that was strung up. Its head flew off and the corpse spun around the bar like a bloody Catherine wheel, spraying all of us with innards and brown stuff that looked suspiciously like runny rabbit shit. Our culling days came to an abrupt halt, for there is a world of difference between fermenting pig poo and the intestinal discharge of a dead, diseased rabbit. Good God, how awful we sound.

The summer of 1977 was a glorious adventure that held the potential, at all times, for calamity. It was when we found a freedom that was more than just a lack of parental supervision; it was the kind of autonomy of spirit that open spaces, endless time and a shared experience affords. I couldn't imagine finding the equivalent happiness in Fulham. The opportunities offered by the green, smelly, *epic* space of Suffolk came with caveats and rules that tapped us constantly on the shoulder, but this was the price of Woolverstone's system, and it brought a reward beyond measure; it was one hell of a *quid pro quo*. My development as an individual was enormous, and that was when the school's ethos paid spectacular dividends. I know that there may be many reading this whose childhood summers were like this always, that endless days in the country, exploring and challenging the environment were as common and as familiar as cornflakes for breakfast, but it wasn't for us, you see. It just wasn't.

School sports day came and went, and being a track

monitor (which meant sitting at the side of the track, moving hurdles, holding tapes, carrying bags, etc), I saw at first hand the wondrous feats of athletes the school had nurtured. Sam O'Garro running the 100 metres on grass in 10.4 seconds is burned permanently in my consciousness, and the close rivalry he had with Neil Rice, both of them in Hall's, was special indeed. These were two sprinters of international class for their age and I don't think either of them gave it a second thought. O'Garro ran exactly like the legendary American 400 metre runner Michael Johnson: straight of back, effortless.

As a track monitor, one would expect me to find little of threat in the day, sitting quietly beside the track, moving hurdles or picking up bits of clothing, yet that wouldn't be like me at all. I found half an old aluminium arrow shaft and sat idly sticking it into the ground. Pushing too hard, it snapped, and as the back of my hand descended past the embedded shaft, the jagged end took out an inch-long chunk of my flesh. I felt nothing at first, but noticed the shiny, speckled filling of the shaft and thought how curious it was, since I always imagined they were hollow. They were: my flesh, decorated with nerve endings, was the filling I saw, and I soon noticed the pumping eruption of blood from my hand, too. Off to sickbay I went, with a wound too wide to be stitched, and one that would take the whole summer to heal because I refused to stop swimming.

In the following year I think I won the throwing the cricket ball and javelin competitions and eventually, I competed in shot putt and javelin in the county championships where in the javelin I came about third, but thinking the shot putt in the bag, I managed to lose to a scrawny waif whose technique was flawless. I strolled into the circle having seen the competition grunt its way to nothing more than measly distances. Flinging the shot several metres further than the nearest previous distance, I noted that only one thrower was left, and he looked incapable of picking up the shot, let alone pitching it any sort of length. Indeed, he seemed to struggle when lifting it and staggered into the circle, but when he held it to his chin, he spun like a whip across the concrete throwing area and sent the bloody thing soaring into the air. All of us, including the judges, watched with mouths open as the shot sailed three metres beyond my throw. I resolved never to underestimate anybody based on appearances.

With Neil Pearson dressed in a cassock and looking for all the world like a clean-shaven Jesus, the school play, *A man for all seasons*, was a hit that went further over my head than the winning shot putt. More on my level, I played the back end of a cow in a puppet show. I insisted on authenticity and invented a rudimentary urinating device, which allowed me to squirt yellow liquid through a hole in the suit. It knocked them dead. Showing off onstage was to be a strong feature of life at Woolverstone.

And so the academic year was drawing to a close. It had seemed so short, full of incident and drama. Rugby was already in our blood, and we were getting used to being winners, something that became evident as we arrogantly sauntered around London in the holidays. Woolverstone demanded we consider ourselves to be the best, and we needed very little encouragement to go along with the idea. The long ten-week summer holiday felt like a reward for making it through that first year's tribulations and as I returned to Fulham I was changed. I know I was. Climbing roofs and pissing off the porters just seemed so terribly mundane after running dares to the Woolverstone marina in the dead of night to steal the sign from the chandlery. And how could a kickabout in the flats compare with a full-blooded slaying of fifteen posh kids from Norwich? In that first summer, my primary school friends and mates from the estate began to melt from my mind as I spent my entire time walking the streets of London with various friends I had made at Woolverstone. We were special. We knew we were. Woolverstone had told us.

The relating of stories in these pages may give the impression that it was all sweetness and light at the school. Memory plays tricks, doesn't it? It is not an exaggeration to say that, on balance, we did not truly relish being there, not when we stopped to think about it anyway. Despite our surprising compliance, some things just could not be accepted easily: the rules, the hierarchy, the control and the traditions. Maybe it was impossible for kids like us to be parachuted into a vast playground of unbounded potential and be expected to get our heads down over a textbook at the same time. My report book after the first year was acceptable, if not spectacular, and there was clear evidence that masters were onto me. It was too early to be concerned, anyway, so I got back to London with a sense of pride and contentment.

Then, as with every preceding school break, people

looked at me differently, as though they expected to find horns had sprouted or hooves grown. Friends on the estate, before I drifted away from them, were full of questions, and their mouths dropped at the stories of punishments, adventures and day-to-day life of a boarding school. These truly were tales from another world. All of them agreed that they would retaliate if a teacher tried to slipper them, and none would accept being told what to do by another boy, even an older one. To them, Woolverstone might well have been a borstal. But none of them had the guts to say that within earshot of my mother.

The remarkable accomplishment that Woolvo could rightly claim as that first academic year drew to a close was the change in all of us. Fulham Court, Eelbrook Common, North End Road market, those things that in my world had always sat proudly at the point where the sky met the land became small, unimportant and insignificant. I felt like an explorer who had travelled beyond the frontier of our domain and had seen things, wonderful things. I felt, too, like a stranger. No doubt some were thinking that I had been robbed of my loyalty to my community and the very neighbourhood that had created, nurtured and provided my childhood. But that is not how I saw it. I sensed an incipient desire to break for that border again and again, for freedom. I glimpsed the limitations of what just ten months before I had believed to be limitless because the inner city had been able to trick me – and those like me – into the belief that its shackles were, in fact, wings. At Woolverstone I took flight that summer, but the restraints still chaffed at my ankles when

I returned home. I suppose that the battle for my future began then, wings beating furiously, trying to pull me from the anchors, but it would be many years before the inner city, for want of a better phrase, would release its son. I sometimes wonder if, in truth, its ties and binds have ever been fully ruptured, but having even the ability to consider it at all must say something.

I had turned twelve in the May of '77, and my interest was firmly shifting towards the opposite sex. We had parties all through the summer with girls from our respective parts of London. I had started doing holiday work in a sweet shop in Fulham, and there I met Alison, the much younger sister of the man who managed the shop. I worked behind the counter with Alison, and my brothers and friends would come into the shop to clean it out. Stock control was cursory since the manager was busy zooming about London in his Porsche and so sweets, cigarettes and sundry other items were on tap in our shop, whose position opposite the police station meant frequent custom from the boys in blue.

Alison had lots of friends, and so I made sure all my pals were frequently around, although with a collective libido the size of a supertanker, they needed little encouragement. We would all snuffle and jostle at the threshold of whichever house hosted the latest party, scanning the darkness for signs of female life: frankly, it was like being at the heart of a pack of dogs stalking bitches in heat, able to locate a fresh, sweet teenage girl at one hundred paces. We were blessed with the *desire* to be urbane, but that's where it ended, since as young boys ourselves, sophisticates we most certainly were not. However, as many of the girls we hung around with would remark, we were definitely *different*. It was during that first summer that I had my first proper girlfriend, Samantha. She was more a fully-formed sixteen-year-old than the thirteen that she actually was, and I was eager to put all the things I had been boasting about at school into practice. She had sisters who called me Voluptuous Volps, which I thought was a compliment at the time. It was a terrific summer holiday, but the looming return to Woolverstone was a nuisance. Still, Samantha would write to me 'every day', which would win me a few credibility points, although several of my Woolvo coterie were busy gallivanting with Samantha's friends, and so I would have competition.

SHOCK AND AWE

Samantha had nice big curly handwriting that took up space, meaning long letters on thick pages of pink writing paper, which were then crammed into thicker pink envelopes that landed on the table with a thud. Morris would give out the post at breakfast, and we always waited eagerly for the arrival of anything from girls we knew or were involved with. Samantha's letters were a treat, and she wrote frequently, soaking her letters in Anäis Anäis perfume and ensuring the outside was decorated with anagrams like S.W.A.L.K. Being mocked by those at table for the soppiness of such letters never struck too hard since it was easy to discern jealousy.

Samantha's letters were in themselves barely entertaining. It was the receiving of them that mattered. I was very fond of her in that intense, new-experience, obsessive kind of way that young men get, but I was never overly interested in the mundane day-to-day reportage of her writings. I scanned the letters quickly to find examples of her love for me, how she felt about me, what she thought of me. Having found them, I would read them out to the hungry audience, busy chomping on cornflakes or chasing fried eggs around the grease on their plates. After a few weeks of gushing over me, she sent a letter, which, on examination, contained frequent mention of someone called Mark, her friend. The next letter she sent made such recurrent mention of the git (who was going to be a pro golfer, incidentally) that she talked herself into dumping me by the end of the second page. Mark *this*, Mark *that*. Apparently, the distance and long periods of not seeing me were taking their toll on our relationship and well, Mark *was* going to be a professional golfer after all. She was sure I would understand and that we could go on being friends and so on and so forth. I've hated golfers ever since.

Samantha's letter coincided with several others to my friends saying pretty much the same thing. There had obviously been a summit meeting of Alison and Samantha's friends, who had all decided that 'saving themselves' for a bunch of boys they wouldn't see for another six weeks was no fun. No fun at all. I composed a stinking reply to Samantha, full of emotional blackmail and angst, pointing out that golfers wore shit jumpers. Soon, a procession of my friends was asking me to write something similar to their treacherous former girlfriends.

Dear so and so,

I have just received your letter telling me that you wanted to finish with me. My heart is breaking into a million pieces and I have not stopped crying since I read those horrible words you wrote to me. God created us so that we might be together for always and you agreed with that the last time I spoke to

*you. What happened? Why did you do this to me?
When I am far away and thinking of you every waking
moment?*

*You have become evil and twisted and a bit of a
bitch actually. I cannot believe I ever fancied you in
the first place now you mention it. You have shit
hair and your arse is fat. Your friends hate you and
Maureen tried to get off with me at the last party
round Alison's house. What do you think of that eh?
Some friend she is. I'll get over you very soon. You'll
miss me more than I miss you I can tell you.*

Bye.

From David/Rob/Simon etc

P.S. I fancy your sister.

Those poor girls would gather together and bemoan the
viciousness of the onslaught. Eventually, Alison, with
whom I was still friendly, told me they realised that one
person was writing all of the letters and that I was the
main suspect. To be perfectly honest, I did take a bit of
pride in knowing that.

Woolverstone life was settling into a pattern, and the
second year was about as uneventful and sterile a year as
I would have at the school. My reports suggest a relatively
happy boy who was taking part in all sorts of new things
such as debating forums, badminton, gym club, drama,
pottery club, woodwork and so on. I have to chuckle at
my involvement in the debating society. Debate, per se,
was not something I excelled at, and I have no memory
of any of the meetings. I can only deduce that I debated

with the same singular and offensive vim that I used in every other discussion I ever had. Pottery club I *do* recall. It was an extension of our art classes, but we could make extra stuff outside of the curriculum. Creativity engaged me throughout school life, but, as with most endeavours, I failed to bring the requisite patience and thoroughness to my work. I tried, I really did try. Working the clay to rid it of air bubbles began slowly and I treated the material with loving tenderness, but after ten minutes I was beating it with a rolling pin. Once done, I set about making my item by rolling the clay and cutting it to shape, getting a finger full of slip and carefully sealing the edges – at least, for another ten minutes. And so it went on. I marvelled at one boy's ability to spend half an hour rolling a small piece of clay until it had the consistency and smoothness of a crisply ironed shirt. He would then skilfully slice it into shape before applying it to his masterpiece. In this way he produced the most exquisitely delicate model of a vintage Rolls Royce.

My own tour de force was going to be a bowl of fruit so life-like that viewers would be fooled into breaking their teeth as they bit into the remarkable facsimiles of pears, peaches and bananas. What I ended up making was half an apple, a dark green and white glazed lump of gnarly clay that adorned my mother's coffee table for decades. It was forever to my frustration that I could *see* what was required, and *knew* what rewards awaited patience, but I just couldn't do it. It was the same in woodwork, a craft I adored but where my dovetail joints looked like an old sailor's teeth; and my mortise and tenon joints required so much packing with slivers of wood that, when viewed from the end, they looked like marquetry. The lathe offered solace inasmuch as it produced things quickly and I once turned two beautiful mahogany candlesticks on it. All I had to do was draw lines where I needed to apply the chisel, and the lathe did the rest in about thirty seconds: no joints, no measuring, just eyes half-closed, a shocking shower of sawdust, *et voila*!

Rugby continued to be a huge influence on our lives, and our success as a team was up to Woolverstone standards. Our back line was scintillatingly good, with Gareth Brunt at fly half, Seaton Jean in the centres and Rich Henry, who had begun as a prop but had been moved to the wing, running in try after try. We played rugby endlessly, either in training, school matches or in house matches, when I got to wear the hooped green and white jersey of Hall's House.

Of course, as second formers, there were now boys below us, and it was time to have our own fun with them. As far as I can recall, instead of bullying them, we chose to sell things to them. As the saying goes, you can take the kid out of the street etc., and so our extracurricular activities involved enlightened enterprise of a kind found frequently in the back alleys of estates in London. We supplemented the pocket money our parents had sent us to school with by renting out porn magazines to first formers and selling them dried banana skins rolled into joints for £1 a go. That was a lot of money even then. It was whilst persuading the buyers that a couple of grams of Fyffes finest was actually the best stuff that I first experienced the placebo effect. Having run off to the bushes with several friends to share his illicit 'narcotic', the junior, along with his squad of willing dope-heads, would return to the house giggling, falling about the place and saying 'man' a lot. Renting 'lech mags' was very lucrative and well-worn copies of *Razzle*, *Penthouse* and *Mayfair* were distributed to boys, priapic with the anticipation of it all, for anything up to £2 per wank. Orders and instructions about sticking pages together were strictly enforced. Being in possession of such magazines was forbidden, and Morris would throw surprise locker inspections in order to find such items or illicit tuck. We kept well ahead of him, though, and the business thrived: on some Sunday afternoons the entire stock would be out constantly. Readers may draw their own mental image.

The booty paid for trips to Ipswich, tobacco and any number of illicit pastimes, including on one occasion a home brewing kit with which we produced some dreadful beer, to be consumed after the Christmas dinner. We had set up the brewing barrel in the bushes on Orwell side. It was terribly cloudy and bitter, but we drank it anyway and it kept the chill from our bones in the dark, wet and windswept shrubs. It would have kept angels from heaven, such was its sinful dreadfulness.

My mood around the school seems to have been pleasant, if masters' reports are anything to go by, but by the spring term I had begun to believe my own publicity, becoming 'loud, arrogant and difficult' or 'critical, slapdash, lazy and disruptive'. You may take your pick.

Paddy, as ever, took a positive view, although even he

had to recognise what was becoming a pattern. In his report he says, 'Michael is a great mixture of energy and enthusiasm on the one hand, and carping criticism on the other. He must not allow this abrasive side to dominate his pleasant nature.' I am not able to explain why there was a sudden change in my behaviour, but it was as clear as day. Confidence might have something to do with it. Rather than clash with every rule and oddity I encountered, as I did in the first form, I had developed a system whereby I could circumvent some of the rules, adapt to others and work out strategies to render the rest easier. General familiarity with my surroundings played a part too. As a result, I think my mind began to wander towards other things, and not just how to survive. Those alternatives obviously included a process of reverting to type.

By the end of the summer term, things had not really improved, and there was a wild inconsistency in my approach to subjects. In chemistry I took 'absolutely no trouble with written work', but in art I showed 'very good work and effort'. Encapsulating my entire character set with perspicacity, my cricket master Kev Young said I was 'an aggressive batsman, a hostile bowler but lacks direction in both'. Despite my Damascene conversion from the ways of physical discrimination against my weaker housemates, I was nevertheless a bit of a handful.

Something was clearly amiss: everybody could see it and for the first time there was concern. It was my erratic nature that drew most alarm, with great swings in attitude and behaviour from term to term. I tend to the view that I was just a growing adolescent with an outlook that mirrored

the wild ups and downs of hormonal growth and development. On the other hand, I was turning into a conceited,
careless and self-destructive shit. I had begun to make distinc-
tions between what I wanted to do and what I didn't, and
I would resist and display my displeasure at subjects I felt
less inclined towards. I simply considered myself to be too
good for them. From time to time, Paddy would call me
aside and give me a few corrective words, and I would fall
back into line for a short time, but I was an incorrigible
attention seeker, and spasmodic effort punctuated long
periods of reactionary, petulant laziness. If I had any saving
qualities it was that I threw myself wholeheartedly at whatever I decided I liked: rugby, drama and being jack-the-lad.

I think I wanted to succeed but was sliding back into the
habit of mistrusting anyone, with the exception of Paddy,
who suggested I could be a success. My second year at
Woolverstone drew just about satisfactorily to a close. I
was relatively applied, not beyond redemption at all when
it came to my behaviour, and I had started to enjoy the
school. Still to arrive was the persistent suspicion on the
part of masters that their efforts were fruitless, but a few
had their eye on me, that's for sure. With his blessed patience,
Paddy said I was 'all over the place, but he has been quieter
recently so perhaps a good year is just around the corner'.

The year ended, we went on summer holiday and I
began to grow some whiskers and pubic hair. I didn't need
the added complication of my endocrinal rampage and
neither did the school.

* * *

It was spring term 1979. I was thirteen years old, not far off fourteen. The first term of my third year at Woolverstone had again been blighted by a lack of control and academic inconsistency. Teenage intensity had crept into my dealings with teachers, and it was becoming harder to forgive my indiscretions. Although I'd had a great term in rugby, I had been sent off in a match towards the end of the season. We had returned back to school after the Christmas holidays, and I was a tiresome, unpleasant bore.

Things were to take a turn for the worse.

With rumours spinning through the school, David Hudson, the deputy headmaster, walked onto the stage at assembly one morning during that spring term in 1979 and, with a shaking voice, spoke two sentences that I recall verbatim: 'Patrick Richardson was involved in a car accident last night in London. He was killed instantly.'

And we laughed. Well, I and a few others did. I remember it. I think we laughed out of shock. The stunning effect of that announcement was horribly palpable, the sharp gasp in the hall sucked the oxygen from the room and my ears began to ring with the awful silence that descended. But a few of us laughed. A short, snorting snigger would better describe it. I think a few announcements were made by other masters, and the head boy said something about it being a difficult time and that we had to all pull together, but it was academic, really. I was horrified and devastated, and I think I even felt angry with Paddy. The effect of the sudden, shocking death of someone prominent in the lives of so many young people is profound. Being there as the jolt blasted through over three hundred boys is to experience something I have never since encountered. Each of us who heard the announcement had their own experiences of Paddy, their own feelings and memories, and was suffering their own sense of loss, but it remained a collective understanding. Our disbelief and upset lifted into the air above our heads and formed into a black cloud that hung ominously over all of us. How could this be true? How could Paddy be gone? Dead? He *was* Woolverstone.

It would take us some while to adjust, although I am almost certain I never really did.

Immediately after assembly, a few of us crept through the gardens behind the old chemistry laboratories and picked a small bunch of flowers. We took them to the back door of Paddy's house and knocked. Jill, his widow, opened the door, and Rob handed the flowers to her, which she graciously took. I can still hear his children in the kitchen, wailing with grief. Remarkably, more than thirty years later, Jill Richardson would come across my name in a publication when she visited Opera Holland Park as a patron. She left me a note, and I called her, telling her that I was amazed that she should remember me after nearly three decades.

'I remember how you came to the door with flowers, Michael,' she said. 'How could I forget that?'

Since we spoke, I have taken the view that even the smallest gestures make their mark at such times, and any urge to resist making them should be overcome. One other thing struck me about our conversation: quite how moved I was to be talking to her, to be recalling those days. As I spoke down the telephone to her, I was choking on the fresh memory of that day, now revived and intoxicating. I was trying not to let it show in my voice. She said it was half a lifetime ago, that she had enjoyed a wonderful life since and that she had fully recovered from it.

Perhaps I hadn't. In the years since his death, Jill and her children had moved on, made other, new lives. We, though, had that screeching halt, the shock – of course as nothing to his family's – remaining as a pungent memory. I suppose we thought their lives would stop at that point too. We were children after all.

The appalling atmosphere caused by Paddy's death hung around the school for months. His legacy was to be found in the individual remembrance of each of us. There may have been longer-serving, even better headmasters than Paddy, but he was the only one I knew, and he was one of the few adults in the world for whom I had an instinctive respect and affection. I understood deference, but I never proffered it without design or consideration, and rarely did I find a natural urge to be respectful, but Paddy attracted my natural regard for all the reasons I have elaborated upon elsewhere.

Paddy's loss also signalled a material change in the attitudes of some of the masters, as well as in many of us pupils; some of them left and new masters, palpably from a different brand of thinking and dedication, joined. For my part, I think the shock of it all calmed me down and subdued my wayward nature for a period, and my report book is good for that term when Paddy's hand is suddenly absent from the page, now replaced by the equally fluid pen of David Hudson. There is talk of me 'turning a corner', and Morris pointed out that I had become 'determined to do what is right'. Hall's won the house rugby championship, and along with playing well in the final, I 'encouraged others to play well too'.

Paddy had fruitlessly attended to my pastoral wellbeing for three years, had watched and worried over me, pushed and pulled me in the directions he thought would be of greatest benefit. All of it was seemingly worthless, negated by my own boneheaded intransigence, yet all it appears he had to do was die for me to take heed.

Individuals like Paddy and those teachers who had been with him were the glue that held Woolverstone together. It is clear now that they had been fighting a rearguard action against politicians whose cruelly pursued doctrines, based on a perverse, inverted snobbery, were slowly making inroads into the school's chances of survival. They had already succeeded in turning the place comprehensive – my year was the last of the grammar intake – and had designs on closing the school altogether. What often seemed to outsiders like anachronistic traditions and principles, often unspoken ones, were carried in the hearts and minds of such people as Paddy and then passed onto us. Of course, we resisted them to begin with and if I were being generous, those at County Hall who hated the style of the school more than we might have done were probably of a view that they were protecting us. But those people were wrong. This is not a debate, to my mind, about comprehensives versus grammar: those two principles now exist in our system when perhaps they shouldn't, and another book is probably required for that. But nobody was protecting me when they took cold and malicious advantage of Paddy's death to further their own aims.

At Woolverstone there was a through-line of expectation, achievement and spirit that new teachers who came and went would either pick up or not, but it was people like Paddy who laid it all out for them. With the arrival of a new regime, there was a slow and unmistakable repositioning of the school's ethos, and lots of us began to give up on it all. But that was some way into the future. For now, we tried as best we could to adjust to the change that had been brutally and suddenly imposed upon us, and the term went on in as normal a fashion as possible. We won the Suffolk Under-14s Sevens Cup, and I worked stage crew for the Rock Prom where Rob and a boy called Holloway sang a passable version of 'She Loves Me' by The Beatles.

Spring term 1979 was potentially the fulcrum of my entire school career. It may well have been the point at which my life could have taken a different direction had I allowed myself to follow it. Everything was still in the balance but I appear to have had a sort of epiphany, and the optimism of masters who had hitherto been depressingly pessimistic about me began to shine through. I had every reason to feel good about myself. But I didn't.

★ ★ ★

Rage.

Rage arrived back at school with me in late April 1979 for the summer term. It was a new feeling that differed from the bad temper that had always been my trademark. This was something altogether more malignant. I don't think that I differed from many boys of that age, yet at times I felt like an alien. When rage took over, I paid no mind whatsoever to consequences, and once I had decided on a course of action precipitated by rage, I would proceed with gusto. Walking out of classrooms, refusing to do what I was asked, total insouciance towards prep and not even half-hearted effort during the end of year exams became the order of the day. I wasn't a disaster in the making; I was already a fully-fledged catastrophe. I found time to do archery, Cadets and Hall's won the house cricket, too, but the word on the street was 'relapse'. I find it almost impossible to remember what was happening at home between terms. I imagine Matt was as dedicated a recidivist as ever, the police probably kicked our front door in once or twice and girls were definitely a focus, an obsession even. During holidays, I fell in and out of love on a weekly basis, which was emotionally exhausting.

Nevertheless, I had developed a nasty habit of meeting fire with conflagration. My violence towards others was still responsive inasmuch as I did not go around punching people for the entertainment, but any affront was met with overwhelming force. I was hit around the ear by a sixth former wearing a plaster cast because he thought I had made a remark behind his back. I was walking with Rob when, out of the blue, my ear was walloped and, looking up to see the perpetrator, I punched him so hard on the chin that he fell flat on his back. Later that night, one of his cohorts came to the house to warn me against hitting sixth formers and I told him to eff off too. I suspect he did not pursue the matter further because he saw Rage. One senior boy took a golf club to one of our number who was a tough, resilient cookie, but even his bones succumbed to the wooden driver and he ended up with multiple bruises and a broken arm. So we went to the senior's room to warn him that any repeat would result in a certain visit to hospital. By now we were strapping fourteen-year-olds and five or six of us were a force to be reckoned with. I say all this because none of what I have just imparted was normally permitted at Woolverstone. You did not hit or threaten sixth formers, and you did not disobey masters. But I didn't care. Rage made sure of that.

In that third year there was a flu epidemic, which really meant only three boys actually got flu and 150 pretended to have it. We developed techniques for duping Matron and most popular was quickly putting the bulb of the thermometer against the hot metal radiator in her laundry room when her back was turned. Sometimes, boys held it a fraction too long, which meant the thermometer reported temperatures similar to those found on the surface of the sun. Matron was inattentive and trusting, but she wasn't stupid, and such mistakes meant you would be sitting in English lessons with only four others whilst your friends enjoyed all day in bed.

Soon after the bogus flu epidemic I actually did contract viral meningitis. As with my broken arm, it went un-attended for three days, during which I lay delirious in bed with a headache registering 5.8 on the Richter scale, unable to open my eyes to the light that sent them into spasms. As it was viral and not bacterial meningitis, I was presumably at less risk, but it wasn't as if anyone was paying attention to know whether that was the case. Dragging myself to sickbay and the doctor again, I was given tablets that I later discovered were soon banned. I have avoided finding out why.

The Butt and Oyster at Pin Mill became a frequent destination. The landlord was a curmudgeonly old goat with a huge handlebar moustache and it will be of no surprise to learn that his nickname was 'Handlebars'. He was also about one hundred and three years of age and hated Woolvo boys with a vengeance, but for some reason he allowed us to sit in the smoke room, giggling and guzzling the Butt cider that was brewed on the premises. We were fourteen, but we had begun to look a lot older, and in rural Suffolk I don't suppose they worried too much about under-age drinkers. Butt cider was syrupy, golden and lethal. Obviously, it was an opportunity to drool over 'Jugs', the voluptuous and sweetly brainless barmaid, who never failed to fall prey to our japes, like phoning the bar from the nearby phone box and asking to speak to Mike Hunt. 'Mike Hunt? Is Mike Hunt here?' she would call through the pub.

One or two pints of Butt cider left us struggling to put on our Wellington boots in the lobby of the pub, falling about the place and shouting, and it was in this state that we had to trudge through the darkness and mud along the foreshore back to school, hoping to get back into the grounds, into the house and under the covers without being caught. Sometimes, a master would spot something going on out of the corner of his eye from the study or whilst on a patrol around the house, and we would have to charge up the stairs and dive into bed. Through the door would crash the master, switching on the lights. If you were lucky, he would go into the wrong dorm first, giving us a few seconds to disrobe. If he chose well, then you were under covers fully clothed with shoes on and I was more than once trapped by the telltale mud on the blankets.

Pubescent, fit and arrogant: our third year at Woolverstone was possibly the most entertaining and care-free of our time there, despite my frequent angry clashes with authority. Work was substantial and, whilst I took a lesser amount of care over it than I might have, I was getting on with it more or less. We were growing up fast and few of us were coping with it as well as we thought, yet Woolverstone was home, even though it was struggling to make us conform entirely. Quite how quickly we were growing up was evidenced by the work we undertook in the school holidays – money, or the pursuit of it, occupied us greatly. Fashion was becoming a factor in our lives and it needed to be paid for. So did football.

Chelsea FC was mine and Rob's abiding passion. School holidays meant trips to Stamford Bridge where I had been torturing myself for several years. The ground was a toilet in the seventies, a large bowl, a swirling wind and a distance between pitch and terrace so vast that it later provided land for hotels and a couple of hundred flats. The 'Shed' is where we squeezed ourselves in, by the white wall, two young kids screaming obscenities. We just screamed when a couple of hundred West Ham fans once announced their presence among us. As we leapt the wall at the front of the terrace, a policeman tried to get us to jump back in.

'Fuck off! You go in and sort it out,' I said.

'If you think I'm going up there, you must be mad!' he replied. The battle that raged involved horses, dogs and the kind of territorial madness that football in the seventies was famed for. I shall never forget the Chelsea fan who sat on the crush barrier imploring everybody not to run and was then engulfed by scores of attacking fans, the scarves tied to his wrists whipping and flowing like flags as, still sitting on the barrier, he threw punches in his defence. Stamford Bridge in those days could be terrifying and exciting in equal measure; in and around the ground there was a tactical war every Saturday, with a malignant atmosphere you could almost smell, especially when other London clubs came west.

Thinking about it, I am surprised that football violence never appealed to me more. Perhaps my desire for tribal aggression was sated by rugby, when we indulged in a class war against those who thought themselves better than us. Football violence was a serious thing in those days, but it was more a spectator sport as far as we were concerned. Chelsea's 'firm' was a significant player in the world of hooliganism, and there was more than a simple male aggression thing going on; it had a fashion, music and a lifestyle all its own. Hooliganism was a social problem inasmuch as it caused a lot of trouble on the streets, but it was never, as far as I could discern, the result of social deprivation, because these people had jobs and normal lives and just liked fighting. We knew all the faces and learned the ebb and flow of a vicious conflict, egging on the participants, whose waves of attacks across the sloped terraces would create undulating, pulsating patterns like those on a medieval battlefield as retreat and clash were acted out. It could be beautiful, in a grotesque and brutal way. We were too young to be of any real use in all this ferocity, but that never stopped us getting swept up in the whole thing. A police horse even bit me once. Anyway, we cheered on the tribe because cheering the team got us nowhere. The awfulness of the later seventies Chelsea was only occasionally punctuated by great highs; wins against Liverpool in the cup spring to mind. Otherwise, a win was always a surprise. Fuelled by Guinness, we enjoyed the camaraderie and the testosterone, but again, it had to be provided for.

The father of one Woolvo boy was the chief of a London fire station, and his men frequently took alternative work on their four days off, so he had contacts with various agencies and was able to find jobs for us in the holidays. At fourteen, I was able to pass for a lot older so spent many holidays working in warehouses, packing goods or heaving boxes. I worked in a distributor of toiletries for a period, on the strap-bander that tightened a metal strip around a box of heavy items. If I wasn't mistiming it and causing the bander to wrap thin air, I was getting my hand caught between the strip and the box, thus binding myself to a carton of Eau Savage.

These manual labours were good for me, and I enjoyed the money they brought, which meant I could visit Petticoat

Lane on a Sunday morning and purchase knocked-off Levi Red Tag garments and Pod shoes. The work was usually easy and paid more money than I would ever get on a paper round. But one job was extraordinarily hard and demonstrated my precocity and self-belief: I got a job as a security guard at the Earl's Court Boat Show. This was no night watchman role but fully-fledged security personnel work, manning the entrance foyer and controlling crowds. Dressed in my full uniform, with a matching anorak and a peaked hat, I looked fresh faced but passed muster.

My first job at this most popular of exhibitions was as a bag searcher in the lobby. The IRA was still very active in London at the time and exhibitions at Earl's Court had been bombed before. Standing at one of several tables laid out in the large foyer, my job was to call people forward, look through their bags and check any small electrical devices. As we were still pre-mobile phone or tablet days, this tended to be tape recorders, cassette Walkmans or calculators. If a visitor showed displeasure or impatience at being searched by a suspiciously young-looking security guard, I would insist that they emptied the entire contents of their bag onto the table and would ask in as officious a voice as I could what each item was.

'Could you tell me what this is, Sir?'

'It's a calculator.'

'Could you switch it on, please?'

With a huff or a sigh, they would switch it on, and I would take it, check the display was active and then hand it back to them.

'Do a calculation for me, please, Sir.'

'What? This is ridiculous,' he would reply, now almost on his knees with exasperation.

'I can always ask the police officer over there to help you, Sir. Just do a sum, anything, so I can see it works properly. Two plus two is fine.'

When not being the security guard from hell, I was put on crowd control duty, which essentially entailed holding back the flow of people coming up the passageway from the tube station below. The tube access opened into the foyer of the exhibition centre, but numbers needed to be controlled so that officious shits like me could do the bag searching.

Positioned in a tiled narrow section just before the stairway into the hall, I would order the surge of people to halt as those already in the lobby filed in. When I got the nod, I would let another couple of hundred through. Getting them to stop was difficult since they all seemed wild-eyed with anticipation at the prospect of a hangar full of white, shiny boats. They would gush from the platform below, ten abreast, only to be met by me in a coat that was too long and a hat that was too big, arms spread wide and barring their way. Some would try to push past, and one or two actually made it. I wasn't averse to a bit of roughhousing if I thought the escapee was pushing his luck. After a short while, I would drop my arms, at which point there was a stampede past me. Within a few seconds I would try again to stem the flow, by now shouting and growling at those who tried to slink past me unnoticed. By the end I was almost charging escapees against the wall like an ice hockey player. It was exhausting and stressful work that on one occasion I had to do for ten hours straight. But it paid well. I can't deny that it was formative, too, because I got a first taste of effort that had a tangible result: cash. Failure to do the work carried a real consequence, which of course meant I had to do it, whether I liked it or not. It was a good lesson, and one I kept in my locker until after Woolverstone.

COLTS AND KANGAROOS

Retracing the steps of this memoir, it strikes me that it would be perfectly reasonable for a reader to deduce that Woolverstone was doing little for me. Less gracious readers might also observe that I wasn't doing much for the school, either. They could well be right.

It is hard to express just how unusual an opportunity Woolverstone was for most of us. It wasn't necessary for us to realise the effect it was having at the time and you can be certain we were as unappreciative as one might expect young men to be. But growing up is never easy, especially when you have to do it in close proximity to 359 others. As I entered the fourth form, I was planting distinctive fences around what I would *allow* Woolverstone to do for me, and the rest I would leave at the gate. For whatever reason, under the influence of something or other, I returned to Woolverstone in September 1979, to begin what was a crucial year with purpose and not a little maturity. Inevitably, it wouldn't last, and the predictable pattern of decline was beginning to look like a habitual sprint to the edge of the abyss. Was I just looking for someone to stop me? Did I feel let down by the rewards for a good term, which amounted to little more than a good report, a pat on the back? What did I expect from a few weeks of hard work and endeavour? Who was I doing it for? These and a hundred other questions still occupy me. But I just could not keep it going.

The school had all of the accoutrements you might expect of a well-funded, highly motivated public school, including gyms, a swimming pool, lots of land, old buildings and an outward elegance, mostly afforded by the main house. But Woolverstone had to face a greater challenge than other such establishments. It was often called 'the poor man's Eton', which is plainly absurd on many accounts, but there was one crucial difference: its raw material.

Children who attend a school like Eton are aware that they are going to do so almost from the moment their ability to speak arrives and from early on in their lives, they are familiar with the notion of educational achievement. Their parents, their brothers, their aunts and uncles will most likely all have received strong educations and been expected to go on to university and a career and to continue the line of wealth and success. The key point is expectation. My acquaintance with educational achievement was only slight, and part of the test for the school was not only to give me that prized education but also to teach me, before anything else, that it was a prize at all. This was a dual role that places like Eton never have to perform.

Woolverstone Hall School for Boys sounded terribly grand, and I loved telling people I went there. 'It's a boarding school near Ipswich in Suffolk,' I would say. 'Really? What did you do?' would often be the reply. So not only did the school have to instruct me that there was a point, we ourselves were constantly suspected of being resident in a place of which Her Majesty Approved. Mud sticks, but it sticks even harder and more resolutely to scum. I should stress that most of the boys who attended Woolverstone from the fifties onwards were aware of academic propriety and many of them went on to lead successful, even illustrious lives, but a good number of us still needed to understand, and then succumb to, the idea that our life at the school was principally intended to furnish us with knowledge. It was a challenge that the school rose to magnificently over the course of its life, but as it related to me it was a job much like the painting of the Forth Bridge: never-ending and inescapable. Had Woolverstone been a school that required its parents to pay fees and took only the finest from society, perhaps it would have felt the urge to dispense with my presence there. I don't think I was that bad, but who knows?

I don't believe, despite my painfully awful report book, that Woolverstone let me down. How pernicious might my early life have been without it? I think my self-aggrandisement at school became self-awareness by the time I was twenty, and it could well be the greatest asset Woolvo gave me. If I wouldn't allow it to send me out into the world with a catalogue of academic grades, it would have to tattoo a record of my truculence onto my conscience and hope I looked in the mirror one day.

★ ★ ★

In the fourth form you became, in rugby terms, a member of the Colts. The Colts even played in a different strip, which had a yellow bar across the chest of the blue jersey. We were on the cusp of the First Fifteen and were capable of playing swift, powerful rugby to a very high standard. Now we could improvise, design special moves, do tricks. It was the team in which you came of age in rugby terms, and our egos were expanding as quickly as our shirts and shorts.

Tony 'Boney' Watkins was the coach. He was the biology master too, but he was a terrific rugby coach who emphasised fitness and fast, running rugby and he had us believing anything was possible on the pitch. Anything *was* possible when we played, and some of it was even legal. I was by now playing hooker, having moved from prop in the second form, and could be relied upon for a good number of tries per season and just as many unseen fights in scrums and mauls. I dare say the victims deserved it.

The style of rugby we played was based very much on the Australian model of medium-sized, mobile packs and quick, deft handling. We even stole a couple of their set-piece moves, too, the most prominent of which was the blandly titled 'Kangaroo'. The move was the epitome of Woolverstone rugby: the opposition rarely saw what was coming before it had steamrollered them. It involved three members of the pack standing with their back to the opposition for a tap penalty and several players would line up downfield of them, preparing to run at angles past this 'wall'. The scrum-half would play the ball to the first man in the wall, and the ball would then be manoeuvred, unseen by the opposition, to the central player or the far man in the barrier. We had a set of codes to denote who was to receive the ball – decoy runs would be made, all sorts of obfuscation devised. I was the man who would burst through the middle of the line, the members of the wall parting suddenly at the very last second.

My running style was best described as abrasive. Ever since we had joined the school and played the game, it had been drilled into us that defeat really wasn't an option, and looming over us was thirty years of high achievement on the rugby pitch. We also had the added incentive of playing, almost exclusively, wealthy private schools whose view of us urban oiks was less than generous. I invested every ounce of inferiority complex, every shred of that fear of failure and every fibre of my considerable arrogance into my running. I was thick-set, heavy and quick over twenty-five yards, after which my speed would settle at around that of a gun-dog trotting to pick up a pheasant. But for those first few yards I was like a darted rhinoceros. Give me the ball ten yards from the line, and I was a cert to score, scattering boys like ten pins. I had a sidestep too, which tended to work because the opponent was so flabbergasted that I should try it. He might know which way I was going to move off my planted foot, but he was too stunned to move in the same direction: it was more Gordon Bennett! than Phil Bennett. Indeed, that famous Barbarians try against the Kiwis, when Bennett began the move by leaving three flailing New Zealanders grasping at thin air, was very much our touchstone try. We all wanted to emulate that style of rugby.

Thus, in the Kangaroo move, as I burst through that wall, I posed quite a challenge for any defender. Without fail there would be one from the other side who would trot towards the wall once the ball had been tapped, always with a slightly bemused look on his face as he wondered what was going to happen next. If the coded call had been 'seventy-eight' when the penalty had been awarded, then *I* was what happened next. The defender would have approximately one tenth of a second to either position himself for a tackle or take cover, but rarely were there foxholes or bunkers nearby. I imagine, rather like my earlier observations with respect to the on-rushing Thommo fist, the first thing to go through his head was a wonder at the size and nature of what was coming towards him.

'What's that rhino doing on the . . .'

No doubt a short life flashed through his paralysed mind, too, but what eventually went through it, with cruel inevitability, was concussion.

Scraping yet another brave but essentially moronic opposition player from my studs produced as much of a sense of pride in me as academic excellence did in others. There were many maddening individuals whose academic excellence was surpassed only by their sporting prowess, but it is of perverse consolation to note that if real academic distinction had been within me, then I would no doubt have found sustaining both too great a challenge. Still, being good at one of the things that made Woolverstone famous in the educational community was about as good as it gets. Despite the long line of academic and cultural achievement the school could boast, there is little doubt that rugby was the shining tower from which most of us wanted to be able to sing. If I required it, rugby would bestow dignity as quickly as persistent misbehaviour divested me of it. Rugby was meant to channel natural aggression, teach us teamwork, strategy and fitness, but I clearly saw it as a means to further express my aggression and to hone my arrogant individuality, which was starting to flourish as profusely as the foreshore ferns in summer.

And I hated losing.

It had happened to us only once, when the opposition ran out of the dressing rooms looking twice as old as us. We were sure they were ringers, so desperate were schools to beat us; and despite Tunji Obasa breaking one opposition leg and damaging another's ankle, we lost by four points. Tunji was one of the smaller players on our team, but, as a full back, his tackling was peerlessly efficient. He had compact square shoulders that he would apply to the lower anatomy of oncoming runners with the precision of a surgeon's blade, and his tackling was a violation of the laws of physics. So abrupt and violent was the deceleration of anything below his shoulder that, anything above it, on account of it continuing at normal speed, was in danger of leveraging bone and sinew to breaking point. And it frequently did. Nevertheless, even with the appearance of stretchers on the field of play, we lost by four points. And it hurt. Badly. We felt hugely hard done by and I am pleased to report that in the return fixture we beat that same team by fifty points.

In the first term of fourth year I did allow myself to achieve something in the classroom as well as on the rugby field. I think I only ever did this to prove that if I wanted to do well academically, I could. Once demonstrated over the course of a term, I seemed happy to put it aside again, justifying to myself that I, and I alone, knew what would be best for me after Woolverstone. I had already decided that staying on to sixth form and university was not going to happen and thus I had two years to enjoy myself doing precisely what I wanted, and nothing more. That first term ended with a glowing school report, and the new headmaster was moved to remark that I was 'becoming a mature and sensible young man'.

The kind of crazy logic that was going through my head at the time I shall never really understand, but every time I grabbed the lifeline being offered by the school, I pulled myself to the bank, only to let it go as helping hands stretched out to yank me up.

Spring term saw the predestined decline in scholastic application, which took greatest expression in the wanton baiting of certain masters. In this respect, we showed commendable powers of discrimination, because some masters would not have any nonsense whatsoever in their classroom, and weren't worth irritating. It is easy to portray my younger self as an out of control little git whose masters ran scared, but that was not the case at all. Oh no, not at all. Once, a huge, red-headed chemistry master, known affectionately as Honey Monster, called me to the front of the classroom and proceeded to hang me like a smoked kipper by the locker key rope that swung from my neck. He hitched me to a hook in the frame of the blackboard and watched me kick my feet furiously for a while before unhooking me and sending me back to my seat. There was a peculiar ignominy to this reproach since I lost the power to speak as I dangled by the throat, and my expression, which could always be relied upon to display defiant insouciance, betrayed me horribly by transforming itself into a look of terrified panic. As ever, I was not to be defeated, and although I never directly confronted him again, I did find ways to make myself noticed by him. The most outstanding example of this was when I opened the gas tap on the workbenches and lit the stream of fumes, sending a jet of flame across the classroom, scattering several boys off their stools as they sought to escape the inferno. He admitted defeat with that one and sent me to the headmaster. It did not occur to me in victory that the only loser in all of this was standing in front of the headmaster with a smug look on his face.

Other masters were never challenged because they commanded great respect or because they were bloody big and not afraid to bring that size to bear upon the person of a scoundrel. Others, however, we circled and attacked like a pack of tiger sharks. Mercilessly. It did not help the master in question's cause if he had a habitual way of imploding emotionally when it all got too much. We simply enjoyed provoking whatever pyrotechnic temper tantrum was in the offing. A French teacher had cracked the wall plaster behind his chair, which would frequently slide at the speed of sound into it as he catapulted himself to his feet to scream obscenities at the class. This only happened after twenty minutes of digging away at him with silly requests to go to the toilet, constant talking and general silliness. His floppy fringe fell across his ever-reddening face, and his hands would be clasped in front of him on the desk, his knuckles whitening as quickly as his face flushed. Then the eruption would arrive.

'YOU BUGGERS WILL STOP BLOODY PISSING AROUND IN MY FUCKING CLASSROOM!'

And we would all cheer.

In the house we were just as cheap with our shots. Morris was a no-go for obvious reasons. But when he was off duty and other masters were supervising the house overnight, we felt freer. Mr Cromarty was our favourite target. 'Crom' was Scottish and a gentle soul. He looked ninety when he was forty and only looked his age when he actually hit ninety. He was an academic of ferocious repute and taught Latin, Greek, Religious Education and anything else considered impenetrable. Crom had an explosive temper, articulated in a wonderful Highland burr, but it took more effort to draw it out of him. When we did so, he would charge into the dormitory as violently as his shuffle would allow and order all of us down to the hallway outside the study for a mass slippering. In we would go, one by one, where Crom would not be able to find it in his heart to hit us particularly hard. Once done, we would rejoin the end of the queue, so when you arrived back at the front of the line, it was fifty-fifty that he would remember he'd already slippered you. The record was three, I think.

I have a sense of guilt as I recount these stories because these were good people. Dedicated, kind-hearted and excellent teachers, they did not deserve half of what we threw at them. They were entirely different from those genuinely malignant teachers who revelled in their power over small boys or who liked their company more than is healthy. Whilst I never heard of any direct pederasty, even as fourteen-year-olds, we knew those whose pastoral care needed watching like a hawk. Announcing open house for nights of baked beans and Radio Luxembourg, one master knew he'd attract a crowd and relished serving the food to all-comers in his skimpy white shorts that only fractionally covered his dangling testicles. He just liked the thrill of it, I think, but if we had had any guts, we would have given him as hard a time as it was possible to give. But he was feeding us extra food so we let him off. But Cromarty's only crime was to be kind and gentle.

Homosexuality was probably no more or less prevalent at Woolverstone than at any other public boarding school. We all seemed to be obsessed with girls, but I suppose some might have affected this out of peer pressure. It was never a real issue as far as I can recall it although we might have teased anyone who was effeminate. Among three hundred and sixty young men, there is likely to be at least a couple of dozen who are gay, and, of course, in British culture, the public school is supposed to be a hotbed of such activity. I am sure, too, that there were inappropriate liaisons between older and younger boys, including those that were not entirely voluntary. Someone in our dorm did once wake up in the middle of the night to find a sixth former's hand on his crown jewels, but the darkness and speed of escape by the offender meant we never knew for sure who it was. Another of our friends once walked into the communal showers to find a boy tootling on the pink oboe of another of the same age. Come to think of it, it was probably rife in the place, but either they were incredibly discreet or I was just blind to it and ignorant.

But as I remember it, girls were our obsession and we

spent most of our time chasing them, either at home during holidays or at school discos when a couple of bus loads would be shipped in from Ipswich. It was about this time several of us began to visit the home of a female French exchange teacher. She was in her early twenties but enjoyed the company of fifteen-year-old young men enough to allow a certain amount of eager fumbling to go on. Visiting her house *en masse*, we took over her living room and kitchen, but some drifted to her bedroom. I preferred emptying her drinks cabinet to fuelling any fantasies and left that sort of nonsense to others less discerning. They obviously considered themselves to be the lucky ones, but I had begun to develop my own tastes in the opposite sex and a podgy French temptress wasn't in the running. Maybe she never wanted to be in the running, but neither of us ever found out.

After one such visit, when we were walking along the main road at the top of the school drive, a carload of locals screeched to a halt after someone had hurled a box of matches at their car. Everyone scattered, and I sprinted up the driveway, which is precisely where the car came screaming in pursuit. My only escape was to dive over the barbed wire fence and into deep, watery cattle slurry, where I lay up to my neck, watching the 'yokels' hunting fruitlessly for me in the darkness. There were four of them, all of them large adults, and I found being soaked with cow shit preferable to getting a shoeing, but that was the dirtiest I ever got visiting the Mademoiselle.

My general behaviour during the fourth year was not overtly obnoxious, despite an emergent and misguided sense of respect and pride that frequently led to me turning into an outraged, righteous bore. You simply did not offend me, whether teacher or pupil, because I wouldn't back down. You either had the patience and humility of a saint to apologise, or you put your fists up. Predictably, there were those who felt the need to invite and then challenge the righteous indignation I carried around with me like a zealot with a prayer book.

* * *

'Just call it off, Mike,' Rob advised. 'He's big!'
'I know, but I don't think he wants to let it go.'

* * *

I have to admit that my sense of righteousness was accompanied by a sense of violence, though I probably wasn't thinking about that when I hit Washburn over the head with a club. It wouldn't have been too bad if he'd just crumpled unconscious to the ground. But he didn't. He staggered backwards, stunned but most definitely conscious, and then came charging back at me. I looked at the broken four-inch stump in my hand, stared up at the bull flying in my direction and nearly pissed in my pants. I had tested that club on tree trunks, walls and a metal gatepost. Yet when I whipped it out from the back of my jacket and brought it down on Washburn's crown, it disintegrated like a cinnamon stick. I was mortified. In movies, the buggers go down. At Woolverstone they just got angrier.

Today I am upset at the way in which I thought nothing

of using such a weapon on another boy, even one much larger than me. I was not sadistic or gratuitously violent at Woolverstone, although this and other stories might bring you to the alternative conclusion, but I honestly think my arrogance is what led me to wield such a tool. To me, it was the obvious tactic, so I used it.

Truth may well be that I would do it again today.

I wielded a small gatepost for the infamous battle of Freston Crossroads. In fact, there wasn't a battle at all, as I shall divulge, but about fifty boys had tooled up for a spontaneous challenge from some local skinheads. Dez (he of the bay tree Afro, which by now was more football size) had reported, late one Saturday night, that we were being 'offered out'. I have absolutely no idea how he would know such a thing, but word was spreading fast through the school. By the time we had begun to gather on the cricket field there was a pack mentality developing. Highly excited but probably intensely nervous, we set off to walk the two or so miles to Freston Crossroads. The destination was simply what it says – a crossroads in the middle of nowhere, channelling four roads in different directions. There were a couple of houses along one of the lanes, and this is where we had been told a party was being held and whence the challenge had first emerged. Our intended silent approach turned into more of a hum, but it didn't seem to matter since none of the houses showed signs of partying or skinheads. I suspect many of our number were breathing sighs of relief when suddenly, out of nowhere, several police cars screamed into the lane with sirens blaring and blue lights flashing. As they did so, the air became thick with wood, chains and sundry weaponry as boys set off running in all directions.

On either side of the lane were wheat fields with waist-high crops and I found myself running parallel to the road through one of them with Rob, Dez and Cyril Offiah. Cyril was a magnificent athlete. His younger brother, who was in the year below me, would become one of the most legendary rugby league players in Britain, but he wasn't a patch on Cyril. Cyril could play cricket, football, and rugby as though he was born doing it. He could have done anything he wanted in the sports arena – which is probably why he became a musician. People whose gifts are so great that the things they do with such ease cause weeping among observers and contemporaries often choose do something else. The effortlessness with which they perform the activity makes it uninteresting: when all around them are pleading for them to pursue glittering careers, the Gifted One is yawning.

In the wheat field, Cyril was a panther, quick as the wind and twice as elegant. Whereas I ran as though my life depended on it, he breezed along as if on a conveyor belt, his running style poetry, whilst mine was coarse rhyming couplet. But relative speed counted for nothing when a disturbed pheasant took shockingly to the wing with a loud squawk. The surprise meant that Rob also took to the wing, but with a 'Fucking hell!', and came screaming past all of us. After fifty yards we stopped and crouched beneath the crop cover. We could see police up and down the lane searching for us, and Dez spotted a friend hiding in the hedge. As he tried to get his attention, I warned that there was a policeman walking along the lane at that precise point. Dez couldn't hear me and continued to call out in a way that he thought was quiet but was, in fact, like blowing a trumpet. I stood up to move closer to him, and as I did so a bright torch swung round to shine directly at me. I froze. Beneath me, at my feet and hidden by the wheat, Dez laughed quietly. 'Don't fucking run, you, we have dogs on the way!' barked the policeman, who didn't seem to need dogs at all. I whispered out of the side of my mouth for my comrades to give themselves up with me. Some hope. The only consolation was that I got a lift back to school in the back of a panda car.

The whole idea of a violent clash with a bunch of skinheads was absurd anyway since the majority of those on the sortie to Freston were in no way equipped for the kind of wild-eyed violence mass brawls generate. A few of us had once encountered skinheads in a collective sense during a school holiday. At a party in a hall in Fulham, we had been set upon by some and Dez had a gin bottle brought down on his skull. It succeeded only in denting his scalp and provoking him into knocking the attacker into next week. But the desire to be on the Freston journey, whatever each of us thought would be at the end of it, was powerful and strong. As ridiculous and thuggish as the enterprise was, it was hugely exciting. Would fifty Eton boys cross the fields of Berkshire in the dark to fight with a load of oiks from Slough?

DRAMA QUEEN

A s I have intimated, there were a couple of activities at Woolverstone that could engage and inspire me to fruitful endeavour. Sport was one, and drama was the other. Neil 'Noddy' Clayton became more of a regular fixture in my life during the fourth year. He taught me English Literature and was the drama teacher who directed and produced the school plays. I liked Noddy, who was a brilliant teacher, full of bright language, and was one of the early masters when Woolverstone was set up. So of course, I set about annoying him immensely.

Serge was a good actor and the year before had stolen the show as a gay art dealer in *Black Comedy*. Noddy liked Serge and detested me, especially my showing off and attention-seeking whilst he was trying to teach us English literature, but he assumed I had similar stage talents to Serge and he wasn't going to let a little hatred get in the way of useful resources. He ensured I was involved in the forthcoming production for which he auditioned me by simply asking if I had acted before. I said I had. That was enough.

That year, things were going to be different and, rather than taking a standard text for subject matter, Noddy had decided that we ourselves were to conceive, write and develop a series of dramatic pieces. Among a collection of monologues of varying coherence and a 'movement' piece where scores of boys wearing stockings on their heads formed a human pyramid to ethereal music was a mini-play about the witch-hunts and trials of the eighteenth century. For whatever reason, I was playing Daniel Defoe, chief prosecutor of a witch played by Helju Sadler, Pete Fart's daughter. I do not recall who of us wrote it, but it was full of florid, decorative language that I naturally luxuriated in, affecting the most ridiculously haughty English accent for which I had taken inspiration from Alastair Sim in the St Trinian's films. I was a horrible ham, but I enjoyed getting the laughs.

I was also the model company member, learning my words and being quiet, attentive and helpful to other cast members during rehearsals. Something very strange had become of me. And I loved the entire process of producing the play. If you gave me a text to read, say, about the effects of glacial erosion, it would pass through my eyes and into a void, where it would evaporate. Give me a script, and the words – both mine and those of every other cast member – would be committed to memory, ordered and filed into neat lines in a strong room from which they would never escape. You were as likely to get a prompt from me as one from the person whose job it was. If you were still forgetting your lines on the second day of rehearsals, I was at you in a trice, criticising your lack of professionalism but offering to help you with it afterwards. So diligently did I learn my part, as well as everyone else's, the rumour started doing the rounds that I had a photographic memory. I did nothing to dispel it although all I did was allow my brain to do what came naturally, which is to absorb information.

I was a fifteen-year-old luvvie who thought the enterprise of producing theatre was as seriously important as drawing up a new Europe. My performance in rehearsals was as committed as it would be when audiences arrived, and Noddy's advice was taken, discussed and put into practice. For once, I was at the head of a hierarchy on merit and I enjoyed the way that others looked to me, asked for advice and commented on how good they thought I was. I was in my element and acting was like being given permission to misbehave. You could play the fool, follow the emotional mood of the moment, pull silly faces and, if the script had it, swear in front of masters without fear of repercussion. The play was the school expressing itself, and it was the focus of the entire term. For once, I was speaking words that could be heard by hundreds of people, but this time they were listening. For the hours he spent taking me through rehearsal, Noddy Clayton behaved as though the sun shone from whichever of my orifices was not spewing expletives.

The school play that year was a rum old piece precisely because Neil Clayton had encouraged us to write it. As a teacher of English, Clayton was able to count Ian McEwan among his past pupils, and as a drama teacher he produced several fine actors, including Neil Pearson, so we should have taken any encouragement he gave. To this day he is immersed in the world of books, buying and selling valuable libraries. Back then, he was thus immersed because his lessons took place in the library. His knowledge was immeasurable and his enthusiasm, when he wasn't teeing off at Ipswich golf course, was endless. He enjoyed having us read Chaucer's *Canterbury Tales* in Middle English and it was his reading of it that ensured half of 'The Miller's Tale' remains with me today, buried in my memory. Some of that might be to do with the fact it is one long fart gag, but nevertheless, Clayton's evocation of its characters brought it vividly to life. I still recollect the relish with which the arse was proffered from the window in his telling of it.

It would have been uncharacteristic of me to positively exploit such a gifted teacher. So I didn't. I just took the piss. And on the recurring theme of looking gift horses in the mouth, I did whatever I could to be thrown out of his class. Clayton was swift to give vent to his feelings about me as I skulked from the library, and although it was often unspeakably rude, it was nevertheless accurate. However, it was not unknown for a contretemps to occur and for us to be getting along like a house on fire a few hours later in rehearsal. Whether Neil found this relationship bizarre and uncomfortable I don't really know, but I never gave it a second thought. To me, it was perfectly natural since I wanted to be doing drama and I wasn't overly keen on English Lit. If the irony of that strikes you as you read this, it is nothing compared to how hard it is hitting me as I write it.

It is impossible to draw a picture of the benign way in which I took to the theatrical arts. The contrast with the boy I have described in this memoir and the boy who showed enormous maturity on the stage could not be wider. I cannot truly explain it. For once, my showing off had a purpose and drew others towards me, as opposed to having the normally repellent effect. Clayton persevered with me in English Lit because he had no choice, but he confidently dragged performances out of me in the play. I wonder at the exasperation he must have felt when trying to get me to pay attention to him in the classroom, when just hours later I would be held rapt by his every word. If there was a perversity to it that Neil found hard to account for or tolerate, he hid it well. On reflection, even I was not aware of the dichotomy these two personas represented, and I can easily imagine a scenario where Clayton felt nauseated by what must have appeared wilful at times. I can assure him that it wasn't.

The first term of fourth year had been pretty good, and the second had been crowned by the school play. The report book shows that things were starting to slip somewhat although I was still hoping to take the English O-Level in the summer (a year early), which was pretty high academic attainment as far as I was concerned. I had already decided that English was one of the subjects I would get an O-level in – the rest, I hadn't decided on yet. The tone of most masters in the book is benevolent and encouraging, so I can only think I was, on the whole, being pleasant around the school. The weeks working on the play had been a soothing factor on my behaviour, and I was still singing in the rugby choir under Derek 'Doc' Thornbery, which I always enjoyed.

Drama Queen

Doc Thornbery was a legend. He was the first rugby coach any of us had, and he had taught hundreds of boys at Under Twelves. In fact Doc wasn't much bigger than the eleven-year-olds he taught to play rugby. Doc also taught English and it would be fair to say he was one of the most radiant and inspirational teachers I ever had. He was unorthodox, too, leaping up onto the desks and walking from table to table as he elucidated some book, text or poem. He was transfixing, speaking at volume, then a whisper, eyes wide open, hands pressed into gesticulating action. If your attention wandered, Doc would spring leopard-like across the desks, grab you by the hair and shake you senseless as he continued to recite Shakespeare or Keats. He wore Doc Marten shoes (hence the nickname) and these helped his balance, the cushioned soles offering rudimentary suspension as he bounced across four desks to his target. In the seventies, we all had long hair, but Adebola didn't. He wasn't interested in Afros so kept his hair cropped short to his head. When Doc leapt across to his desk one day, he scratched away at Adebola's head trying to get purchase on the hair that wasn't really there. After a short while of trying, he took hold of his ear instead and shook him by that. I often think of that little vignette as a metaphor for my school life – when shaking me one way didn't work, somebody tried something different.

Doc was just as inspirational as a choir master, but I never saw him shake anyone by the hair in rehearsals. I don't recall how I came to be in the choir – I must have auditioned – but I was a member of the junior choir in the first form so I was singing throughout my school career.

I was only marginally less attentive and dedicated to music than theatre, enjoyed singing immensely and in my senior years I recall performing in various sections of the choir, ranging from second tenor to second bass, so my range was acceptably wide. Our programme was challenging and varied, too, and we gave concerts not just to the school but also to the community at large. Doc had a remarkable ear for voices and could spot a flat note from a thousand paces when he would suddenly crouch low and stare, pointing accusingly at one section of the choir.

'Everyone stop, stop! First basses, on your own, quick!' Having narrowed down the section, he would set about singling out the culprit until one poor soul would be singing solo, sounding just like the drain Doc had heard above the din of forty other voices. Being that person was unpleasant because a flat note sorely tested Doc's patience, and he would make you sing the part repeatedly until he was satisfied you had mastered it. I'm bound to say that the choir could sound magnificent, and its peak for me was the performance of Handel's *Messiah* when a local girls' school and other choirs joined us to provide the full range of voices required for the piece. We really let them have it with that one.

Despite the choirs at Woolverstone, the school had become musically less ambitious than its earlier years. Weber's masterpiece, *Der Frieschütz,* is a complex, beautiful opera but requires considerable vocal and orchestral forces, not to mention complicated staging since magic and all sorts of nonsense is involved. It provides a huge challenge for any professional company, but I was astonished to discover, on looking through some Woolverstone archives, that the school had produced the opera in the early sixties. Along with it, they had also performed some Britten (the composer actually visiting the school to see the production), Mozart's *Magic Flute*, Verdi's *Requiem*, Menotti's *Amahl and the Night Visitors, The Mikado* and even Smetana's *The Bartered Bride*. These are hugely ambitious pieces, and the rugby choir was just a remnant of what had been a glorious musical and theatrical history. In 1962 alone, the school mounted productions of Bertolt Brecht's *Mother Courage*, the aforementioned Smetana opera and finally George Bernard Shaw's play of *Androcles and the Lion*. Other years were equally challenging and remarkable. Perhaps the swinging sixties brought about the demise of such high classical endeavour, but the school certainly continued to produce, with seriousness, classical music and theatre. It must have required huge dedication and commitment on the part of masters too, in particular the music teacher Barry Salmon, although having the pupils in school twenty-four hours a day must have helped a bit. To bring young boys like us to the doorway leading to such high classical art is almost unimaginable today, I suspect. It is likely the boys involved never realised that, when they took on *Frieschütz*, they were producing one of the great German operas of all time, but they would come to appreciate their enlightenment later in life. That was Woolverstone: anything and everything was possible, and I can imagine the masters sitting down to devise the latest theatrical or musical wheeze, nobody wasting time wallowing in their cleverness.

Except for me.

On stage, I could indulge all sorts of haughty, high stepping self-glorification and nobody would criticise me for it. Theatre and everything attached to it was my academic high point, and it was the one place where the dull, hard, battleship grey of my educational prospects took on a patina in which you could see the potential for something approaching bright lights reflected.

* * *

The fourth year was punctuated by a skiing trip to Italy. Mum couldn't afford it, so I would have to earn the fare by taking various holiday jobs. Skiing was impossibly exotic to me. I longed to do it and loved the Alps, having passed through them by train whenever we travelled to see the family in Italy. Most of all, it was another opportunity to show off, since I had deduced that being a decent ice skater would stand me in good stead.

Bardonecchia in the Italian Alps was full of other school-children from England. It was late in the season, which meant it was cheap. Adebola experienced hair tugging again when a chattering group of Italian school kids, having never seen a black boy before, encountered him at the mountain café and proceeded to play with his hair.

Naturally, within minutes of arriving on the slopes, we had attracted the attention of a group of public school boys who proffered their school boxing champion, 'Johnny', as upholder of their school honour. I don't recall why this happened but it was just like the rugby: they thought we were beneath them. We were in most respects, but it wasn't their place to remind us, we thought. If Johnny and his pals were expecting a conflict under the rules of the Marquis of Queensberry, the rain of skis, sticks, blocks of ice and fists quickly disabused them of the notion. Having asserted our dominance of the mountain, we set about hitting it as often as possible.

I first hit it as soon as my second boot had locked the binding shut. Without a pause, I was on my back. Ice skating was clearly no apprenticeship. True to form, lessons were nothing but a trial, mainly geared around preventing us flying off the side of cliffs as we tried to emulate whatever Austrian or Swiss nutter was star of *Ski Sunday* at the time. We paid no attention.

I was determined to master the parallel stop, which I had seen the locals execute with effortless ease. I particularly wanted to be able to do the version where snow sprayed in an arc into the air as you looked nonchalantly back up the mountain holding both sticks in one hand. I was nothing if not determined, and I tried and tried, crossing my skis so that I crumpled head first into the snow, or, more painfully, when trying to bring them together, sending my skis further apart. I only finally managed to achieve the parallel stop under duress. Heading for what looked like a terrifying precipice at breakneck speed, I had no option: fail to produce a shuddering stop and I'd be a goner. So I did. And it was a brilliant one. So brilliant, in fact, that my skis were immediately stationery, but unfortunately, I chose to stay upright rather than lean up the slope so the rest of me carried on and I went over the edge of the precipice anyway. It was my lucky day because what had looked lethal was merely an injurious ten-foot drop. I landed with a clatter, broke a stick and damaged my hand. But I had done it, and I was ecstatic.

Now that I had mastered the parallel stop, I practised the looking up the mountain bit. For a while I would rotate to look back and continue to revolve until I did a pirouette and landed on my arse. But I got to the point where I could look like I was gazing up the mountain, but really, under cover of my dark glasses, I kept a beady eye on the tips of my skis. Charging down the mountain at high velocity could now be achieved since I knew how to stop. What I did not bargain for was the imperfections in a ski piste, which would make the stylish halt redundant because I had already used the better part of my face to slow down. A kindly ski instructor gave me a nugget of advice that essentially said: you could only truly ski when you could descend a mountain as *slowly* as you wanted.

The skiing trip was also an opportunity to find girls. Italian girls, I had warned my friends, were not like your average English strumpets who gave out at the first opportunity. Italian girls usually had backup in the shape of their father's shotgun, so best to avoid them at all costs. This was easily done since there were plenty of English girls ready to give out at the first opportunity. I vaguely remember one occasion when Rob was snogging two girls at once, but I don't recall how he managed it. In any case, I was too busy perfecting my parallel turns to worry about such things, and when not on the slopes trying them out,

I would work on my theories of trigonometry and physics to accomplish the perfect turn.

I also saved someone's life.

The fact that it was I who had jeopardised his life in the first place was of little consequence to me then, but it was of critical importance to him. It happened on the chairlift one afternoon as we descended the mountain. Being late in the season, there was no snow below the ski station to enable us to ski back to town and so we had to take the main chairlift back to the valley floor. It was a two-man chair lift and to mount it required a simple but crucially important technique.

We were lined up in pairs ready to go down, and I was with a random sixth former who, in my memory, had a flashy one-piece ski suit. We would hand our skis to the attendant, who would put them in the holders on the back of the chair, and we were to hold our ski poles in our hands. The idea was to stand side-by-side, wait for the next chair to begin to swing round the large wheel and then step across to be in line with it. When it got to you, you just sat down and let it carry you away as you swung the safety bar down and locked it into place. I was on the left so I had to take two steps to my left to be in line with the far side of the chair, and my partner on the right needed to take two steps to be in line with the right side of the chair. Simple.

Except as the chair swooped around towards us, I took only one step to my left which meant he had to set off running to get around me in order to sit on the other side. Ski boots are not especially good for quick manoeuvring, so he had his work cut out. He began his charge for the other side of the seat with an 'Oh fuck!' and managed to incorporate a small spin in the middle. He reached the other side just as I sat, oblivious to his suffering, onto the wrong side of the chair. Unfortunately, his arse never connected, but the small of his back did, and he was hanging by his elbows as the chair continued towards the edge of the platform. At the edge was a large cargo net, designed, one supposes, to catch dropped skis, poles or people riding a chair lift with me. By now I had awoken to the struggle for life to my left and had grabbed the collar of his ski suit.

'Jump into the net!' I advised, somewhat unfairly since the net was mounted over a void of frightening proportions.

'OK, OK. No, I can't!' he wailed.

'Oh for fuck's sake!' I moaned.

As this episode unfolded, we could hear the gales of laughter from our friends at the chair lift. Or at least I could. My partner was already frozen in terror and could probably only hear the pounding of his own heart. However, when we sailed over the net and my partner's legs were still hanging free below the chair lift, the laughter stopped and we could hear the eerie swirl of the wind across the mountain, even above the screams and pleadings of my partner.

I gripped his collar with my left hand whilst holding my poles in the right. At this point, I too was in some danger since he could have dragged me off the chair. By now, we had traversed the flat run below the lift's first fifty metres and had passed over the ridge that dropped to at least 100 feet below. If I let go now, he would die. I considered letting go so that I wouldn't die with him. His elbows were on the edge of the seat behind him, and he was craning his head as far back as he could to provide some counterbalance to the enormously heavy ski boots that were fighting hard to drag him in the opposite direction.

'Don't let go of me,' he pleaded with an intensity I still recall vividly.

'Of course I won't let go, you stupid idiot! Just get yourself back up on the seat because I can't hold you much longer!'

Fear was the reason for my lack of sympathy, but he was starting to annoy me.

'Look, let's wait till we get to a low bit, you can jump down and maybe you will only break a leg,' I suggested.

'I don't want to break a leg!' he replied.

'Well it's better than fucking dying you stupid fucking idiot! I'm trying to save your fucking life here!'

Even at such a moment, the words struck him as somewhat perverse.

'It's your fault! Just pull me up, pull me up!'

'I can't!'

And so it went on for an eternity, but somehow, and I honestly do not remember how, I got him back onto the chair, and we dropped the safety bar. My heart was pounding and I couldn't shake the visions of him falling to his death. He sat staring ahead for a moment, his breathing rapid and shallow. Neither of us spoke for a while until he broke the silence.

'Jesus Christ, Volps. You got a fag?'

It is a fitting footnote to report that he went on to be a ski racer and instructor for the army.

* * *

The spring term had ended with our customary triumph in the Suffolk Sevens tournament. I loved Sevens because it gave me a chance to run with the ball. We had a superb team, to be perfectly modest. We trounced everybody, which is a testament to the coaches at Woolverstone, because everybody was bigger than us. Mum actually attended this tournament, which lasted the entire day at some school in Ipswich. She wasn't able to visit frequently because having no car meant a tiresome journey on the train, but she would arrange to come down in the car of other boys' parents when it was convenient.

She'd watched me play very little rugby – in fact, I think this was the first time – and her reaction to it was predictably hysterical. Standing on the touchline with absolutely no clue of what was going on, she merely cheered and clapped when everybody else did. But on a run along the line, an opposition winger leapt onto my back and tried to bring me down.

'FUCKY LEEVIMALON!'

My mother was foaming at the mouth with bag in hand, ready to strike.

'Bastardo!' she screamed.

The poor boy who tackled me ran off in the opposite direction as I tried to assure Mum that it was OK and people were allowed to jump on me. I forgot to mention that this was, in fact, the final, so there were lots of people watching. Mum's interventions wiped away some of the gloss from the victory since Sevens tournaments gathered together in one place all of our vanquished opponents. For a star player on the winning team to have his mother squeal obscenities at anyone who dared touch him was not the stuff of strutting champions. It was the only time I hated getting a laugh.

* * *

'Despite Michael's attempts to blame everybody else for his troubles, it must now be clear to him, as it has been to the rest of us for some time, that at present he is on a disaster course. He has done almost no work this year; he has upset a lot of people by his rudeness and behaviour. Fortunately, it is still not too late. I hope he can get his attitudes sorted out quickly next term – if he can, I wish him well for the future. JM'

I reproduce, in full, John Morris's end of year entry in my report book. Soon after, he left to join another school. It is a salient entry because not only does it chronicle my slide, it also demonstrates, yet again, the way in which masters at Woolverstone never seemed to give up on me. His encouraging note at the end was surely given in the full knowledge that indeed, it was too late, but he gave it anyway because I don't think he felt able to write me off.

If I am honest, I could scream when I read it. I could slap the boy he is talking about. There was one bright side to it all: I did take my English O-Level a year early and would later find out that I'd passed, but that only makes my refusal to tackle other subjects with any real effort all the more unforgivable. I managed to prove my then English language teacher, Mr Taylor, wrong when he predicted in the report that although the exam was easily within my reach, I had probably blown it. The infuriatingly erratic self-destruction continued unabated.

Neil Clayton, who was, in that fourth summer term, my cricket coach, brought the curtain down on the year:

'Cricket – He was a nuisance because he could not keep his mouth shut. The promise he has, which is considerable, will never develop unless he can control himself.'

He could have been talking about almost any subject.

BRINGING THE HOUSE DOWN

*'Ridiculously self-centred. He should stop clowning
and start working.'*
J.M. Hyde, Geography

'Alas, he hasn't bothered. Does he care? I doubt it.'
Neil Clayton, English Literature

*'School play. Absolutely first class. Utterly reliable,
co-operative, sensible and a good actor. Well done!'*
Neil Clayton, Drama

Entering what should not have been, but which I had
determined would be, my final year at Woolverstone,
the promise and potential I had shown at primary school
had less than ten months to produce the goods. Not
that it stood much of a chance while my rampant adolescent hormones were in charge of my behaviour. As the
above extracts from the autumn term report show, the
signs for the end of year exams were not good, and I
wasn't placing academic effort high up my list of priorities. Roughly in order, my priorities were me, myself
and I. John Morris had left Woolverstone, and the new

housemaster was Dave Morgan, the metalwork teacher. I got on well with Morgan and on the whole I wasn't behaving particularly badly, I just had the most remarkable impudence and, if I am honest, the foulest, most explosive temperament. It showed itself moderately infrequently, but when it did I could send a ripple through the school. I got into an almighty battle of wills with my physics teacher, whose loathing of me he did not even bother to disguise. Once he had found a reason to exclude me from the classroom, he decided I was never to return, which even I knew wasn't allowed. I approached the headmaster for advice.

'Return to the classroom, Michael, I will talk to him,' he said.

The next day I entered the room and was instantly challenged: 'I thought I told you never to come into my classroom again, Volpe?'

Knowing I had cleared things with the headmaster, I was not in the mood to show any form of contrition for past misdemeanours: politely, but with undisguised self-righteousness, I told him I had seen the head and that he should speak with him if he had a problem. And then I sat down with my back to the blackboard and began to do the mock exam that sat on the table as the master stormed out of the room. Ten minutes later he stormed back in and halfway through a question on refraction I found myself looking at the ceiling as the master, now livid after what had obviously been a fruitless discussion with the head, dragged me bodily along the floor and flung me into the corridor. He slammed the door behind him as he leapt back into the room. He leapt because I was halfway onto my feet and coming towards him. Rage had returned, but this time he'd brought his pals Fury and Murderous Psychosis with him.

I charged for the closed door with wild abandon, screaming like a banshee, but the door had a strong lock and reinforcement on account of it being a physics lab. I took off, feet first, with the intention of kicking the door down, thinking that nothing would withstand my weight and power. Except, as it turned out, the reinforced door of a physics lab. The soles of my shoes connected with it, and the rest of my body carried on, crumpling up behind my feet until my arse was the next thing to hit the door. Without drawing breath between volleys of invective, essentially because it had all been knocked out of me, I dragged myself to my feet and continued to gasp obscenities through the small head-height window whilst banging my fists furiously. I think I stood there, puce of face, for about ten minutes shouting and hollering and banging the door until I got hoarse and my hands hurt. My arse and feet were already painful. Something else was niggling me: my shoulders were bruised and scratched, so violently did he grip them when dragging me along the floor.

He had crossed the line, in my eyes. It was unquestioned that I was not the world's greatest student, but, paradoxically, I was respectful towards teachers in the normal course of things. It was part of my internal code of conduct: you treat me with respect and I will return the gesture. I could get exceedingly haughty about it too, and, on the whole, teachers were clever enough not to patronise me. This particular master had reduced himself to my level, his challenge was physical: in the mind of a truculent, hormonal fifteen-year-old boy, he had forfeited his right to respect. This was a view I would express most graphically as he returned to his classroom after break.

I had waited for him, and as he walked with Coulter, the art master, I offered him the chance to upbraid me physically once more, only this time whilst I faced him and had the help of a garden spade. Coulter – bravely, I would say – challenged me, telling me to stop it and to put the shovel down. I continued to hurl righteous indignation at the physics master over Coulter's head, until the proximity of his pleading drew my attention and I shouted at him too. I threw the shovel to the ground and walked away.

The disgraceful nature of this episode would have come as no shock to some, but as I travelled home on the train to begin my one-week suspension, I knew in my heart that something, somewhere had gone seriously awry. I cannot recall spending more than a few minutes trying to wonder what it was, but nevertheless, it nagged at me as I pondered the pleasures of an unexpected return to London. Waiting for me at the door, Mum glared, although she didn't throw anything at me or wallop me in the corridor. She had complained officially about the master's behaviour, but the disappointment with me was evident. My brother Matteo, fresh home from his latest stint as a guest of Her Majesty, sought to lecture me about throwing away opportunities. After a period of resistance, I burst into tears. Perhaps for the first time I became aware of the people I was letting down: I don't think, at that stage, that I was aware I was only truly letting myself down, but I hated being the way I had become.

My brother's lecture was probably the first that anybody had given me since Paddy died. For two years since that day, I think I had been waiting for someone to show an interest in me beyond remarking on my failures. As ridiculously self-centred as teenage boys can be – and I was certainly that – it is often the case that their behaviour is merely a ploy to grab as much attention as they can. The pub-psychology of that statement does nothing to render it less true.

'You are at that place because we don't want you turning out like me,' Matt said, proving that at least his self-awareness had developed during incarceration. Serge, who had left the school by now and was working, was disgusted with me. He had always got along with the master at the centre of the row and couldn't understand the animosity towards me that I had reported.

'You are never in the wrong, are you, Mike?' he said.

There's no mistaking the sound made by a breaking wave of shame.

★ ★ ★

I had the school play to look forward to in the second half of autumn term. It would be my last, and Clayton had made me the star. Knowing that nobody else had stood even the faintest chance of usurping me in the lead returned me to my full, strutting pomp. With perhaps a little irony, I was cast as the eponymous hero in *Jack Sheppard*, a play about the infamous eighteenth-century London thief; it was a wonderful version by the British actor Ken Campbell, full of characters with names like Dribbling Wilf. The production was elaborate, too, with a two-level set, and would involve me climbing from the ceiling onto the stage. With great relish and my usual enthusiasm, I would attack the part; I would even work on the stage crew after rehearsals had finished. This was to be my crowning glory.

I was given the script and immediately set about underlining in red all of my dialogue, along with the few lines before mine, which I underlined in blue. The almost frenzied way in which I learned my lines was of course another huge contradiction in my general approach to study. By the time rehearsals started, I wanted to be ready and prepared: struggling with my lines would only hinder my showing off, and I had both my part and much of everybody else's entirely committed to memory within a week. I didn't have a particular technique for learning a script, but began by reading it several times through so that I fully understood every scene and plot turn. Should I ever get into trouble on stage, I could at least make something up that loosely followed the tenet of the scene. Forward planning on such a scale is uncommon in teenage boys, but impossible to imagine in me, and there was seriousness about my approach. It was a big cast, and my character was on stage virtually the entire time, which meant rehearsing with almost everybody in the play at one point or another. Abilities would vary, yet I would find myself encouraging and working with those whose acting tended towards the stiff and actually discovered that gentle cajoling worked so much better than impatience and irritation. One boy was struggling to deliver just two lines of dialogue in a convincing manner, but Clayton and I worked with him for what seemed like ages until, suddenly, he unleashed a cod northern accent of such accuracy and timing, I found it hard to rehearse with him from then on, so funny was his new character. Corpsing was a bit of a weakness of mine (it still is), and I would often hold up rehearsals so that I could compose myself. It was behaviour that in other circumstances would have resulted in admonishment, but onstage, Clayton seemed happy to go along with it, only intervening and calling us to order once it began to seriously affect the work that needed to be done.

Jack Sheppard's claim to fame was that he could escape from prisons. In the play I went from carpenter's apprentice to common thief. I find it hard to remember the entire plot, but suffice it to say the end of the play saw me executed. The opening scene was a comic monologue that required me to walk alone to the front of the stage and introduce myself. There were many such moments in the play, when I delivered narration between scenes, then other characters would appear and the drama would be played out.

It was sweet nectar to deliver those first lines by myself, and as the play proceeded, the laughs would grow louder and more frequent. The script was my insurance, but my delivery was the thing in my mind. If these were my own words, they would be even funnier, I thought, but I invested every ounce of emotion I could muster into that prose. This was my best incarnation. I knew it, the audience knew it and most of the school's masters knew it. Woolverstone could smile to itself when it saw me on stage. It had made *something* of Michael Volpe.

My hamming and mugging during each performance was ceaseless, but despite not being satisfied that the script already made me the centre of attention, I was still a generous performer. I added several new things to the play every night, and watching me must have given Clayton some worrying moments. The desire to elicit laughs led me into all manner of over-acting. I relished every single moment of stage time and cursed every curtain call.

School plays at Woolverstone were very professionally produced, and calamity was largely kept at bay, but it would be unlike me to fail to seed a success with the potential for disaster. At the beginning of the second half came the moment where I climbed from the ceiling of the hall above the lights, down onto the stage. I was escaping from a prison, and a rope made from blankets and sheets was dropped into the spotlight: from the darkness I would appear, delivering another narrative solo. I had tied the sheets and blankets together myself, reinforcing the knots with string and testing the rope all through the rehearsal period. Rob was stage manager, and it was his job to escort me up the ladder and onto the ledge that ran around the high windows. The rope was tied to the ceiling rafters, and I was to begin my descent once Rob ensured I got onto the rope safely. On the first night, after the interval, the cue came and Rob dropped the rope. The audience were silent, and I heard a ripple of laughter as the line appeared suddenly in the spotlight. With hardly a pause, I then appeared, at terminal velocity, landing on my arse and making a sound like an elephant landing in a skip. The roar of laughter washed onto the stage like a tsunami as I rose to my feet, ad-libbed a bit and continued my speech.

On my descent, a few feet from the top, I had seen the knot in front of my face begin to slip apart. I had frozen and watched it, rather than having the presence of mind to climb quickly to the bottom before it finally separated. I had looked up at Rob, who even in the darkness I could see sniggering hard; he too had seen the knot begin to slip. Time had stood still. And then the sudden, sickening partition of sheet and blanket had sent me hurtling to the stage. In my mind, I had made the whole thing look deliberate, like a well-worked stunt, but I was kidding myself because everybody knew what had happened. I still lapped up the laughter.

Jack Sheppard was a great success, and I was lauded and applauded from all quarters. But my end of term report made scant mention of it, except when it was used it to illustrate how badly I had performed in everything else. There was no doubting that the contrast between my attitude to drama and everything else had become more stark and inexplicable. Rugby was another area where I had let myself down. Having abused a fellow player in the first training session, I was kicked out of group and deprived of what would have been the inevitable hooker position in the First XV. After a couple of weeks I was asked to return, presumably because it was considered I had learned my lesson, but I refused out of indignation at having been banned in the first place. If I could be bothered, I turned out for other lesser teams, only to end up fighting in virtually every match. It was a grotesque waste, and it is among several aspects of my school life that fill me with regret and shame. Swallowing my pride was all it would have taken to be returned to the Firsts, but whatever it was that turned me into a righteous bore saw to it that the humble pie being offered to me in only small pieces would remain uneaten. The truth is that my success in *Jack Sheppard* had essentially convinced me that I had triumphed, that the play and my part in it had gloriously topped out almost five years at school and little else was necessary.

By now, I had reached the firm conclusion that I wasn't too keen to achieve many exam passes. I had passed English a year early, and art was the other exam I wanted to pass. The others were going to have to fall by the wayside. I didn't tell anyone this, of course, and masters just continued to implore me to work harder and fulfil the potential they said I had. My behaviour in the house was good, according to Dave Morgan, although he delivered a stinging rebuke for my academic listlessness. After the school play, it appeared that my Woolverstone career would peter out with a whimper, not a bang.

THROWING IT ALL AWAY

Once I had made my decision to forgo the exam process that was looming in the summer, Woolverstone life would really only consist of fun and games. Going to Ipswich for club nights, listening to music, playing football and visiting the pub were my principal activities for the spring term. Home life during holidays was girls and working to raise money for clothes and other entertainment. I still had about me the lofty air of a Woolverstone boy: my pride at being at the school never left me. But I was unforthcoming about the secret resolution to throw five years of academic endeavour, such as it was, down the drain. I knew the stupidity of such a decision well enough to keep it to myself.

The thinking behind such a choice was fairly simple. There was no doubt in my mind that achieving good grades was well within my capabilities, and despite the reports of lack of effort, there were many subjects I did enjoy, and I absorbed much of what was put before me in a lesson. However, I had become convinced that examination passes were just pieces of paper; back then there was still talk of achieving your aims in life without grades or university. I was full of self-confidence and bravado, so I would leave Woolverstone and still become a millionaire. Now, of course, I can look back and think of all the possibilities I had laid out before me. Indeed, Clayton had even arranged for me to have an audition at RADA, such was my ability as an actor considered to be. No surprises that I thought the concept of three years of further study bordered on the hilariously impossible. To be perfectly frank, that particular misstep doesn't haunt me at all since I continue to meet out-of-work actors.

To my mind, with decades of distance between my adult self and the mid-teens version, it seems obvious to me that Woolverstone had not – yet – cracked the nut, hadn't broken the spell of my fractured urban background. Given the choice between succumbing to the intellectual restrictions of a no-hope life and the limitless possibilities my school facilitated, I went with the street, because I thought the possibilities *were* endless in my council-estate-market-trader-no-socks-dirty-fingers world, which bore little relation to the real one being laid out on the table for me by Woolverstone. I wore Woolverstone like a coat, but I was still wearing my old clothes underneath. It would be possible for me to do any kind of work when I left school, and it mattered not whether I had exam passes. It took until three years after I left for the penny to drop, but as my fifth year wore on I became more convinced by the day that I was right and that thirty years of miraculous academic achievement at Woolverstone was wrong. I had simply reverted to type. I had travelled full circle. I was certain – and there was nobody in my world who was going to draw my attention to the folly upon which I was about to stake my entire post-school existence – that I was embarking on a course of action that would see me do anything I wanted in life. My confidence was only surpassed by my inanity. Is this the mindset of all bright children whose social background labels them? We can achieve in *our* world, not 'theirs'?

My ill-advised self-assuredness meant my disposition around the school and my attitude towards lessons was very much take or leave it. New masters continued to join, but few of them seemed to have a clue how to deal with us and nor did they have any affection for the school as it had once been. By now, it had completely changed from its original premise and was essentially at the start of a decade-long, politically motivated demise.

For my part, respect for these teachers had become a cosmetic enterprise. I had none that was genuine, but I would approach their dealings with me as a shop assistant might talk to a difficult customer: with politeness, but also scarcely disguised loathing. One such youthful master had clearly decided he was going to pull me down a peg or two. Either he was aware of my nihilistic tendencies and wanted to provoke them, or he was a blithering fool who thought he could pull me back from the edge of the precipice, but I find it hard to believe that he never saw that I would pull him over that edge with me. If that were the case, he deserved the humiliation I would visit upon him, which involved threatening to throw him out of a window after he got a little physical when disciplining me. I could give you the full gory details of the events that led up to the exchange, but I find it too awful to recall.

Episodes such as this were not happening on a daily basis. In fact, this was the only such event in my last year at Woolverstone as far as I can remember. What characterised me through the spring term of 1981 was sullenness and uncooperativeness. I thought I knew where I was going in the world but was finding the journey exceptionally dreary and tiresome. In truth, I think I knew that my chosen course was the easy one. I had copped out, bottled it. There didn't seem a way back, either, since my academic efforts had withered to nothing. I drifted around the school like a dour ghost, materialising into recognisable human form only when angry or doing something I wasn't supposed to. I often wonder if what really made me reach the decision to jettison my chances of academic qualification was a doubt that I could actually do it. I honestly don't recall ever thinking that, but maybe hormones and the lack of a guiding hand were enough of a diversion to justify it to myself.

Back home, Serge was working in childcare, my eldest brother Lou was a photographer's assistant and Matt, when he wasn't in a correctional institution of some kind or another, was working on a barrow in North End Road market, dreaming of becoming a painter and decorator, and taking heroin. I thought I would surpass all of them. I had always been the most gregarious of us four boys, the loudest and most belligerent, but now I was also the most self-confident and arrogant too. Whilst I can analyse myself and recognise the possible influences on my behaviour, I can't genuinely feel any sympathy for the person that I was. I suppose a reader who might be a sociologist or behavioural scientist would apportion all manner of blame to several factors in my life. But when it comes down to it, I was as self-aware as any teenager has a right to be: I remember feeling so cocksure of myself. I didn't need sympathy and understanding, I needed a kick up the arse, but of course, the last person to try that was threatened with expulsion from the nearest window.

I do have a shred of a theory as to why I lost it so completely with that young teacher who wanted to teach me a lesson, although I can't say it has been thoroughly examined, which is naturally in keeping with the way in which I approached everything back then. It is that to me and those like me at Woolverstone, the wrong things mattered too much: respect, being the toughest, being the bravest, being the loudest. It's the same today with the youth who are busily carving each other up on London's streets. The things that bring out the worst in us carry an importance that supersedes all that would make us productive and successful. To me, what mattered was being respected and being thought of as a sophisticate of sorts. I could act, I could play rugby, I could fight and I thought I had the mouth to win me riches and success. Sure, it might be handy to have a few academic achievements to throw into the mix, but if not, so be it – what really mattered to me, and what that young teacher hadn't shown me, was respect. It's really that simple, and so entrenched were these views, nobody could get beyond them to articulate the potential benefits of academic endeavour. These attributes weren't entirely bad, and I certainly had the expressive nature to win friends and influence people

because I was bright and engaging (though those charac-
teristics might just as easily also qualify as bullshit). I
suspect those without at least these qualities are the ones
who stand no chance in life at all, and I also had the
example of a brother to know that I didn't want to be a
criminal either.

The spring term report included a comment from Tony
Watkins about me being a confused individual. If he knew
something I didn't, I wasn't prepared to give him the credit
for spotting it. Morgan noted that my goodwill in the
house had evaporated, and Jim Hyde condemned me as
bone-idle and silly. In art, I was excelling but I had of
course decided that art would be the only exam for which
I would make the effort. I had one term left at Woolverstone
and to write me off at that stage would have been the
sensible and almost humane thing to do. To his credit,
Woollet, the headmaster, still encouraged me to change
my attitude because it wasn't too late. He wasn't to know
that I had decided it was too late several months earlier.

* * *

And so summer term of my final year at Woolverstone
had arrived. Most of my friends were dreading it because
at the end of May would come the long stream of exams
to sit. Riding on the results would be their ability to stay
on for A-Levels, a concept that seemed completely alien
to me, although I would have been allowed to stay in order
to resit O-Levels. But that was just another opportunity
I would fling back into the face of those offering it. The

fear and trepidation of those around me merely added to my smug self-satisfaction that I needed to have no such concerns. Summer term 1981 offered nothing but fun and entertainment before I left to take my rightful place in the world.

Most of the term was spent playing football on the patch of grass outside Johnston's house in the evening. I had decided to get fit and would go for regular runs along the foreshore, returning to play footy or squash or just hang out in the rooms of pals. Lessons and revision were given scant attention, and playing pranks in the house was more important to me. I kept singing in the rugby choir, and I spent a lot of time in the cricket nets, even though Pete Fart had decided to carry on the previous term's rugby ban into the cricket season. The frequency of visits to the Butt and Oyster grew, and it would often be after such imbibing sessions that our ridiculously puerile behaviour in the house took flight.

Pranks are important to schoolboys and university students. I have no idea why, really, but when I sit and reminisce with friends from Woolverstone, it is the pranks we recall most frequently. Every schoolboy has stories of such jollifications; ours may have had an edge on account of us being able to pull off jokes and stunts at night, but essentially, we are all the same. The best pranks, of course, are those that focus on an individual and expose them to the full force of our wit and invention. Bluntly speaking, it's bullying.

Each landing of the house had a huge red fire hose perched on the wall. The roll of thick rubber pipe seemed to be more appropriate for the lobby of a skyscraper, as if the school had bagged a job lot. There was a mighty red nozzle at the end of the pipe, and we suspected that the water pressure was significant because from time to time we would turn the stopcock on the wall and see the heavy reel of hose jerk and lurch as water surged into it. We had never, however, opened the nozzle, but several pints of Butt Cider encouraged me to do so one evening when the house was silent and sleeping. A boy who had always been the recipient of much japery was sleeping silently in his private room off the landing. He was fair game because, like some of the masters we tormented, he had a very entertaining way of reacting to adversity. He screamed. More specifically, he screamed like a small girl.

So as he slept, we concocted a prank that would surely elicit such a response. Unfurling the hose, I drew closer to the door of his room, opening it quietly and creeping in. Rob and another friend, Sean, were on the landing, and as they opened the stopcock I could feel the powerful rush of water through my hands. Although I was struggling not to laugh, I managed to feed the hose into the opening at the top of the boy's sheets. He was sleeping on his back, mouth wide open, gently snoring, oblivious in his dreams to the rudeness of his impending awakening. I considered opening the nozzle into his mouth, but even in my inebriated state, I knew this might result in instant death. I opened the hose, and a geyser of water erupted from the nozzle, almost throwing me backwards. I let go of the pipe, which continued to fire a jet of water that could have cut concrete into the depths of the boy's bed. He continued to snore for what seemed like quite a while until suddenly he awoke with an ear-splitting shriek, kicking wildly at his covers, not knowing in the almost pitch blackness what was happening.

His frantic efforts to escape knocked the hose out of the bed and onto the floor, where it continued to writhe, spraying countless gallons of water around the room, up the walls and onto the ceiling. I stumbled out of the room and slipped on the wetness of the floor, crashing to the ground of the landing, which I noticed Rob and Sean had vacated. Rather than turn off the stopcock I bowled through the door of the long dormitory, laughing heartily to myself as the victim continued to scream and wail over the roar of rushing water.

The wanton spitefulness of such a prank never occurred to me, not even when Morgan gated the entire fifth form of Hall's House for it, but the boy wasn't one for remonstrations, and so the enjoyment I took from it was allowed to stand unchallenged.

★ ★ ★

When the timetable of examinations was given to me, I took note of them with barely a cursory interest. I would attend the exams because I did not want the hassle of being chased around the school for not registering, but this I considered a huge inconvenience since there was plenty else I could be doing rather than sitting in a hot gymnasium for three hours trying to answer questions I hadn't bothered to study for. As the term approached its climax, I began to feel more and more alienated by my lack of revision. My friends were all stressed and buried in books, writing notes for history, geography, biology, maths. Even people I thought took the same approach to exams as I did were getting their heads down, which I found to be something of a betrayal. People's patience with me was short. I wasn't prepared for how it made me feel, which was shit, actually. I was faced with a choice; cram the revision, do my very best and go for it or forget about it, accept it was too late and look forward to leaving school.

Yep, you're right. I took the second option.

So I sat through my exams. I pretended to write. I even answered one or two questions when I got bored, but if it is hard to imagine such a breathtakingly sinful attitude towards exams, it is even harder to fathom the lack of guilt I showed. No, it wasn't guilt I felt. What I was feeling under my bravado, my negligence, my disgraceful betrayal of everybody who had ever believed in me, was anger. Anger at myself. I was angry because I hadn't had the guts to turn the tide when it was still possible and I was furious that I could have elected to take that path. And I was livid that I still felt it necessary to keep up the outward charade that I didn't care. I was a mess. Screaming inwardly at myself for my stupidity was evidence, I suppose, that I knew what I was doing, but it doesn't make it any better. Decades later, I still feel awfully sick to my stomach.

So that would be my legacy at Woolverstone: an actor, a rugby player and an idiot. Masters would look at me with pity as they collected my obviously incomplete exam papers and I could see it in their faces that they didn't hate me or take pleasure in my failure: they had that disappointed commiseration in their eyes that appears when they see waste, squandered promise that they knew was inevitable, but hoped wouldn't be. So hard is the memory to bear, I don't even want to keep writing about it. So I won't.

Leaving Woolverstone *was* a wrench, although I pretended it was the one thing I longed for. On a warm June day I trudged, for the last time, along the drive to the bus stop and waited for the transport to Ipswich station. I looked around me: at the village hall where puppets club had taken place, at the small house where the master with the dangling bollocks had cooked beans by the gallon. I squinted through the sunlight at the fields full of cows and the road along which the school bus would hurtle on the way back from rugby matches and I thought of my five wondrous, formative, hormone-filled years of fun. I smelled the summers, I felt the harsh, frosty air of Sunday mornings by the foreshore. I heard my bragging to friends of how *we* did Oxford and Cambridge Examination Board O-Levels, not crappy old London ones, the *easier* ones.

'We'?

What do you mean, 'We'?

I recalled how I first felt driving into the school on that damp September night all those years ago. I shuddered at Mum's fight in the flats, protecting her honour and pride that we should be at such a place, and I shivered at how I had sailed, deliberately, onto the rocks.

I didn't want to leave. I wanted another chance.

Let me have another go, I thought. I could, couldn't I?

This time I won't be a loudmouth. This time I'll show you that I'm not a waster. I won't show off. This time I'll take the opportunity with both hands. Please?

My adult life was about to begin, and I had ensured it would be harder than it ever had to be, or ever ought to have been.

What an idiot. What an unconscionable fool. What a thief. I stole an educational opportunity from those who trusted me and dumped it by the roadside.

Fuck.

IDIOT

The last page of the previous chapter is the first time I have admitted to myself what was going through my mind as I trudged out of those gates in 1981, and I am being truthful when I tell you that I really can remember precisely how I felt at the time, it is no romantic invention to embroider the story.

How effortlessly the memories tumble from the past. I can so much more easily recall a day from over thirty years ago than I can a moment from last week. Such is the nature of memory. Do these reminiscences serve anybody but myself? Who'll learn anything from my errant child-ishness, my profanity, misbehaviour and negligence? I have retraced my life at Woolverstone and evoked my inglorious adolescent self, in love with its reflection. I'm not Stanley 'Tookie' Williams, who turned many gunslingers from crime and was the saviour of countless LA gang members whilst languishing on Death Row. Williams pumped out confession after confession, but that didn't stop Governor Arnold Schwarzenegger from pumping him full of lethal chemicals. Confessions that seek redress or look for brownie points tend to fall on deaf ears these days, and this whole exercise has not been an effort to change my ways, either. I haven't the slightest hope of an epiphany; I'll always swear and cuss and continue to tell people that they are idiots. My way is set.

But Woolverstone *hadn't* failed. It is not so much that it would return to weave its spell but rather that the magic itself was woven through me. It planted little pictures in my mind that offered alternatives whenever I was contemplating my future. It gave me (often ignored) options.

This book began as a record of a school through the eyes of one pupil, but it soon became clear to me that to understand the miracles Woolverstone performed, any reader must also understand the material with which it had to work. Travelling through my early childhood has not always been a fun exercise, and I had never before held up for examination the two parts of my existence (pre- and post-Woolverstone); I still know that boy from Fulham Court, he is still in there and appears regularly, but the stage upon which he performs is the thing that surprises, and I know people often look at me and wonder how I got from there to here. I do too. But while I can't claim a eureka moment – a moment when I suddenly decided that opera was the thing for me, I can give you the reason why I ever thought it might be a possibility: Woolverstone. I am convinced too that, thanks to Woolverstone, the contrast between my worst potential life option and where I am now, is far, far greater than the disparity between the present-day me and a wealthy stockbroker.

I know that whatever happens with this memoir, no matter how many read it, it will not, on any one of its pages, contain a Wildean phrase, a nugget of Freudian insight, not one epic Sewellian paragraph, filled to the edges with instruction, knowledge and balletic prose. Most depressingly, neither will it have a phrase that is 'polished until it catches the sun', as Clive James once described his style. Actually, I say 'depressingly', but I don't suppose I mean that because I am aware that a genius with words is as inbuilt and natural as a talent with numbers. I don't scold myself for having neither. I tend to suppress more than express anyway, and I am sure I can do *something* better than all of those I mention. Furthermore, I am as convinced as I can be that this is probably the best I could ever have done, which is commendable, since giving my best to anything is not an event that frequently punctuates the story of my life. What distinguishes great writers is not only what they say on a page but the pool of knowledge and learning from which they choose the appropriate words that eventually get turned into ink. They will travel along the rank and file of their minds, of thought and knowledge and influence, judiciously picking those that suit the purpose. More is left behind than is brought forward for us to share. I, on the other hand, round up everything I have, do my best to tidy it up before throwing it out into the world.

That's the difference between them and me. At Woolverstone; I never, ever, allowed myself to absorb enough of what was thrown *at* me. I never had the sense to examine more closely the things that I deemed uninteresting, so that they might actually become interesting. To me, everything had to have a point, even though I was too youthful or just plain stupid to know what was, and what wasn't, pointless. Everything I considered unimportant had the door slammed in its face.

I know better now. I know that everything academic or cultural – especially cultural – in its way, has a part to play in our journey. Variety is most certainly the spice of life in this respect; I feel the juddering impact of opera in the same way that I luxuriate in the vocal wonder of Bobby Womack; I can be irritated by the tone of a book but appreciate the author's idea, and I remain able to enjoy the blissfully exquisite lilt found in both Grieg's 'Varen' and John Martyn's 'Solid Air'. That's a privilege, for sure, to have the capacity for both and all things in between.

I thank my lucky stars for the all-consuming passion I have had for music since I was knee-high to a small Italian opera composer. My response to music is essentially an emotional, visceral one; at a push, when colleagues in the office at Opera Holland Park, taught in college that continental reactions to music must be treated with the sharpest of suspicion, I am able to hold my own in opposition. But more often than not, I will merely suggest they are talking bollocks. I suppose I was, and am, the antithesis of what E.M. Forster called the 'underdeveloped heart' when referring to the public schoolboys of England. Contrary to his thesis, I was, am, all heart; my mind and body were the things that struggled. And I am Italian, am I not? A race whose well-honed positives are as well documented as their weaknesses? I am an unquenchably emotional and anxious individual, there is no 'off' switch – just a dial that turns it up or down. I'm melodramatic, too, and Woolverstone never managed to curb that side of me at all. Did my life make me like that? Did I learn my anxieties from my mother? A psychotherapist once told me that I had, and I don't know for sure if he is right, but I choke and weep at films and operas and almost everything in between. I am, however, keen that few should ever notice.

So whatever, wherever or whoever I am, I am probably just a product of all the things that formed the corridor of my life's journey up to this point; nothing particularly exceptional there then. When, at sixteen, I walked out of Woolverstone for the last time, I was certain, convinced, absolutely bloody sure that I knew precisely where I was going and what I would do. I'd flunked my exams deliberately, so I had to believe that, didn't I? I was still a Fulham boy on the surface of it, and that's where I wanted to go. The big wide world was to be my domain.

The big wide world, in reality, meant going home to live with Mum, who was undoubtedly wondering if my next step would be an illegal one. She had expressed disappointment that I had dismissed my exam prospects, but she was more concerned – frantic even – that I should get a job, any job.

Rugby still held me in thrall and, quite quickly after leaving, I received phone calls from people working for the (still amateur) clubs in London and who knew masters at the school. I didn't do anything about it for several months, but eventually I was invited to a training session with Rosslyn Park Colts one Thursday evening. The pitch was waterlogged so the session didn't involve any playing but would be a fitness workout, and they asked if I would go back in a couple of weeks. In the meantime, another player from Epsom and Ewell RC asked if I would go and play for them and agreed to pick me up in Fulham for training sessions and matches. I was pretty puffed up about the fact that clubs seemed to be after me, so I took the opportunity offered by E&E and at the first training session, faced with a group of behemoths, I said my favoured position was wing forward because there was no way I was going into a front row with that lot. It wasn't improbable either since I loved to tackle, was quick across the ground and very aggressive in both. They started me off in the fourths or fifths, I can't recall, but I do remember scoring quite a few tries in each game and twice being promoted to the next team up.

At around the same time, and just a year after leaving, I remember going back to Woolverstone for what was a regular Old Boys' reunion and meeting Steve Halliday and Adrian Thompson, two fantastic players who were playing first class rugby at Harlequins and were my team-mates against the First XV when I was invited to play hooker for the Old Boys. Outside the Butt and Oyster, both asked me if I was still playing, and Adrian Thompson, almost certainly unaware of the dangers, said to the gathered throng that I would be England hooker one day! With such a commendation ringing in my ears I returned to Epsom and Ewell ready to prove him correct. However, my neck, twice badly injured during my school career, was playing havoc, and I went to see a specialist. His verdict was unequivocal: 'Well, Michael, you can either walk or play rugby, the choice is yours.' It was devastating to have a burgeoning sports career curtailed at eighteen years old, and to this day it still smarts.

Ludicrously, I then worked in a trendy hairdresser for a few months. I had begun to hack at my friends' hair whilst at school; I don't know why, but it was probably because I just thought I was good at everything. Some of us had done holiday work washing hair in Scissors, the single trendiest hairdresser in London at the time, so it may have come from that and I thought it was worth a try when I left. So, I became a junior at Annie Russell's salon on the King's Road. I did have a talent for it, apparently, but the whole thing didn't suit me at all. Some of the female clients were foul-tempered, rude and whined about having sensitive scalps or bad necks, and their perfume was of the expensive type that weirdly, always had a note of sweaty body about it. It wasn't long before I had worked out a system of scalding them accidentally at the washbasins or being a little vigorous in my scrubbing. The final straw came when I was asked to make a cup of coffee for Reginald Bosanquet, who was as drunk as a lord as usual and who, because he lived in the flats above the shop, was in almost every day. On this day he was in Bloody Mary mood and abused my coffee-making abilities. Time to leave, I thought. He died a couple of years later, which came as no surprise to me whatsoever.

Despite the apparently wasted six months Annie Russell's represented, it was my first experience of wealthy clientele, and the conversations in the break-room among the gay staff were instructional in many ways. Everybody was impossibly trendy, and after a while I didn't feel like a fish out of water, but goodness me, I felt like slapping some of the staff. I had never really seen an adult tantrum until I'd worked there. (An interesting footnote: I still know how to cut hair and even have my prized pair of Solingen scissors, purchased at great expense and which are still in mint condition, never having needed sharpening in over thirty years.)

I left Annie Russell's, chuckling to myself at the thought that I had ever imagined hairdressing offered me a path to fame and fortune. I'll go for something more my cup of tea, I thought, and ended up at a builders' merchants in the sales office, where I would take large telephone orders from building firms. This was more my style, I decided: doing deals, using my wits and outsmarting people. I enjoyed it because I got the chance to barter and argue over prices, and one afternoon, I negotiated a huge order with one of the biggest builders in the country. I put the phone down with a flourish, punching the air in triumph. Dave, the dour sales manager of Polish extraction, congratulated me until he took a look at the sales sheet. He wanted to stab me when it became clear that my lavish brokerage had clinched a deal that committed the firm to selling a mammoth order of plastic guttering at less than cost. Soon after, they moved me into the yard, where I was taught to drive a forklift and got very fit lifting and carrying bags of sand and cement. I rose to the giddy heights of timber foreman in a matter of weeks, but there was no getting away from the fact that it was manual labour, however high I got. I had already taken a step backwards.

In south London, where I worked, there were plenty of people in the yard who were ready to mock my 'public' school past. I never denied it or ran shy of it since I always wanted to appear different from them, but the contrast between us in that yard was not as marked as it had been during our respective educations. I was kidding nobody but myself. How could I tell myself I was different from them when I was sitting in the same hut, drinking the same tea, trudging through the same mud and enjoying the same bawdy, wilfully offensive humour? I beg you not to misunderstand me because these were not people I looked down my nose at. They were straightforward, working class individuals, honest and lacking in pretension and from precisely the same background as me, but they had not been offered the chances I had. And there were things in my head, experiences, put there by Woolverstone, that I could neither ignore, nor shake. I liked theatre and classical music, I had sung in choirs, I had studied books none of my workmates had ever heard of. I was a bag of contradictions, and I could sometimes spy on the faces of my fellow labourers a look that asked: 'why are you here?' George, a lecherous old soldier who supervised the yard, stung me one afternoon with a comment he may or may not have intended to have much impact, but it struck home like a sniper's bullet. As I trudged back into the hut, soaked and tired from stacking ten tons of sandbags onto pallets (twenty five bags to a pallet, ten pallets), he snorted in derisory fashion, his feet by the paraffin fire, a cup of tea in his hand.

'I bet you never thought you'd end up doing this.'

I looked at him, not sure how to respond, but I brooded on his remark for the next twenty minutes. Eventually, the lights went on. That hut, perched under a railway arch near Clapham Junction, was the scene of my revelation and I do mean a revelation. Bells rang, horns sounded, shame and regret and embarrassment consumed me. *I'm better than this.*

So I found some words for George. I'd like to think that the glint in his eye as I said them was because he saw himself as a mentor, that he had given me the awareness to take my opportunity, but to be honest, it was probably because the eye was a glass replacement for the one he'd lost in Aden.

'You know what, George? I *am* better than this. I didn't go to that school so I could be told what to do by an old git like you or to stack bags in the pissing rain."

He took it well as I got up from my ragged, reclaimed armchair, walked out of the hut, out of the yard and out of denial.

The story from there is long and winding, but suffice to say I read, I listened, I thought. I decided to repay the debt that I owed Woolverstone. The pride of being at the school returned to me, and my eyes fell open – wide open. It is hard to say what I actually did to change things other than taking more interesting and challenging jobs, including working for a group of local newspapers selling advertising, which turned into a cushy number writing travel features and going on press trips. I curbed my belligerence a bit too, and from various bosses learned the art of ordered thinking; I took broadsheet newspapers instead of the *Sun*;

I listened to Radio Four instead of Radio One and began to attend theatres and concerts, dragging bewildered Fulham girls along for dates. (Admittedly, when Tchaikovsky failed to get me within a mile of their action, I had to revert to pub bands and discos.) I am aware that this all seems ridiculous – like *Educating Rita*. I find it a little embarrassing to impart the information to be honest, but what it did do is enable me to feel normal about having had an education; that to know and appreciate things beyond the environment in which I lived was, in fact, something we are all capable of and nothing to be ashamed of. My sense of self-worth had never left me inasmuch as I had always thought of myself as being 'equal' to others. My precocity had never dimmed either, but the ambition that Woolverstone instilled in me had been squished and mangled to fit my old Fulham mindset. I had, in this respect at least, reverted to type and what my awakening did was simply recalibrate my self-image to a version of myself that Woolverstone worked hard to put there in the first place. When I left school I thought anything was possible, but it was within a boundary set by my little world. Now, I was ready to try the one everyone else lived in.

That was 1984.

OPERA HOLLAND PARK

The story of the rise of Opera Holland Park probably deserves another volume all of its own, but I would be remiss not to explain why, after so often being cast as the well-intentioned pariah of any company I ever worked in, I have managed to sustain a quarter of a century in this one job.

In 1989, after moderately successful stints in newspapers, the hotel industry, advertising and marketing, I ended up at the Royal Borough of Kensington and Chelsea on the strength of a scant CV and the gift of the gab – and that is really all I had. I had no knapsack of qualifications to offer employers, but I was fortunate to be in a time when 'talent', if it was discerned, was allowed to flourish. Along with the experience I had gathered in my other jobs, I also had the knack of being able to learn quickly, to absorb, draw on things I had learned at school and to create an apparent whole. So I convinced Kensington and Chelsea to let me loose on their cultural portfolio. Indeed, they had in fact pursued me when the job had failed to attract a suitable candidate, although I had turned down the offer of an interview to take up a post in a marketing agency where within a couple of months I realised that scratchcard promotions and working from a hideous office on the North Circular was never in a million years going to satisfy me, nor, if truth be told, was I ever going to satisfy them.

Now living hand to mouth in a tiny but expensive Chiswick flat with my girlfriend Alison, who would become my first wife, and with our mortgage rate going through the roof, it was a desperate time, and the letter repeating the invitation to interview came at a good moment, and although the meeting didn't go well on the surface of it – one of those interviewing me was dozing through half of it – I must have been the best of a bad bunch. The first incarnation of my life at the Royal Borough saw me in a pioneering role as a marketer of the libraries and arts services, which seems an odd thing to say now but which nevertheless rang very true at the time, when libraries had never previously felt the need to actually persuade people to use their services. I was also required to promote and publicise the cultural offering of the borough, which had a surprisingly vibrant portfolio of museums, galleries and what was known then as the Holland Park Theatre – it was inevitable that I would find the latter of greatest appeal.

Simply acquiring some press for the venue was enough to take its audience from 14,000 in 1989 to 25,000 in 1990, my first season. I even persuaded the BBC via its GLR radio station to become media sponsor. Opera was a large part of the theatre's summer season, provided by visiting companies of varying quality, but there was a rich programme of dance – contemporary as well as an annual residency by the Royal Ballet School – theatre and even puppetry. Birmingham Rep brought two productions to the festival, including *Cider with Rosie,* which remains one of the most vivid memories I have of anything on our stage.

Opera, though, was the big seller, and Mick Goggin, the then theatre manager, had developed a roster of companies who generally produced the pops of the repertoire. At the same time, I was being pressured into acquiring greater levels of sponsorship of a financial kind, but I was increasingly exasperated by these demands because I knew that no sponsor worth its salt would invest in something that had the pong of amateurism about it. I don't want to insult these companies because they were not all amateur in the least, but they didn't always give us the finest productions. When a chorus member in *Aida* has not only a real tea towel on his head but one with the word 'glasses' emblazoned upon it, you know that something needs to be done. That production was given by a company called Opera Lirica, which had at its head the conductor Joseph Vandernoot, who was irascible, as old as the hills and conducted at half-speed, but he had enjoyed a distinguished career, notably as music director for Ballet Rambert. He had also given the first UK performance of Puccini's *Edgar* under the auspices of the Fulham Symphony orchestra, and I always admired his dedication, learning an awful lot from him whilst he growled and spat at me. It was, however, possible to knock twenty-five minutes off the length of any production he gave when he allowed his assistant to conduct a performance. So these were not the best productions our money could buy and, after several years of listening to my colleagues bemoaning the fact, I proposed a radical solution: we should start our own producing company, an idea that went down like cold vomit, to be fair.

By 1995, six years had passed, and I had immersed myself in the process of opera in the same way I once immersed myself in memorising lines at Woolverstone, learning its distinct producing dynamics, the personalities of its proponents, the details of delivering it and, most crucially, the technicalities of the singing and playing at its musical heart. I had also begun to explore the repertoire beyond the core pieces, and my tastes were becoming well defined. I had experienced opera at Woolverstone and had sung throughout my time there, and had a facility for the theatre in general. But meeting and working with singers and directors, designers and conductors meant I could absorb so much more. I was essentially, once again, educating myself. What I knew for certain was that the nuts and bolts of putting on a production were simply not for me and held no appeal beyond being a horrifying matrix I could admire and understand. So in arguing for the creation of our own company, and pressing home the idea that every penny we spent went not into the pocket of an independent producer but onto our stage, I also insisted that we engage someone to do the legwork. The council agreed.

By the autumn of 1995, we were fully engaged in creating the company Opera Holland Park, and it had strong ideals that we still retain. The intention was to give emerging, British-based performers the opportunity to sing and work with more experienced and established artists, and to that end we engaged Anthony Besch and Peter Rice to direct and design our inaugural production of *Un ballo in Maschera*. The production sat head and shoulders above anything we had done previously, and we acquired the support of American Express for the run.

Suddenly, we had a brand, and this enabled me to envision a future that saw development and growth, rather than merely sustaining a cute but ultimately half-arsed festival. Most of these plans I kept to myself for fear of terrifying the council, but if I could maintain the company for three years, I thought perhaps it would build a momentum of its own. Already, I had begun to nurture the idea that we could ape the old Camden Festival by reviving rarities that London seemed at that time to be starved of.

My time in the Royal Borough's employ had been characterised by an innate and instinctive unwillingness to succumb to the rigidity of council practice; officers and councillors who remain with the Royal Borough will freely attest to their frustrations with me. If I couldn't beat it, I worked around it; if I couldn't work around it, I moaned on relentlessly. As ever, I was *always* right. What is obvious now is that I had stepped into another environment that was naturally allergic to someone like me, but one I was determined would eventually accept me. I was certainly an unusual beast; forthright, even cheeky to the politicians and never afraid to tell them categorically what I believed they should do, but I was loyal, honest and dedicated. It was these qualities that I think stopped them booting me over the threshold. There was, of course, a proper way to deal with the council, a process and a strategy and I am much more adept at it today but if I am perfectly honest, words are still often had in my shell-like.

Anyway, it will not have escaped your notice throughout this book that ideas were never a problem for me, but the strategic patience to deliver them (and to *gently* coax people into sharing my vision) most certainly was, so after our successful launch it might have been more wise to table a longer-term plan to deliver the concepts I was percolating gently. Obviously, I didn't, and having scoured old libraries and books for late Italian rarities, my attention was drawn to *Iris* or, as it was initially put to me, 'Mascagni's Butterfly'. At this point it would have been prudent to walk away because the opera was monumental, with a very large chorus and an orchestra featuring four or five percussionists. It also required, I believed, sumptuous costumes, a ballet and a soprano who had to pretend to be sixteen but sing like a Wagnerian. And it had not been seen in London for ninety years. Yet I had been listening to the Domingo recording of the opera and was in love with it, so, whilst we were actually running our inaugural production, I was already planning to take a mighty plunge.

In 1996, one of my other responsibilities – Leighton House Museum, a glorious architectural wonder in Holland Park and the former home of Lord Frederic Leighton – was celebrating the centenary of the artist's death. As part of the programme of events, we recreated the interior furnishings of the house as a backdrop to a dramatic interpretation of his life. The decorative accessories and costumes were designed and made by the couturiers Charles and Patricia Lester, who work in silks and hand-tinted fabrics of exquisite beauty and refinement.

Their work is also powerfully orientalist and it didn't take much for me to see their creations being translated into Japanoiserie for *Iris*. The problem was that their clothes tended to cost a lot of money per item, and we needed about sixty or seventy of them. Having got to know them during the Leighton centenary, I and the director, Tom Hawkes, went to see them at their home and workshop in Abergavenny, where they generously agreed to provide the costumes at an enormously reduced rate. As artists, they relished the project, but even with the Lesters' effective sponsorship, I was still looking at a budget beyond anything we had ever conceived. I returned to London that afternoon for the evening performance of *Ballo* in a weird mood, excited at everything *Iris* promised but glum at the growing prospect of having to ditch it.

As I stood on the balustrade, deep in thought, Mick tapped me on the shoulder, handed me a business card and said, 'An expensively dressed, important looking bloke just asked me to give this to you. He wants to talk about sponsoring a production.' If fate ever smiled on me (and I was generally of the view that it only ever scowled), this was the moment. I searched the theatre for the owner of the business card, John Grumbar, managing director of the London office of Egon Zehnder International, one of the world's biggest executive search companies, and found him having a picnic with his party of friends. Why Mick didn't just point him out to me, I don't recall, but I still chuckle at the memory of Mick's description and my ability to use it.

John explained that he wanted to have an exclusive evening during the following season to which he could invite 800 guests for his company's annual get-together with clients and colleagues. An Opera Holland Park performance seemed the perfect thing, he said, and asked what we were planning for the following year.

'I have just the thing for you, John,' I said, scarcely containing my glee, 'It's an opera that nobody has really ever heard of and which hasn't been done in London for over ninety years. I would say it is perfect for you.'

John's grimace didn't deter me from persisting, even when he said, 'Haven't you got anything more, erm, *popular*?'

Desperation leads you to many misdemeanours, and I took the view that I couldn't really lose. I suggested I sent John the CD of the opera: if he liked it, he could sponsor it – and I assured him it would be one of *the* events in London – but if he didn't, we would happily produce a *Bohéme* or *Tosca* instead, even though I was almost completely consumed with the idea of *Iris*. Neither did I tell him that OHP were planning to produce *Tosca* anyway, as well as *Onegin*,

John, to his eternal credit, loved *Iris*, agreed to sponsor the production and even purchased hundreds of copies of the CD for his guests. We persuaded Sony to reissue the CD, selling it directly to our patrons. Sony later told me that had those sales been transacted in shops, the album would have been, by far, a number one in the classical charts. Liberty, which sold the Lester's clothes in London, devoted their windows to the production, and there was as much fashion press about the opera as there was anything else. It was a hit. Such a big hit, in fact, that we revived it immediately in 1998, when we also produced Cilea's *L'arlesiana*. The die was cast for the company, and ever since we have mined that repertoire relentlessly.

It seemed clear to me at the time that nothing quite like the concept for OHP that I envisaged existed; an opera company that was genuinely accessible but also produced operas that went beyond the top twenty and that would exist in a static venue, seeking audiences in their tens of thousands. There were of course companies with accessible aims like English Touring Opera, which in its former incarnation of Opera80, under David Parry, was known for touring interestingly challenging productions in the core rep and developing many talented artists who still thrive today. If opera is considered rarified now, despite the enormous amounts of work that has gone into making it less so, it was ridiculously parodied back then, even whilst the main houses claimed some egalitarian principles. At Ireland's Wexford Festival, rarities from the sort of repertoire I had my eye on were frequently produced, including *Iris*, which it had given some years before, but in the UK, there was nothing like OHP that I could discern. One had to look to New York and Teatro Grattacielo for inspiration. Indeed, it was a member of that company, visiting London for our production of *Iris*, who first put me onto Montemezzi's *L'amore dei tre Re*, an opera it would eventually take ten years for us to produce but which inevitably became my favourite of them all. Teatro Grattacielo have gone on to present many of the operas that we ourselves have either done, or wish to do.

By the turn of the millennium I was ten years into a career that my family still couldn't quite believe. Mum and her best friend Giovanna would occasionally visit the opera and pass judgement. ('Dey speaka fucky shit Italian.') Serge was a senior social. worker operating among the worst horrors the world can throw at children, Lou was an IT engineer and Matt was punctuating infrequent decorating stints with spells in rehab. I was the odd one out, and my brothers never considered me to be in serious employ. OHP was still a growing entity, trying to establish itself as a serious operatic enterprise, but our budgets and our planning methodology were such that the council would, every season, consider the reduction of expenditure on what still seemed like a luxury nobody cared too deeply about. Added to that, our administrator was not terrifically wedded to the idea of budget control, and despite the successes, I was still getting regularly beaten up about budget over-runs. At the same time, by then ten years into the world of opera, it was abundantly clear to me that the problem was overwhelmingly to be found in the nature of operatic hierarchy. Directors, designers and conductors, to one degree or another, seemed to be in charge, laying down the law to what I realised was a compliant administrator. I would find out, often too late, that a budget over-run had occurred because a designer had insisted on something for which there was no real production need but which nevertheless satisfied his artistic desires. It was a situation that had to stop and whether because I was applying greater pressure or because he saw what was coming, the incumbent decided to leave.

To me, the way ahead for OHP was clear. The management would be in charge; we pay the bills, we call the shots. Someone with a history in opera, who would likely subscribe to the traditions of deferment to the artistic personnel of a production, could not be the replacement. So we set about searching for a candidate with experience of producing in theatre, but not opera. With me and an interim specialist administrator, any new producer would have plenty of in-house experience to fall back on, but, crucially, if we chose right, would have no idea what the opera hierarchy was about and was thus less likely to succumb to it.

When James Clutton, fresh from the theatre producer Bill Kenwright's company, turned up, we seemed to be onto something. He knew almost nothing about opera but plenty about producing. It was a risky but promising combination, and with just three months until the festival, he was thrown into producing the entire season of six new productions. He would either sink (and the company with him probably) or he would swim. He swam, and whilst I think at times in that first season the old adage, 'He's drowning, not waving' was applicable, we got through. We had also acquired magnificent sponsorship from Cadogan Estates and this enabled us to engage the Royal Philharmonic Orchestra as our resident band. One of the aims I'd had in the early days – an ambition, really – was that the company could make opera accessible whilst providing challenging repertoire, and still manage to have an orchestra of some repute (although the RPO eventually spread itself too thinly and we engaged the City of London Sinfonia, who remain our house orchestra to this day).

Woolverstone had always taught me that the impossible was no such thing, and I can recall having no doubts that we could achieve our aims. Today, we have not only reached our goals, but continue to march beyond them with an army of supporters and a whole new set of ambitions. A single chapter on OHP cannot do justice to its history or achievements because so many people have passed through our doors, there have been so many great productions, we have had both challenging and gloriously fulfilling times and literally hundreds of people come to mind in remembering it. From our eager, seat-of-the-pants beginning, we can now present seasons full of international singers, directors and conductors.

It is indisputable that Woolverstone has contributed hugely to whatever success I may have personally had in creating and developing Opera Holland Park. The growth of the company, and the people and organisations with whom we have become associated certainly led me to a level of social and financial interaction wholly distinct from one you might expect a boy from my background to have in adult life. Such is the world of the arts I suppose, where the love of music and performance bind people of every social and economic hue. I have not changed my accent, and I am still foul-mouthed most of the time. The cockiness, identified and then assertively (but largely unsuccessfully) suppressed by masters at Woolverstone, has played its part, but so too has my enduring propensity to consider myself worthy of almost any station just shy of royalty. The reputation of OHP as a welcoming and accessible festival almost certainly comes from the backgrounds of the people who run the place; perhaps we believe ourselves to be the perfect illustration of the potentially universal appeal of the classical arts?

I have learnt to manage and manipulate my impetuosity, although for many years (and still) the frustrations of operating within an environment not designed for running opera companies pitched me into conflict with countless individuals and systems. Councils, by their nature have short planning and budgeting cycles, and they tend not to speculate, either. The arts are a risky business and local authorities are averse to risk these days. In the end, I think it is simply passion, belief, working with talented people all through the company and a bloody minded ability to articulate my desires that have helped me establish and to then contribute to the sustenance of OHP and help it thrive. The idea that a council like the Royal Borough of Kensington and Chelsea should tolerate me in their midst for so long still amazes me; conversely, it is fair to say that their support and belief have also brought some rewards for them and the residents they serve. I have at least spared them overt embarrassment or controversy of the type I delivered to Woolverstone on so many occasions, and perhaps my school can claim to have given me the tools to negotiate the perils. In every respect, the council can truly claim to be uniquely ambitious because its commitment to cultural enrichment is almost unheard of in municipal circles.

As for opera itself, I still believe in its power, in its relevance, despite growing concerns to the contrary in the modern digital world, and I am still devoted to the effects it can have on people. The role of the arts seems to be forever questioned in the UK, but if I represent my old school with dignity in any way, it is in demonstrating the worth of culture in young lives. I am more modest these days, too (a relative concept, I know), always prepared to give room to those many artistic egos we encounter and which have yet to self-reflect to the degree that I have been forced to over the years. I was once like that, and knowing it probably explains why I am more tolerant of them. But the angry, sharp-tongued beast is forever fighting to free himself from the cage. Despite that, I take the greatest satisfaction from the successes of others, am more able to offer guidance without manipulation, and have less inclination to the necessary Machiavellian manoeuvres of OHP's early years. I sound like a Teddy bear.

Two and a half decades is a long time to spend in any single place. For almost two of them, OHP has existed and flourished, close to the edge and never dwelling on the past, but I am often personally forced to do so, because what I can't ever deny to myself is the truth of my nature, its attraction to melodramatic denouements, with only cursory consideration of the consequences or outcomes. Memories of Woolverstone, therefore, serve to constrain my ever-present truculence.

AND THE POINT WAS?

There is no doubt that the confidence that Woolverstone gave, the belief I drew from it, has enabled me to engage with a variety of people who patronise Opera Holland Park. Our risky programming and the challenges we set ourselves may have something to do with my schooling – or maybe it is arrogance again? In any case, I have something of which I can be proud. The journey from Woodstock Grove to Holland Park is short in real terms – half a mile perhaps – but from where I was in relation to where I am is a greater distance by far. I have felt shame and embarrassment whilst writing this volume – but maybe because I realise what damage I might have done to myself, as opposed to what I could have done to others. I told you I was selfish and I meant it.

But . . .

On this journey, I have been increasingly angered when I think of the eventual demise of Woolverstone. Politics have now been fully embroidered into the fabric of our education system, and a procession of politicians from every party talk unexpurgated drivel on the matter, proposing and re-proposing ideas, putting forward new 'targets' and standing tall with platitudes. I cannot think of one idea in the last twenty years that wasn't a serious contributory factor to the poor condition of education. Indeed, it was political doctrine that destroyed Woolverstone. Educating our children today is very much a process of reaching the lowest common goal that we can. Too often, we teach *down* to our children, their aspirations only stretching as far as the classroom door. Culture, as it is presented in the classroom, is one-dimensional, trendy and narrow; so much of the great art on our planet is scandalously neglected or served in idiot-sized portions.

Throughout my life, I have countless times been written off as an ill-educated oaf, not because the person doing it has any evidence of it, they just assume it, normally on the turn of my London accent. Maybe I do just come across as an oaf. Maybe I *am* an oaf. Yet, it frequently amazes them to discover what it is I now do for a living. More frequently still, it really bloody annoys them. They are out there, these people, who consider those of our society who are from the other side of the tracks to be unworthy of the enriching, inspirational wonder of the classical arts. Still worse, there are just as many, if not more, on the 'wrong' side with us who would tell us that we should never try and make the crossing.

Woolverstone, I believe, was the reason I have been able to see the course ahead of me as clearly as I have done since the age of nineteen at least. If it could never teach me to believe fully in Shakespeare or Chaucer, it taught me to believe in myself. Well, it encouraged me to continue to believe in myself, anyway. Academic achievement as measured by pieces of paper and qualification was something I actively sought to avoid, and I am sorry, I have no logical explanation for that and I wouldn't recommend it to any young person today. You, the reader, might have reached some conclusions of your own.

Don't be fooled, however, by my behaviour, because I received a full and thorough education. You could be forgiven for thinking, after getting so far into this memoir, that for me to proclaim such a thing comes as a bit of a shock, but this book isn't a treatise on the wonders of Woolverstone's curriculum: it is a documentary of how a boy did everything he could (often unknowingly) to look squarely into the mouth of the gift horse. I have told you of my approach to exams, but that is distinct from the process of getting me to them. Unquestionably, knowledge imparted to me had a struggle finding an unimpeded route into my consciousness, yet I was nonetheless exposed to a quality of teaching that from time to time would break through the truculence. Woolverstone's prospectus advertised the school as, 'A boarding school for boys from the London area who are suitable for an academic education' and that is precisely what it gave prior to being turned into a comprehensive. I read an article, which quoted the school's final headmaster, Richard Woollett, who said that of the sixty boys being admitted annually in later years, 45 of them would not have qualified for entry pre-1977.

Despite my attitude towards academia, I still recall enriching lessons by some of the brilliant teachers we had. I cannot hear mention of the town Hexham without recalling, almost verbatim, Jim Hyde's geography lessons on the development of modern urban conurbations. My son, who studies geology, was shocked to discover during a holiday in Greece that I knew all about rock formations and screes; that was Jim Hyde again, and this was a teacher whose lessons we often spent firing spit-balls of paper from pen tubes into the back of Adebola's head, or at the black, metal globe hanging from the ceiling. The point is, even as we behaved so miserably, we knew *where* Santiago was on the globe when we challenged each other to hit it with the sticky pellet. When Mr Shakeshaft, our explosive, floppy-fringed French master. wasn't erupting, he was drilling French verbs into us in compelling fashion and taught with an animated passion that means I can actually hold a moderate conversation in French when drunk. In history, John Morris led us to Culloden, Ypres and tremendously evocative projects on Tudor England.

You see, it wasn't just the nature of the curriculum that gave Woolverstone educational potency, it was the quality of the teaching and the hugely talented and academic individuals who stood before us and delivered our educations in that old fashioned, in-front-of-the-blackboard method. They encouraged discussion, but they spoke to the classroom in a way that evoked images, and you absorbed, even against your will, what they said. How else do I recall the anatomy of plants as taught by Tony Watkins and Mr Hawes? Tony Watkins wrote copiously on the huge blackboard at the front of the biology lab in a beautiful hand, and I was often transfixed by that alone. I can recall the process of osmosis, photosynthesis and electromagnetic fields and I know verse from Yeats, Keats and Shakespeare.

It is important to remember that our home situations and our backgrounds were a secondary issue once we arrived at Woolverstone. The majority of boys there had been selected because they had passed the eleven plus exam and were considered bright, so that is generally how our teachers approached lessons. My education was vivid and eloquent, not delivered by text book alone or by individuals following a set script, but by people who were brilliant, often among the best in their fields. Of the thousands of hours of lessons I received, I only missed a couple of hundred of them whilst standing outside the room in disgrace, so I had plenty of time to absorb their instruction. Above all else, however, I believe I was taught *how* to learn so that when, post-school, I did finally wake up and look in the mirror, I knew where to begin again. Those lessons demonstrated, even to this reluctant scholar, that I had ability of a fashion, an enquiring mind and yes, even a Machiavellian, artful-dodger intelligence that could find more useful expression than just in tricking someone. I knew, even as I turned my face against academic achievement, that there was space set aside for more knowledge than I had, and the processing power to understand and explore it.

Do schools today teach children at a level where they might fail dismally at first, then improve and ultimately succeed after being dragged through the elevating stages of knowledge and culture? Or do they teach as little as they have to so they can fill a box on a government form once a year? Setting a bar so high that a child might at first fail is considered beyond unholy these days. There are grammar schools that claim to have higher aspirations, but such places, with their unseemly parental scramble every September, pick and choose from the glut of children who are often outwardly able only because they have been relentlessly coached in the eleven-plus exam. Yes, Woolverstone was selective, but it was a model of schooling that should have been adopted and taken forward and made available to as many as possible. If you have a talent – and Woolverstone believed that everyone did – then the school would find it and develop it. It seems to me that Woolverstone embodied an idea that took the concept of grammar education to another level. Poor kids sometimes get a chance to try out for the local grammar nowadays, but Woolverstone featured another layer of opportunity, it said that not only would the boy be pushed and elevated, but he would be given a further dimension of experience and facility; Woolverstone went the whole bloody hog.

When the authorities began to send far more troubled and troublesome boys to the school, it began a descent that ended with its closure and acquisition by Ipswich High School, for Girls. After the doctrinaire conversion of Woolverstone to a comprehensive in 1977, the school shifted its criteria for selection, and by the time a *Forty Minutes* TV documentary called 'The poor man's Eton' was aired in 1987, the school was in a battle for survival. Woolverstone had essentially become a safe haven for at-risk boys from London, whose social risk profile, rather than their educational potential, appeared to be the primary consideration. Unquestionably, Woolverstone provided such boys with a rare opportunity, but the school was there in order that they could be removed to a place of safety in many cases. The costs spiralled and the educational cost/benefit ratio came under scrutiny from those at ILEA who resented the fact that only forty out of nineteen thousand annual secondary school starters got the chance to go to the school. It went wrong not because the boys they eventually sent there were less able – because this wasn't even a factor for selection, and few seemed interested – but because they expected less of them, and allowed the structure of the school, its traditions and practices, to fall away. No doubt the environment enabled many of these boys to receive a better education than may have been possible if they were left in their home situations, but the target had been lowered.

The decline began when the principles of excellence were jettisoned. What the change to a comprehensive did was remove the core idea that those boys who had real promise, but who came from poor or deprived backgrounds would, from the first day of Woolverstone life, understand that they could indeed elevate themselves by the mere fact they *had* been selected. Eventually, Woolverstone selected boys for very different reasons, expected little of them, and consequently gave the officers at ILEA an out by being able to say that such troubled and threatened boys – by then 'a mere forty of them'– could be educated at other facilities with whom the authority had arrangements. Had the school continued to blaze a path for excellence and achievement, as opposed to performing as a safe-haven, such cursory and dismissive financial pen-pushing would have been far harder to justify.

Public schools educate the wealthy and middle and upper classes, they ensure the status quo, but Woolverstone sought to turn that on its head, and there is a perversity to Woolverstone's demise that is hard to fathom. It was made comprehensive so that it would become egalitarian, a decision which itself failed to recognise the purity of the egalitarian principles the school's creation embodied. Working class boys had, the thinking went, no right to consider themselves better than *other* working class boys, and neither should they be afforded greater opportunities. In washing away the bright colours of Woolverstone's uniqueness, those in power at ILEA created a school that became a distillation of the problems they sought to prevent, and which the original school performed miracles in diverting. Having created the monster, ILEA soon realised they had to kill it. I find it hard to forgive them.

What Woolverstone showed was that if you expect great things of children, in everything that they do, then invariably they will deliver, rise to the challenge. You do not need to dress the curriculum in modern hip-hop clothes or draw pictures to accompany the spelling of words. Children, including those from impoverished backgrounds, have the facility and the capability to understand the tenets of Roman society, or the wonders of ancient Greece and the glory of Renaissance painting, or any number of things that seem to have been given only cursory presence in the classroom. If parents do not fill their child with the desire to learn, then the school and its teachers should do so, rather than dismiss all sense of responsibility for motivating their charges. Some children will always possess more intelligence or natural talent, some will always fight the system and some will always 'fail'. But the journey is all-important. If you aim low, then they will lower their sights with you, guaranteed to fulfil the pessimistic prognosis.

And the Point Was?

Woolverstone forced us to participate in a regimen of discipline that probably helped us develop a sense of responsibility. The debate on corporal punishment I will leave aside for now, although it is clear to me that being slippered was the first time I ever fully knew what consequences felt like.

We must enable our young people to believe that their paths are not set from birth, that our world, with its class divisions, its prejudices and inherent injustices, has loopholes that all of us can exploit. If you believe the man who condemns you to ignorance, crime and social inactivity, then you will, as sure as eggs is eggs, fulfil his prophecy. Indirectly it is a tragedy to report that those who condemn today are our education system, our government and even our community leaders. The principle of education and cultural exposure for the pure, unalloyed pleasure of it is alien and rarely put into practice, and hopes for our children are lowering by the day in order that successive governments can claim their plaudits.

Nobody is fooled by it of course. Eye-watering amounts of money are thrown at education in the form of consultancy, curriculum, sports buildings and fancy new ecological schools with windmills and Plexiglas canteens. We spend billions on it. But our school leavers are less literate, less numerate and a have a narrower cultural spectrum than ever before. Woolverstone was condemned as being too expensive, but how much does crime, income support and the consequences of ignorance cost us?

Self-confidence, self-belief and a refusal to succumb to the command that told me which social pigeonhole I was going to fit into have been my determining influences since leaving school. I have had some luck, I came under the influence of good people at the right times and had enough sense to listen to at least some of what they taught me. It is also true that I could have done so much better in my professional life if I'd exploited more of what my school provided for me, but fifty per cent of Woolverstone is exponentially better than none at all. I didn't turn to crime, although the temptations were always there, and I thought it was beneath me anyway. Arrogance? Confidence? Does it matter? How was Woolverstone responsible for it? I honestly believe it may have been as simple as repeating the mantra that we were, could be, had to be the best. Eventually you start to believe it.

So can Woolverstone be replicated today? Well that is a silly question because there are hundreds of private schools that operate along similar lines. What is different is their raw material, but only because those who attend can afford the fees. Which brings us back to the very reason Woolverstone was created. Promise, intelligence and achievement – none of it has anything to do with how wealthy you might be. And discipline comes not come only from the whack of a slipper or a cane, it comes from the collective desire to achieve and it becomes self- policing.

I recently read of schools being set up in central New York that have very strict regulations. They are getting remarkable results with poor, urban children. But it is not control that makes a child want to fulfil their potential – or at least believe they have some potential to fulfil in the first place. No, it's the aspirations that their teachers have for them that do it. And to be perfectly frank, that has nothing to do with money, does it? If you teach a child to find Spot in *Spot the Dog*, and they succeed in the simple task you set for them, they will be comfortable with their lot. If you set them something more challenging and they struggle, but you persist with them, lead them through it to enlightenment, then that child's self-esteem will grow with the additional understanding and knowledge that he or she has acquired. It's not rocket science.

Enough of this rant.

I was spectacularly, ungratefully and magnificently lucky to attend Woolverstone. This is no rags to riches story for sure, because I was never in rags and I am certainly not rich. But my school, with its weird customs and other-worldliness, ensured I had a choice. My friendships today, the closest and most meaningful, were made and nurtured at Woolverstone, our collective experience no doubt being a glue of sorts.

My children have shared in the writing of this volume. Leanora, my eldest daughter, possessed of a dedication to learning that surpasses mine by light years, has rendered her parents proud by graduating from Oxford in English literature. My son Gianluca, who, when small, giggled at my behaviour as reported herein, has grown into a fine musician and performer. I have been able to point (usually with red-faced shame) to chapters featuring my failures and misdemeanours and he has often been brought up short by the harshness of the outcomes. Woolverstone has, then, played a role in his upbringing too, even though I feel forever pained that he could not experience a childhood like it. Now my youngest daughter, Fiora, named after the main character in *L'amore dei tre Re*, excitedly asks her Daddy to tell her stories of his school days. I keep it clean, but already I see the value of explaining what it all meant.

* * *

To those of us who went there, Woolverstone is soaked into our being. The same applies to many of my ex-masters, some of whom I have had contact with during the writing of this volume. More than one has expressed the almost misty-eyed sentiment that Woolverstone was, for them, a remarkable experience also, and virtually all seem utterly depressed by the fate that befell it.

When I telephone a master after some thirty-four years of no contact, it is with trepidation and squeamish hesi-tancy, and I am astounded that not only do they recall me, but most at least affect the attitude that they do so fondly. One spoke quite gravely of his regrets that at times he felt he'd been a little vindictive to some boys, which produced a frisson of 'I told you so!', a mental fist pump in celebration of the confirmation that I hadn't always imagined the persecution. John Morris, who went on to become headmaster of Hymer's College, was the call I found the most nerve-wracking, but I needn't have worried, because he didn't recall me as a particularly recalcitrant boy. Dave Morgan, the housemaster who followed Morris, was equally soothing, so was Barry Salmon, the remark-able music teacher, and David Hudson, the deputy head who delivered the awful news about Paddy Richardson. I asked David if he recalled us laughing when he told the assembled school the news; he didn't and I was relieved.

I have kept in most regular touch with Neil Clayton since leaving Woolverstone and he still calls me a fool, still has a theatrical humour to his conversation and often throws withering judgement my way. For my part, I continue to cringe at the almost criminal contrast in my dealings with him now and whilst at school. During a recent conversation, I happened to mention that my fiftieth birthday was about to pass and his response pitched me back several decades. 'Ah, Volpe,' he said, as if preparing to deliver a Shylock speech, 'to me you will never be fifty. You will always be that thirteen-year-old fucking menace to whom I had to teach Chaucer.'

Above all, this recent contact with ex-masters has given me some pause to contemplate the idea that perhaps I wasn't as bad as I thought I was. I think I was a compassionate, if robustly abrasive, young man, but I would be lying if I didn't admit to a sneaky resentment that I hadn't made quite the impression I thought I had. As ever, behaviour of the kind I report herein tends to affect most profoundly the person who is delivering it, but boys like me need an audience to work through our confusions, and the chaos we create gives validation.

Today, when we gather together, my friends and I revert to type: as with fame, which dictates that a person remains at the age he was when he found it, we Woolverstonians appear to be as silly and as childish as we were in the common room, or on the bus to Felixstowe. And we talk about the school a great deal, apparently aware of what we may have become had we not been caught in its embrace.

This common emotional attachment runs very deep in all of us and one can't easily define why that should be so. Our experiences there were both joyous and traumatic, so perhaps we believe we *survived* Woolverstone, as well as benefitted from it? Whatever it is, we have bonds that are unbreakable, we understand each other, never judge one another and we never, ever, tolerate boastfulness, no matter what the success.

Rob is still a close friend and we share holidays together from time to time. He remains deeply empathetic as an individual and we are as close to brothers as non-genetically related people can be. He runs a beautiful estate in Somerset for the designer David Mlinaric and has a son, Marshall, who loves to hear stories of our escapades.

We are all middle-aged men now and we understand more of what we are and have become, but we all know that Woolverstone shaped and moulded us; that we all still fall back on the experience when things get rough. I doubt that a more tremendous tribute could be paid to a school.

As for the school itself, after it closed in 1990 it was acquired by Ipswich High School, for Girls. Hall's and Johnston's house have been demolished and a beautiful brick sports block has been built in their place. The irony of it being full of girls always gives me cause for a chuckle, but there is something satisfying in knowing it wasn't turned into a health spa or hotel. Many old boys make frequent pilgrimage to the school to see their old stomping grounds, usually with children, wide-eyed in wonder that their fathers ever attended such a place.

AFTERWORD

In the introduction to this book, I suggested that I had no idea where it would take me, nor what conclusions I might draw from the process. I still don't, really, but it does seem appropriate that I should try to bring you up to date with my story. I also alluded to the fate of my parents and siblings, and in the course of the past eighteen months both of my parents, as well as my brother Matteo, have passed away.

Lou now lives with his wife Tracey on the edge of a loch in Oban, Scotland, where they built a large eco-house. Sergio resides with his wife Kristin and their two young children in California. My own children, Leanora and Gianluca are beginning their life journeys with a proud mother and father looking on. My second wife, Sally, and I live in London with our daughter Fiora, who, like Gianluca, has already performed on the Holland Park stage.

Matteo's death I have reported elsewhere in these pages, but its effect on me has only really now formed into a whole, cogent concept, followed closely as it was by the deaths of my father and mother. Matteo was really the heart and dominant feature of Mum's life; if anybody epitomised the threats and risks our family was vulnerable to, it was him. His birth was tinged with disappointment, his early years were framed by dad's first wanderings; and if Mum's struggles could be defined in any real way, it would be to the course of Matt's life that we would point. His death was withheld from Mum who at that stage, ravaged by dementia, was scarcely aware of herself, but I was not prepared to take the risk that in there, somewhere, was cognisance. If fate had been less unutterably cruel, her grief would have known few boundaries, and so nothing was to be gained by inviting the prospect that she might feel the loss, but be unable to express it or even understand it.

My father's death came ten months after Matt's, and its consequences are still unravelling in my mind – and literally. I received a call from Corrado (his son by the other woman), my brother and a man to whom I had never spoken in my life. We all knew about Corrado, even spied him from a distance sometimes when he helped Dad on the ice-cream van as a teenager. He was our brother, but our loyalty to Mum ensured we never sought him out or had a relationship with him. But when Fiora was born, it suddenly became clear to me that her attachment to her siblings was no less powerful because she had a different mother, and so my guilt about our neglect towards Corrado began to grow.

Soon after our father had died, I had a conversation with Corrado which revealed that he never knew, until the age of fifteen or sixteen, that he had four brothers, all living close by. He did not even know that he was older than me. Dad's passing closed a few chapters, but it opened some new ones and Corrado attended Mum's funeral, something that was previously unimaginable. His many questions signified so much about our father that was unpalatable, but Dad's death resonated powerfully, not least because I was the only one of his three surviving sons by Mum to attend his funeral. With Matt's death I felt an indefinable loss, a visceral experience that still shakes me, but at Dad's funeral there was only sadness and regret that his life should end so unrewarded by family unity or even the slightest relationship with his grandchildren. His life was scarcely celebrated, but the absence of extensive mourning contributed to a picture of my family that regenerated the tragedy of Matt in my mind.

Mum's passing, just two weeks before I am writing this, has resolved the picture I have been trying to identify during the past eighteen months. Dad, Matt and Mum, on the surface, represented the tragic dysfunction of our clan and, somehow, their collective deaths within a short space of time is perhaps fate's way of ending our misery quickly. Their lives were intertwined as stories of lost opportunity and struggle, and it was not until Mum's death that the tragedy finally resolved. At Matt's funeral, attended by a great many people, I tried to celebrate and value his life. At Mum's, I attempted to talk to her in a way I had wished I'd done when she was alive and sentient, I elevated her life, made it noble. And it had been.

Throughout this book I have told you how selfish I was, how we had all driven Mum to despair and anguish countless times, and, when she died, after she had suffered several years of horrific mental decline, I became desperate that she should have known what an honourable life she had led. I wanted her to know that everything she had done was worthwhile and had produced wonderful results. Perhaps, more than anything else, this book is about Mum.

I cannot bring myself to go back to incorporate more of their lives into this book and so, as testimony, maybe even as conclusion, I reproduce their eulogies, delivered by me through many tears. Because in many ways that's who this book is about; not me, but Matt and Mum. Matt, because my life could have so easily looked like his, if I hadn't been lucky enough to be given a chance. And Mum, because without her, none of us would have had a chance in the first place.

Matteo Volpe

Matteo Volpe, son of Lidia and Francesco, husband to Nikki, brother to Lou, Serge and Michael, uncle to Matthew, Leanora, Marcella, Gianluca, Fiora and Jack, friend to and much loved by countless others. And it has to be acknowledged, sometime frequent guest of Her Majesty.

Matteo emerged from the womb ready to rumble. His life was never going to be simple, never straightforward, forever dynamic in one way or another. As the second born of four boys, Matt grew up a quarter of Mum's responsibility but at least half of her worry. That was Matt.

As a child, my earliest memory of Matt was of him pulling stitches from his latest injury. What we often call curiosity in children was called lunacy in Matt; why else would he light a banger and put it in his own pocket? Why else would he jump onto a pile of plate glass, cutting his feet to ribbons? He was, until his final day, a complex jumble of contradictions, a man who was difficult to predict, who could often surprise, who didn't ask for much but for whom life itself was often not enough.

As children, Matt was the boldest of us, the bravest at times, the biggest risk taker. Like all of us, he had demons and he danced with each and every one of them until the last. I believe he grew to feel safer with them rather than cast them out when he had a chance. Perhaps these demons were somehow his friends too?

I always remember Matt's teenage years, the parade of

*girls knocking at our door, upset because he hadn't asked
for a second date or phoned them. I remember his friends
and their partying at our house. I looked up to him, wanted
to be like him. Whatever Matt could at times be, I will
always remember the Matt I grew up proud to call my
brother; good looking, good at football, good at pulling
a fast one. Pretty good at just pulling too. Matt was cool.
The challenges he would eventually present his family with
were still to come, but even those times, through the struggles, the danger, they were part of what made Matt what
he was. He worried about Mum all the time he was driving
her mad, he worried about me, his little brother. He lectured
me after I had been suspended from my boarding school,
unhappy, angry, disappointed. I was amazed that he should
be lecturing me and I told him so, pointing out that HE
had only just got out of prison. 'We sent you to that school
because we don't want you turning out like me,' he said.
So whatever path Matt was on, he knew what it was and
couldn't change it, but there was awareness enough to
ensure I didn't follow him.*

*Even with all the hard times with Matt, the memories
that return to me are good ones. I remember our holidays
in Italy, I remember his desire to get as brown as it is
possible to get in the sun, oiling himself up with local
olive oil. I remember him trying to persuade his girlfriends
to let me, his younger brother, cop a feel because I had to
learn, after all. I remember him betting us he could knock
the local copper's helmet off from forty yards with a football and then actually doing it, and all of us having to
run away fast. I remember him whacking a bloke who*

had scared a woman in North End Road market so much that she nearly went under a bus. Matt took off his wooden clog and walloped him with it. I remember Matt leaping off the boiling hot train at crazily busy stations to get water as we travelled to Italy and not being back as the train began to leave the station. I remember Mum wailing hysterically, me copying her and then Matt strolling back into the compartment without a care in the world. He had just got back on further along the platform. I was very young, maybe ten years old, and I recall the feeling, the awful panic that we had lost him forever.

And now, as we gather here, we all feel as if we have really lost him forever. But as I speak, have you all been remembering similar things? Do you smile to yourself as you recall one event or other? A good time that you shared with Matt? If you do, then we haven't lost him. He lives on in our memories, and what constitutes our lives is really just that bundle of memories in any case.

They say that people like Matt, who sail close to the wind, walk the line and leave us young, represent a tragic waste. I used to agree. But what do we mean by waste? That their lives were not what WE would expect them to be? That they somehow threw away what could have been but wasn't? Matt didn't waste his life. Matt lived his life the way he wanted, maybe even the way his demons said he must. But Matt made a mark on those who knew him. We knew that whatever he may do, Matt was, to his core and in his troubled heart, good and caring. This full church tells us that whatever Matt's life was, we were all touched by it. And that cannot be a waste, can it?

So now we move on. We always have to move on.

Nikki, who loved and cared for Matt for so long, will begin a new phase of her life, and we must encourage her and wish that she has the best because she has earned it for what she gave to Matt. His brothers will remember Matt for the dramatic soul he was. From time to time, we will wish that that things had turned out differently, that being a brother to Matt hadn't sometimes been so challenging, that one day we could have all sat round a table with our grandchildren and laughed about that copper's helmet. But perhaps we always knew that was not to be. We all loved Matt; sometimes it was tough love.

Fly free Matt. Those demons can't touch you any more.

★ ★ ★

Lidia Volpe

I want to speak to you today, Mum. I haven't really been able to for so long and I want everybody here to listen to what I have to say because there are things that we maybe should have said to you before, but didn't.

Lidia Volpe, née Perillo, you were mother to Lou, Matteo, Sergio and me. You were grandmother to Matthew, Leanora, Marcella, Gianluca, Fiora, Jack and Lily. You were aunty to countless others and a surrogate mother to many, many more. Here with us today are the children of your dear friend Giovanna Volino who you will have no doubt begun an argument with already.

You came to this country from poverty, and it was in

poverty's grasp you would remain for some time. You trusted your life to the father of your children, but it wasn't to be. And so your life was hard and it threatened to crush you at every turn, but you fought and fought. You worked up to three jobs at a time. You faced your challenges, you protected us and you stood fiercely in the path of threat, sometimes literally. I remember you beating the woman who said that Serge was in a borstal when actually he was at a fantastic boarding school. You were so proud that he had gotten into that school, and that I would also join him, and nobody was going to sully that fact. Matteo was in the borstal, but not Sergio, and that mattered. It mattered a great deal because you had, in your mind, saved us, achieved something with your guts and your fight for life. That is all you ever asked for; not favours, or hand-outs, charity or pity. You only wanted a chance, for yourself and for us.

You became the cook at Brook Green Day nursery and so thousands of children in west London grew up on lasagne, gnocchi and so many other delights unimaginable today. People of my age will still remember you, will know the smell of pasta al forno. But one job was not enough, you needed to provide us with more, be more certain that food would be on the table and that clothes were on our backs, and so you gave loyalty and dedication to others who had unimaginably more than you ever did but who never looked down on you. You would never allow that. And they loved and cherished you for your care and service.

We children grew up without the luxuries of life but we knew we were loved. You could overdo the love sometimes,

Mum, I have to be honest, and it made you worry a bit more than you needed to. But we are all parents now, so maybe we understand that better than we did then. My childhood memories are full of people who passed through our lives because you chose to help them, even when they were not worthy of it. You just did that sort of thing. All my friends remember the food at our house, how you would almost force them to eat an enormous breakfast or dinner. My friend, who was named Easter, will remember how you smiled when you first met her and said, 'Allo, mya name is Christamas!' I am sorry Mum, it used to really annoy you when we imitated your accent. I might do it again before I am finished. A thousand other people will remember you, because you were different, made of something so few of us are made of. You always kept your dignity and of all the things I may have ever learned from you, it was this: to keep your dignity, no matter what becomes of you. You were forgiving, generous, allowed people their failings and their mistakes. When all around you said it was a lost cause, you always gave one more chance.

And so it came to your later years, as the great joy of grandchildren arrived, when you should have been enjoying the burgeoning of new life, life that wouldn't face the privations that your own children suffered. You went out with the kids and Lou one day, to Greenwich, Tower Bridge, the London Eye. At the end of the day you said to Lou that you had never realised London was so beautiful – that was fifty years in this city living your life looking after others, with no time for yourself. In that fifty years, even though your English was excellent, you still struggled at times with the London vernacular. When Serge once told you that he had been to see a man about a dog, you looked sternly at him and said: 'I tella you Sergio, I'ma NOT having a dog in dissa house!'

But even your great spirit was overcome by your illness and we watched your very being ebb away. I remember when I realised how this great unconquerable image of you that we all had, this indestructibility, was under threat. The day was Mother's Day, but you didn't know it. Your body was there but we didn't know if your spirit was or where your mind had gone to. We found it hard to visit you, because you looked but didn't appear to see us, you listened but we never knew if you could hear us. Your grandchildren kissed you but did you feel it? If only you knew how excited Fiora was to shout 'Hello nonna!', but she was four and she didn't mind that you never answered her because she knew you were Daddy's Mummy and had never known you any differently. The older grandchildren preferred to remember Sundays at your house, with forbidden treats secretly placed in their pockets, pasta fagioli and all of that food. You only ever wanted your family around you, but later, when we were, did you even know we were there?

You didn't deserve what happened to you; after all those years of hard work and sacrifice. Perhaps you finally had the tranquility that life saw fit to so frequently rob you of, that you could not feel the anxiety and worry any longer, but I wonder if maybe you would have liked nothing more than to feel it again?

You left us some time ago, Mum. We never said goodbye then because we stood at your bedside and waited for you to take your body with you. Now that you have finally gone, we can search again for those memories of the indomitable, incomparable woman you were, who would fight like a lion for us, even when we didn't show you how grateful we were for it. We can banish the recent past and give new life to the happy memories of you that it is your absolute right that we should have above all others.

There was one blessing, Mum, when you were suffering. It was that we never had to tell you that your son Matteo had gone before you, that the boy you had shed so many tears for, suffered so much pain for, hadn't made it, hadn't outlived you. You would have felt that to be a failure, I know you would. But you didn't fail, Mum, we want you to know that. If only you could have seen what we have all achieved, what your grandchildren have attained and what they have become. They will never know the hardships you knew, because you suffered them for us, and for them, and should they ever fall upon difficult times they can remember you and take from you the example of stoicism and sacrifice that you represent.

You see, Mum, I want to tell you that it was all worth it. I want to tell you that your fight was a good fight and that you won. That you had a fulfilling, worthwhile life, as noble, as distinguished and as glorious as any other. That your struggle was not in vain.

You did it, Mum. You made it.

Your granddaughter Lea wrote a poem about you. Its final words I want to read to these people here because it reminds us how we should remember you. She composed it to remind your sons of what you did for us. In it, she tells us, this child of mine, what we should know, she stands up for you and your memory, and I can hear the force in her voice as she says;

> *I know it feels like not even you can*
> *Remember the sound of her voice,*
> *But it is up to you to remember her,*
> *And carry on singing the song she wrote*
> *Because she wrote it for you.*
> *It was always for you.*

We will sing your song, Mum. Now go peacefully with all our love.

ABOUT THE AUTHOR

Michael Volpe, the youngest of four brothers, is from an Italian immigrant family and has three children: Leanora, Gianluca and Fiora. He is married to Sally Connew-Volpe and they live in London. Michael joined the Royal Borough of Kensington and Chelsea in October 1989 and founded Opera Holland Park in 1996.

Michael is a Chelsea supporter, and a fervent advocate of cultural engagement for all – neither of which is necessarily related.

Stories . . . voices . . . places . . . lives

We hope you enjoyed *Noisy at the Wrong Times*.
If you'd like to know more about this book
or any other title on our list, please go to
www.tworoadsbooks.com

For news on forthcoming Two Roads titles,
please sign up for our newsletter.

enquiries@tworoadsbooks.com

TwoRoadsBooks